JAPAN

JAPAN

In the Land of the Brokenhearted

MICHAEL SHAPIRO

HENRY HOLT AND COMPANY   NEW YORK

Copyright © 1989 by Michael Shapiro
All rights reserved, including the right to reproduce
this book or portions thereof in any form.
Published by Henry Holt and Company, Inc.,
115 West 18th Street, New York, New York 10011.
Published in Canada by Fitzhenry & Whiteside Limited,
195 Allstate Parkway, Markham, Ontario L3R 4T8.

Library of Congress Cataloging-in-Publication Data
Shapiro, Michael, 1952–
Japan : in the land of the brokenhearted / Michael Shapiro.—1st ed.
    p.   cm.
ISBN 0-8050-0395-9   BT 19.95/10.79 - 5/89
1. National characteristics, Japanese.   2. Japan—Ethnic
relations. 3. Americans—Japan.   4. Hearn, Lafcadio, 1850–1904.
5. Japan—Description and travel—1945– . 6. Shapiro, Michael, 1952–
—Journeys—Japan.   I. Title.
DS830.S33   1989
952.04—dc19   88-39282
                                                           CIP

Henry Holt books are available at special discounts
for bulk purchases for sales promotions, premiums,
fund-raising, or educational use. Special editions
or book excerpts can also be created to specification.

    For details contact:

    Special Sales Director
    Henry Holt and Company, Inc.
    115 West 18th Street
    New York, New York 10011

First Edition

Designed by Claire M. Naylon
Printed in the United States of America
10   9   8   7   6   5   4   3   2   1

For Susan
and
In Memory of
Jonathan Maximon

ACKNOWLEDGMENTS

This book would not have been possible without the assistance of a good many generous people.

I want to thank my interpreter, Seinosuke Nakakita, who did far more than translate words for me: again and again he pointed me in the right direction, explaining what was being said, clarifying meanings in a language which often strives for obscurity. My research on the life of Lafcadio Hearn was aided by Professor Yasuyuki Kajitani and his student, Shinji Sasaki.

I want to thank Leron Lee, Tim Ireland, Randy Bass, Greg Wells, Mark Brouhard, and Ikuo Ikeda for their tutelage in the ways of Japanese baseball, as well as Gordon Leman and Yasuo Furuya in the ways of Japanese religion. John McIntosh introduced me to the Korean community in Osaka. Shunsuke Nomoto and Aizo Murakami taught me much about human rights in Japan.

Miles Corwin, Simon Holberton, Donald McNeil, Elisabeth Rubinfien, James Shapiro, and Jill Shapiro read the manuscript and aided mightily in improving it, as did my editors, Jack Macrae and Amy Hertz. All writers should be lucky enough to have an agent like Barney Karpfinger, and parents like Herbert and Lorraine Shapiro, who are quick with a reminder that this sort of work is also supposed to be fun.

This book would not have been possible without Eugene Matthews, Tatsuo Shigeta, Leon Lee, Kathy and Jun Morikawa, and Armin and Evelyn Kroehler. I was fortunate indeed to have found them and fortunate, too, in the generosity they extended to me, despite all the questions and time spent together. My thanks, too, to their families and friends, especially to Pamela Lee and Derek Lee, Margaret Kroehler, Ken Kroehler, Kaye Kroehler, and Iris Kroehler.

But of all my debts the greatest is to my wife, Susan Chira, not only for her wise counsel, incisive editing, and unceasing support, but for keeping me dreaming. The greatest pleasure in my life is sharing those dreams with her.

1
Yokohama

There, outside and beyond me, was Japan.

I saw patterns developing. There were lines and shapes and circumstances familiar enough to be predictable. I could anticipate. Though there were dark, narrow alleys around so many corners I could, faintly, spot light. Things made sense. The place felt accessible. A neighbor said hello. I pounded wet rice with a big wooden mallet at the local rice cake-making ceremony. The grocer remembered me. I took a long train trip and chatted with my compartment mates, all by myself.

But pleasure was fleeting and when it passed, when I felt a door as heavy as a cathedral's shut on my nose, I thought of what Leon Lee told me. Leon, who came to play baseball, said, "Playing baseball in Japan is like going through a black hole in space. You begin on one side and have a certain view of things and come out on the other and find that everything is the same except it's completely different."

I had not planned to come. I was sent, with my wife, by her employer. But I did not mind. Work was transferable and Japan held possibilities. I registered for language lessons at an adult extension course. I was keen on getting started. I practiced my vowels. The teacher, a Japanese woman with a girlish giggle, said something about "Japanese without tears," and that sounded fine to me. The teacher then started calling on those who did not raise their hands. I began cutting class. Pop quizzes seemed inevitable and I felt it unseemly being subjected again to past humiliations. Though I would arrive in Tokyo barely speaking a word—fearful of snickers and guffaws lest I try ordering in the more atmospheric restaurants, I lived for three weeks on room service tuna sandwiches—the class served a purpose beyond teaching essential greetings and apologies: it introduced me to the enthusiasts. Six months later, after a string of false starts and evaporated possibilities, it would be the enthusiasts who would lead me to a window through which I could see.

I hated them. They soaked up the language like fat, restaurant-kitchen sponges. They took copious notes. They wore looks of such zeal, such innocent passion. They were so earnest that I wanted to throttle them. Japan was not going to be fun for the enthusiasts; it was going to be an experience. Tokyo was not Paris or Rio or an island in the Aegean where you swilled enough retsina with the locals to think that maybe you were going to write something significant with all those impressions you'd gathered. The enthusiasts would seek a Zen master. They would study tea. (You didn't study the tea ceremony; you studied tea.) They would search for the essence. The enthusiasts would quickly learn—because they wanted to know—that you did not pour *sake* for yourself but waited for someone to pour it for you and that the cup was to be rested on the first three digits of one hand while the other delicately held the little vessel. And oh, the looks they'd give the oafs who did not know, the fools who gave all foreigners bad names by tramping through the countryside with dispositions as obvious and manners as crude as muddy boots on a white carpet. The enthusiasts knew better. And when in the company of those who did not, they gave any offended Japanese knowing glances, as if to say, "The lout is not with me."

The enthusiasts learned sensitivity. The enthusiasts wanted to please. Sometimes they succeeded. Japanese people seemed to like them. Or at least they invited them along. I'd be left sitting at the next table, looking about, studying the setting, seeing significance where none existed. I'd turn to watch as the enthusiasts and their new friends switched from beer to *sake* to whiskey and water and began smacking their glasses together in endless toasting to motherhood and the end of trade friction. And when those new friends could no longer hold their dinners, when they weaved to the door and out to the street, the enthusiasts were there, extending sympathy and understanding with a hand on the shoulder and a look in the other direction.

The enthusiasts connected with Japan. I did not. I saw the look in their eyes and could not understand the attraction. Japan seemed pleasant enough and at times attractive. But this passion, this desire for intimacy, this I could not fathom. I held myself back.

I came to Japan in 1984 having been warned that I was not going to be transported by what I found; but I wanted romance just the same. Few sensations are as deadening as traveling a long way only to find a poor approximation of what was left behind. I had seen the photographic evidence: Tokyo would disappoint me. I'd find a big, bland city built primarily of steel, concrete, and borrowed ideas. Yet I could not help myself. As the plane descended through a cloud and banked over green fields I pressed my nose to the cold window, looking for something new in the terrain. On the long bus ride into town I saw woods and rice fields and a man in high boots walking along the side of the road. I wanted to believe that this man went home, took off his boots, put on a kimono, and gave his wife the nod that said it was time to fetch the Book of the Pillow. (His wife's hair was twelve feet long and her face was powdered white. They never watched TV. They never ate the new, cellophane-wrapped cuisine—instant potatoes, corn potage, and Chocolate Sand cookies. Never.)

Two days later my wife Susan and I went to watch the teenagers rebel. They looked like plausible rebels, though heavily influenced by America in rebellion attire. The boys snarled, combed back their hair in oil-soaked ducktails, and wore leather jackets that read NEW YORK BROTHER and PEP BOY. The girls wore chiffon dresses and aprons and looked like truck-stop waitresses. They danced to re-cordings of Bill Haley and the Comets. People came to watch.

The rebels stood in circles and danced when their leaders blew their whistles. The leaders wore capes and stalked about like drill instructors. The rebels kicked and waved their arms in unison, danc-ing less with a keen sense of outrage than with an eye for getting it right. They maintained form. The looked like subjects in a sleep deprivation study. In the middle of the circle were their big radios; and next to the radios were shopping bags filled with school uni-forms. The rebels arrived in their uniforms and changed into their rebellion clothing in subway bathrooms. They put their nasty clothes in their shopping bags and put on their uniforms so that they'd be dressed appropriately when they got home.

Mild as it was, the Dance of the Rebels hinted at dissimilarities deep and profound. I could dismiss any number of inconsistencies: En-glish that wasn't English ("Let's Play Tennis with Potato," "My Life, My Gas," "Let's Sports Violent All Day Long"); electric toilet-seat warmers with automatic bidets in new homes built without insu-lation; French bistros serving potato on a bed of spaghetti and topped with melted Gruyère. I could hit my forehead with the heel of my hand, chronicle the impression in a letter home (". . . and you won't believe this one either, folks, but grown women carry 'Hello Kitty' handbags—ha ha") and wonder why the Japanese couldn't have just left things the way they once were so that newly arrived foreigners might have their romantic illusions fulfilled.

But there was another class of impressions, impressions that beckoned like a beam of light at the mouth of a mine shaft whose depth and content are a mystery. These were impressions that could make Japan feel like home. Then they made it feel nothing like home. They could do both, at the same time. They made me want to see more. For me, they were the DX Gekijo.

The DX Gekijo was a theater where women danced naked in front of strange men who then performed sexual intercourse with them on a revolving stage. The DX was small, dark, and filled with men in jackets and ties. The men kept their overcoats on. The dancing had a menacing edge: a woman dripped candle wax on her belly; another played the flames of two torches along her back. The men watched in silence.

Then the dancing ended. An elderly man swept the stage clean. The house lights come on and with them, the new music, "Zippity Doo-Da" and "It's a Small World After All." The women took turns prancing about the stage and compact runway. They stopped and squatted before a group of men, spread their legs and displayed their womanly attributes. The men leaned forward. Their jaws fell slack. They peered at the women like first year medical students in an Introduction to Reproductive Anatomy class. One woman produced a penlight and a magnifying glass.

No one laughed. No one spoke. Everyone kept to himself, everyone except for the man who climbed from the spectator section onto the revolving stage. A woman came to him. She was especially thin, with long reddish hair that did not seem to be her own. Her back was covered with tattoos. The chief tattoo, from shoulders to waist, was of a Buddhist deity. The woman removed the man's pants and folded his underwear. The man, with dark socks on and a necktie knotted at the throat, was swabbed clean. The woman kept alcohol pads and condoms in a case that looked like a little girl's lunchbox.

They spun around and around and as they did, the tattooed woman did her business with speed and dexterity. She led. She wrapped her gray jacketed lover in her arms and as he fondled and suckled and, briefly, coupled, she looked up at the sound and light man and gave him a quick smile. Her man took no initiative; he waited for instructions. And when she was finished with him, the tattooed woman sent her man away, his pants and drawers in his arms. He pulled up his pants at the back of the stage.

The women took one more tour around the stage, offering themselves for foreplay. Fingers were proffered, meekly. They were swabbed, sheathed, and briefly inserted. One man was so mesmerized that he had to be taken by the wrist and guided. No one had to remind him to stop when his woman said stop. No one had to keep him, or anyone else, in his seat. In the DX Gekijo there were no bouncers. They were not needed. The women were in charge;

7

and the men acquiesced. They looked up and into the women with wonder and awe. They were tentative. When their turn at foreplay came they did not look at each other with licentious eyes. They looked at what they were doing. They did not smile. The women did not smile at them.

The DX Gekijo did not arouse me. It was too nonsensical to be arousing. At home you could watch naked women dance. You could pay to mount a woman who could make you feel like a fool. But when doing so in the company of other fellows you might want to pound your chest a little or offer a rebel yell. It would not be seemly, playing the lamb led to the slaughter in front of the guys.

The DX Gekijo was the apotheosis of all those impressions that confounded me, confounded me because just when I thought I saw something I recognized, the form altered just enough so that when I looked again I saw an image I could not recognize. I could not dismiss it, but I could not understand it. I wanted Japan to add up for me, and it was not adding up. I was feeling as if I were traveling a path that led to a fork with arrows pointing in opposite directions, either of which was the right way to go. If the men of Japan were the dominant gender, why were they cowed into submission and silence by the DX's women? But if the women of Japan were not as docile as they seemed, why did they talk and dress and giggle like schoolgirls?

If I were as remote as I imagined myself, why could moments that irritated me no end also please me? Why was I reacting viscerally, and in contradictory ways, to the same stimuli? Little boys would approach and ask for my autograph for no reason other than my foreignness. I smiled and complied, seeing in the encounter an innocence I never saw at home. Yet when those boys of the same age and intent called out to me, "Harro, harro," I wanted to grab them by the backs of their collars, lead them home, and explain to their parents that foreigners were not mere objects of curiosity.

Yet I found the innocence seductive. It seemed so well-intended, so guileless. When a Japanese friend invited us to an outdoor dance festival and insisted that Susan and I wear kimono, I demurred. He insisted. I relented and changed. Passersby stopped and stared at me. But I did not cower. I strutted. I tucked my hand in the fold of my kimono and walked the way the TV gangsters walked when they wore kimono.

Our friend's daughter was among the dancers at the festival. Dressed in her bright kimono, her hair adorned with a pink ribbon, she danced a fishermen's dance with the young girls in her dance club. They danced high above us, on a red wooden stage. Our friend's daughter looked down at us and smiled as she glided past.

I fanned myself, as the other men did. They tucked their fans in the back of their cotton belts, so I did, too. People nodded at me. Some smiled and I smiled back.

It was more than innocence alone, however, that drew me in. What it was I did not know. If I could not make out the form, I could still feel its presence. I felt it at unexpected moments, at one encounter in particular so seemingly banal that my inclination was to dismiss it. It was easy watching without feeling, I told myself. I slept better. In my sleep I remained peacefully ignorant of what that one curious moment foreshadowed.

The encounter was with my barber. I offended him. At least I thought I offended him. I could not be sure. Nor was I sure why I was even giving the matter any thought. It began when I started telling him I was in a bit of a rush. I did not want to hurry him, only to cut down on the shampooing administered by his young and enthusiastic apprentice. The shampooing took half an hour. After half an hour of shampooing with your head suspended backward, at the neck, over a porcelain basin, the back of your skull feels as if it were about to give way. I could take no more. I had to hurry, or so I said.

The shampooing time was cut in half. My barber saw to that. But in the chair I sensed something was wrong. He chatted, but in a desultory fashion. He worked quickly, but then he always worked quickly. Was he working more quickly than before? And why didn't we talk about baseball? We always talked about baseball. We always squeezed ten minutes of conversation out of baseball, which was the best I could manage with my meager Japanese. And what about the beard trimming? I touched the beard once, then again. That was all the suggestion ever needed. But the hint was ignored. Or maybe the shop was a little more crowded than usual. It was a Saturday, which explained why he didn't have time to trim my beard. But then, what about the door? He always walked me to the door and bowed me out. Not every customer was bowed out, and I liked to think that my exit was accompanied by envious looks from less privileged patrons. Instead, I got a wave.

It happened again the next time—no trim, no bow. Could I ask what I had done wrong? But what did it matter even if I had? This man was cutting my hair. He was not a relative or family friend. Perhaps I had leaned too hard on the apprentice. Or perhaps by asking him to hurry the apprentice I was, by extension, asking the barber to repudiate everything he had taught the boy about shampooing. I vowed to endure any shampoo. Let him scrub for three-quarters of an hour. I would breathe deeply and go with the pain.

There is a moment when, in the midst of such fretting, you catch a glimpse of yourself in the mirror and wonder who the stranger is, looking back. Was I really that concerned whether my barber was offended? I do not think I would have thought twice about it at home. And if I did think I'd been rude I could simply have asked, "What's eating you?" In Japan the option did not exist. Nothing's wrong, I would have been told, nothing at all.

In time, the baseball talk resumed, as did the beard trimming. We walked to the door, together, my barber and I. And as I descended the stairway he bowed and smiled, as mysterious to me in his courteousness, as he had been when he had cut me off. Or so it had seemed. The more I thought about what had happened, the more the world around me seemed covered in a pea-soup fog. Headlights appeared and vanished, leaving me lost and wondering when the next ride might appear.

Was I seeing in an ever-stronger and richer Japan the future of civilization? And if so, was it the Japan of the $50 billion trade surplus with the Americans alone, or was it the Japan that stood rather than take the empty seat next to me on the subway because I was a foreigner and foreigners were known to smell funny? Was it the Japan that was forever lamenting that it was "a poor island nation with few natural resources and no ideas of its own" or the Japan that appeared one night in the form of a bureaucrat who, after a few rounds, warned me that if his nation was ever pushed to the wall by the blowhards on Capitol Hill it might well react as it had before. He raised a finger, jabbed it at the air as if it were a dive bomber, and said, "Midway mentality."

I was also intrigued for less ominous reasons. All around me, packed close together, stood tall buildings where once there was only rubble. I heard stories about the first winter after the war, when city people rode the train to the countryside and dug for sweet potatoes because they were starving. Now there was a Tour d'Argent in Tokyo, to go along with the replica of Maxim's. Maxim's was in the Ginza, where the property values were the highest in the country, where government ministers drank in private clubs, where you could still hear the sweet potato peddler singing his hawking song. He pulled a cart and sang his song and even before you heard him you could smell the potatoes, roasting in the oven on top of his cart. He sang the song all the sweet potato peddlers sang—"Sweet potatoes, stone-roasted sweet potatoes . . ."—a curiously mournful song heard every night in every neighborhood when the cold weather came.

I met a man who showed me the scroll of his family history. The history was 1,100 years old and unbroken. The man knew the name of his first ancestor. I knew my great grandparents; but I knew nothing about who came before them. This man knew where his progenitors had lived. He used to go there in the summer when Tokyo emptied itself as people went home to pay homage to their ancestors. They were joined, the Japanese I saw and met, with those of a thousand years ago. They lived in the same cities, sometimes in the same districts, and almost exclusively in each other's company. No foreign armies had despoiled the countryside and altered the gene pool, no foreign armies except one, forty years ago. And now, a generation after its only defeat, Japan was surpassing its conqueror.

I was intrigued as I watched, intermittently, from eight in the morning till six at night, six days a week, the three houses next to ours being built in quick succession by teams of men who permitted themselves few breaks and fell asleep when they did; when the supermarket elevator lady bowed me on and off and made the same speech of welcome from the first floor to the second, over and over, thousands of times a day, never showing boredom or fatigue because this was her job and no matter how excruciatingly dull it was she was going to do it right; when I set my watch by the Tokyo subway—not as a test, but as a reliable time check—and found myself believing that there was nothing these people could not do. Then, late at night, as office lights switched off and hostesses helped prosperous men into their limousines, I watched other blue-suited men stagger into alleys, throw up on their shoes, and slump to the ground. Asleep with mouths open and heads between their knees, they convinced me that I had it all wrong.

That was when I stopped hating the enthusiasts. I did so selfishly, with a plan in mind. While I was holding myself apart as the gentleman in the grandstand, the enthusiasts were falling in love. Then they waited for Japan to love them back. They tried so hard. They did everything right. Japan smiled and looked away.

The relationship was not even very complicated. The nation made no secret of its belief in inside and outside and the impossibility of crossing the two. Always, it was *"Ware, ware Nihon-jin desu,"*—"We Japanese"—an identification, I was to learn, that had less to do with the name of a nation state than with an idea, a self-defining concept two thousand years old.

A non-Japanese could be admired and cared for. But he would have to accept the premise that can so sting a would-be lover: limited expectations. He could stay. He could look. But he would not be loved.

My hatred dissipated as I began seeing the enthusiasts as I might see a friend who falls in love when he shouldn't. He hopes that one day the object of his desire will turn and see that she can be better and happier loving him back. She never does. She says that she will always like him as a friend. He asks you what to do and you say, "Forget it," and he says, "I can't." For the life of you, you cannot see what he sees in her. But now you are curious, curious because even if you are happy and contented, the power of that sorry love is infectious and universal and makes you remember how you felt when you thought you could not bear to live another day.

I wanted to see the object of the enthusiasts' unrequited love. I wanted to break it down to components, hoping that all those inconsistencies and conflicts that had so intrigued and confounded me might come together and assume a recognizable form. Maybe then I might learn what possessed me to know, even, I thought, if I could not feel.

But first I needed the relationship defined. I needed a path to follow, the trail of a romance from happy times to sad times to the point of resolution. One day in a bookstore, I stumbled upon it.

That day I discovered that there existed, in eleven books and countless letters, the journal of the emotional odyssey of a short, moody, one-eyed man, long departed and, except in Japan, largely forgotten. He was the enthusiasts' patron saint. His name was Lafcadio Hearn.

No one, I would learn, loved Japan better. No one, I sensed, could have felt such bitter disappointment when he saw that Japan was not what he wanted it to be. But that is getting ahead of the story, which began long before the April morning in 1890 when Lafcadio Hearn sailed into Tokyo Bay, saw the frosted cone of Mount Fuji, and announced, "I want to die here."

Poor Hearn. He came with all the wrong assumptions, assumptions that had less to do with Japan than with his idea of romance. Hearn was not for this world. He was for a world that existed far away and long ago, if it ever existed at all. For twenty years he wandered and struggled, searching for a place and people that embodied his ideal. Then he came to Japan. Japan was simply the next station on a long and futile journey.

Born in Greece, raised in Ireland, he bounced from London to New York to Cincinnati to New Orleans to Martinique. Along the way he established himself as a writer of some prominence: a splashy crime reporter in Cincinnati; the chronicler of Creole life and translator of romantic French literature in New Orleans; the author of a book on life in the Caribbean. He would come to a place and fall in love, blindly, desperately in love. Then the place would cease being the place he loved and Hearn's love would turn to hate. When he was in love, he wrote lavish, rapturous prose. But when he was disappointed, he railed, and his damning attacks were of the sort punctuated by veins protruding in the forehead and occasional sprays of spittle. Moderation was not Hearn's strong suit, and this made him, in crucial ways, all wrong for Japan. At least it made him all wrong for the Japan he found in the last years of the nineteenth century.

In 1890, Japan was already a generation along in its absorption of Western ways and looks. The country's 250-year self-imposed isolation had been ended thirty-seven years before in the waters off Shimoda by Commodore Perry and his fleet of "Black Ships." And while some in Japan saw the coming of the West as nothing less than the invasion of all things barbaric, many others found it the breath of a new world. Hearn was not among the latter. He had lived in the West and had no further use for it. He arrived in Japan forty years old, homeless and searching for paradise, which was odd because he had never displayed more than a passing interest in the place.

He wrote of Japan occasionally in letters. He studied Buddhism. He visited the Japan exhibit at the 1884 New Orleans World Exposition, returning several times to look at the collection of prints, cotton and paper insects, and pictures of kites against the sun. It was not Japan that beckoned Hearn, but what he held Japan to mean. Japan meant the Orient and the Orient—he used the word over and over—was a symbol for all to which he aspired. "I'm trying," he wrote to a friend while still in New Orleans, "to find the Orient at home." *Harper's* magazine was interested in stories. The Canadian Pacific Railroad offered to pay his way in return for an article about the voyage. Hearn had a book in mind, a book about life among the Japanese. He thought he would stay for a year. His announcement on the morning of his arrival, however, was remarkably prescient.

He leaped in. On his first day in Yokohama he deposited his bag in his hotel and set out in a ricksha. He marveled at the small houses and the narrow streets and the ideograms written on signs, banners, and his ricksha driver's coat—"figures that cry out to the eyes, words that smile or grimace like faces." The day was an introduction filled with promise. At his first Buddhist temple the monk spoke English and talked with him about the concept of the soul. At his first Shinto shrine he saw cherry trees covered with white blossoms. People smiled at him. He stopped himself from going into shops because he wanted to buy at each one.

"What you really wanted to buy is not the contents of the shop," he wrote. "You want the shop and the shopkeeper, and the street of shops with their draperies and inhabitants, the whole city and the bay and the mountains begirdling it, and Fujiyama's white witchery overhanging it in the speckless sky, all Japan, in very truth, with its magical trees and luminous atmosphere, with all its cities and towns and temples, and forty millions of the most lovable people in the universe."

Years later, after finding the notes from his early days, he wrote to a friend, "I asked myself, 'How came you to go mad?—absolutely mad?' It was the same kind of madness as the first love of a boy."

But on that first day he decided immediately and surely that the West paled in comparison to what he'd found. The alphabet could not compete with ideograms. Western paintings "valued at more than the worth of a whole Japanese street" did not contain as much "real art" as a Japanese print selling for less than a penny. Even the Western foot, bound as it was by stiff shoes, had little to recommend it aesthetically compared to the sandaled foot of the Japanese. He was so taken by what he saw, and so weary of what he'd left, that even in the simple act of kneeling he sensed a grace in the Japanese that Westerners could not match.

Yet he was not beyond an Occidental mistake. When an old priest brought him a bowl of hot water—the shrine could not afford to offer its guests tea—Hearn dropped in some coins. But even the error could not spoil the sense of being someplace otherworldly:

"Everybody looks at you curiously; but there is never anything disagreeable, much less hostile in the gaze; most commonly it is accompanied by a smile or half smile. And the ultimate consequence of all these kindly curious looks and smiles is that the stranger finds himself thinking of fairy-land. Hackneyed to the degree of provocation this statement no doubt is. . . . To find one's self suddenly in a world where everything is upon a smaller and daintier scale than with us, —a world of lesser and seemingly kinder beings . . . a world where all movement is slow and soft, and voices are hushed, — a world where land, life and sky are unlike all that one has known elsewhere, —this is surely the realization, for imaginations nourished with English folklore, of the old dream of a World of Elves."

The day ended with a dream. Hearn dreamed of Japanese ideograms rushing past him. They pulsated, as if alive. Earlier in the day, as he walked down a shrine's long stairway, he thought of the moment when the priest had brought him before the altar. Expecting a god's image, he had found a mirror. In the mirror he saw himself.

"Then the mockery of the mirror recurs to me. I am beginning to wonder whether I shall ever be able to discover that which I seek—outside of myself! That is, outside of my own imagination."

He journeyed, as always, alone. First he severed himself from the past. The means was his temper, which was quick to ignite and volcanic. Hearn got angry at his editor at *Harper's*. He decided he did not like the terms of their agreement and the way his work was edited and the higher fee being paid to his illustrator. He wrote a poisonous letter. He followed up this letter with nastier ones. *Harper's* responded tamely. He wrote, "What do I care about your vulgar Magazine, anyhow?" *Harper's* got upset. Hearn replied, "Please to understand that your resentment has for me less than the value of a bottled fart, and your bank account less consequence than a wooden shithouse struck by lightening [*sic*]." Then Hearn broke with a friend who once supported him. He decided the friend was cheating him. There is no clear indication why Hearn reacted this way toward his editor and his friend other than that they appeared to have bothered him. But then people were always doing things that bothered Hearn.

When the spate of angry letters ended, Hearn was cut off, with no means of support. He tutored a boy in English. Then, hearing that the Japanese government was looking for teachers, he found an appointment in Matsue, a small town on the western coast of Japan.

"I am afraid I must resign myself to melt into this Orient and be buried in it," he wrote. The tone was strangely wistful; the locale was just what he had had in mind.

Hearn would find in Matsue Japan as he wanted it to be. Later he was forced to move on. Matsue reappeared in moments. The moments passed quickly and when they did, Hearn rushed to find them again. But the further he went from Matsue, and the longer he lived in a Japan that did not resemble the place of his dream, the more desperate his search became.

And if that other Japan, the Japan that was "telegraph lines and newspapers and steamships" was plainly visible in Yokohama, he did not see it.

"Here I am," he wrote to a friend, "in the land of dreams. . . ."

Had he been alone in his compulsion, Hearn could have been dismissed as an aberration, albeit one with a tale to tell. But he was not alone, just exceptional.

Yet to find what he saw when he looked at Japan, and what all the enthusiasts after him still saw, clearer heads were necessary. Unfettered passion has its attractions; but seeing an object of desire through unquestioning eyes is like seeing life refracted through not a prism, but a kaleidoscope.

I looked for those in whom the passion had cooled a bit, who cared for Japan but who understood the limitations. I looked for people who were troubled, who might have had their feelings hurt, people who had gone beyond the romance in its adolescent form.

I looked and found five people, each of whom intersected with Japan at a different point. One was a baseball player. One was a businessman. There was a missionary couple who had lived in the same small town for thirty-seven years. There was also the woman from Pittsburgh who did not want to be fingerprinted. And I had my map, the trail of poor Hearn's heart.

In Yokohama Hearn first saw Japan, and in Matsue he fell in love. In Kumamoto that love turned to hate, but in Kobe he sought reconciliation. Finally, in Tokyo, came Hearn's attempt to find in a make-believe world all that the real one could not offer. The stations may have been Hearn's, but the phases were universal. The baseball player, the businessman, the missionaries, and the woman from Pittsburgh had, without knowing it, followed Hearn's worn path. Each had known the joy of Matsue and suffered the disappointment of Kumamoto. Each would seek a peace with Japan, the peace Hearn tried making in Tokyo.

I set off with my map and five guides. I did not want to be seduced. I wanted to see.

✎ ✎ ✎ ✎ ✎ I met Leon Lee when he was on top of the world. He was the best player on a good baseball team, the Yokohama Taiyo Whales. His teammates were his friends. Children lined up for his autograph. He and his wife and children lived in a big house on a hill near the ballpark. Leon played golf at the Yokohama Country Club.

The Whales were his team. Leon sang and drank with his teammates and invited them to his home. Leon was sure that his teammates liked him because when one invited him out to dinner and Leon had to explain that he had dinner plans with another, the rejected fellow said, "But you go out with him all the time."

We met in Yokohama, at a hotel coffee shop, where Leon's face was known. Leon explained to me that just because baseball in Japan looked like baseball at home did not mean the two games had anything in common. Leon knew enough to be confounded; but he was not upset. He was brimming with feeling that comes when life is delivering on all its promise. He looked the part. He was tall and muscular and he smiled easily. He dressed in a purple sports shirt and slacks and the gold on his wrist and around his neck was not ostentatious. When we left, the waiter wished him good luck for the coming season. But there was no luck for Leon Lee the next season, his eighth season in Japan, the season the Whales broke his heart.

Leon thought he had done everything right. He did not threaten. He did not push. He did not laugh—at least he did not laugh out loud—when he heard his manager say, "I want to get away from the rational theory of baseball and try different things"—this following his call for a pitch-out with the bases loaded, thereby automatically walking in a run. Leon knew better than to ask "Why?" When he came to the Whales Leon made himself part of the team. On the road he stayed at his teammates' hotels, rather than the fancy hotels where the foreigners were lodged. When his teammates invited him out to eat Japanese food he refused nothing. And when they saw that he would eat raw fish, they invited him to go singing with them. Leon had a special black suit made so that he could attend teammates' weddings in the appropriate attire. When new foreign players came to Japan they were told to look up Leon, because he could tell them how to behave.

I saw Leon again two years later at the filming of the *Pro Baseball News* quiz show. He was still in Japan and was invited to be a guest, which made him feel good. Foreigners were not invited to be guests on the *Pro Baseball News* quiz show. (*Pro Baseball News* was fifty-five minutes of highlights and items of interest shown every night of the year, even during the off-season when the hosts visited training camps and filmed footage of rookie pitchers fielding sacrifice bunts.) Leon had seen other foreigners on other quiz shows from time to time. But they were Professional Foreigners, those who could dazzle an audience with their fluent Japanese and knowledge of local customs, but who were nonetheless portrayed by their hosts as something akin to dancing bears. "How long have you been in Japan? Twenty-six years? Do you like Japanese food? Can you eat with chopsticks? How very dexterous of you."

Leon wore a gray three-piece suit that was stretched tight across his broad back and shoulders. He wore glasses and looked worried. But in the green room he saw the baseball players. They greeted him with loud hellos and talked with him about pitching and hitting.

When he could not find the right words in Japanese, Leon held his hands as if were holding a bat and demonstrated what he meant. Everyone understood Leon. The shortstop from Hiroshima, a notorious kidder, came up behind him, grabbed his head in an armlock, leaned close to his ear, and started giggling. Leon asked in Japanese, "Who is it?" and the shortstop loosened his grip, pulled back his head, and smiled at him. An old teammate reminded him that he still owed Leon a steak dinner.

The quiz show host wore a gray plaid sports coat and his hair was done in a permanent wave. He talked very quickly, which only made things more unsettling for Leon, who told his interpreter that while he did not get nervous before baseball games he worried before he went on television. The interpreter explained the format, and when the players took their seats on the guest panel she sat by his side.

A practice round was run before they went on the air. The questions came in rapid order. Leon looked lost. He rolled his eyes as if he'd just gotten off a roller coaster. The producers decided to show him the questions in advance. It was the first advantage Leon had ever gotten in a game against the Japanese.

The stage manager said, "Okay?" and they were on the air.

The studio audience was filled with young girls who applauded on cue and laughed with their hands over their mouths. The set was filled with bright lights and had a bright green floor shaped like a baseball field. The host engaged the players in benign chitchat. Leon sat on the end and when the host came to him he asked, "How do you like Japan?" as if Leon had arrived the week before. Leon smiled and said that he liked it just fine. The host joked with the interpreter about getting her phone number.

The contestants were asked to identify a mystery player through clues given by his young son. The son appeared on a videotape and read a story about his father, to the accompaniment of a nursery jingle. Leon listened and picked a name. The others all chose another.

The host said, "Leon, you are the only one who chose him," and Leon offered a weak explanation about hearing something about the player having thick eyebrows. Not only was Leon wrong, but the correct choice was a friend.

The host smiled and said, "Leon, you have no points so far."

He missed another. The host said, "You guessed wrong." But soon Leon found his rhythm. And as he began guessing correctly, the host said to him, "Good thinking."

"*Toki doki*," Leon said.

"Sometimes," said the host, translating Leon's Japanese into English for no apparent reason.

The questions came even faster now; but Leon, with his hidden advantage, answered a few. He scored points, retained his composure, and finished second. The winner was presented with a trophy, a fur coat, and a space heater. The host asked Leon, "As a foreigner, what did you think?" Leon said it was "very exciting to be invited."

He had accepted the role and, as always, played it as was expected. He was grateful, polite, and, despite his edge, finished second, not first. Everyone was pleased with Leon. Afterward we met backstage and Leon asked, "Did I do okay?" I said I thought he had. But that was no longer enough.

Leon still wanted to know why after doing "okay" for so long and in so many ways he could still be hurt the way he was. He believed that there had to be an explanation for this. Leon wanted to know why a romance so sure had gone so wrong.

Eugene Matthews wanted to meet me on Wednesday night, in Tokyo, at the Rocking Chair, his bar. Wednesday night was the early night at Think Laboratory. On Wednesday night Think's sixty employees were supposed to go home to their children and wives. Most everyone left the office by six o'clock instead of eight-thirty or nine. A lot of men went out drinking. Eugene loved Wednesday nights. He could get on his motorcycle or on the commuter train and be in Tokyo in an hour. Tokyo felt about a light-year away from Kashiwa, the bland little town where Eugene lived and worked.

Eugene was a celebrity in Kashiwa. The Kashiwa magazine wrote about him. Salesgirls and checkout girls in town knew Eugene because he flirted with them. If they did not know his name they knew his face because it was rare in Kashiwa for a tall and handsome black man to flirt in Japanese. The girls giggled when Eugene flirted. Flirting was good for Eugene because it eased the considerable tension of being the only foreign employee of Think Laboratory. Flirting was good but Wednesdays were better. On Wednesdays Eugene came to Tokyo and lit up. He smiled his broad smile and his voice got loud and he struck up conversations on the street with women he did not know. It was hard to imagine Eugene without Wednesday nights. Eugene sometimes seemed a likely candidate for spontaneous human combustion. He could not stand still. Eugene would say, "I'm on a mission."

At the Rocking Chair Eugene ordered gin. Then he switched to rum and coke. He told the waitress to tell the owner that Eugene, whom she knew five years ago when he was a model, was here. Eugene drank his drink and lit a cigarette and said he had a story to tell, the story of the company trip to the hot spring. Whenever Eugene told a story about the company he talked about Tatsuo Shigeta, who owned it.

Eugene had been at Think for a year. He had come with a plan. Eugene, who came from a steel town, Sharon, Pennsylvania, had graduated from Harvard and Harvard Law School and then went to work at a big Philadelphia law firm. Eugene liked the people at the firm. But at the firm Eugene was one of many. Even if he made partner he would be one of a few. Eugene wanted to be one of a kind. Rather than practice law, Eugene began thinking about business on an international scale. That is what brought Eugene to Japan.

Eugene Matthews in Japan, however, made no sense at all. His deportment was all wrong. He was twenty-eight years old, broad and tall and quick to smile. Eugene's face was round and handsome and when he smiled, his mouth and eyes opened wide. His voice, impossible to miss, escalated to a shout when he was excited. Eugene had no facility for masking excitement. He had been in Japan once before, on a fellowship for a year after college. He studied the language, learned karate, lived with a Japanese family for six months, and then found a place of his own in Tokyo's Roppongi district, where the foreign models went to be admired. Eugene dated the models and even worked as a model. But Japan confounded him because people did not react the way he wanted to see people react, which was spontaneously and effusively. Eugene liked being outrageous. This made people look at him as they might look at a man who'd fallen asleep in a bowl of spaghetti—a response that made Eugene want to tweak the public nose. Once, on a subway with some friends, no longer able to tolerate the remoteness around him, Eugene started clapping his hands. No one claps his hands on the subways of Tokyo. No one plays "Ramona" on the saxophone or solicits funds as they might in the great cities of America. At night, people will get drunk and retch on each other. But they do not clap. And they most certainly do not chant "hey, hey, hey," which is what Eugene did to accompany his clapping. Soon he was parading up and down the car, clapping, chanting, and exhorting the half dozen passengers to join in. And for perhaps only the second or third time in recorded history, they did. When the train stopped and more people got on, Eugene, whose demeanor was infectious, got them to join in, too. Now the whole car was clapping and chanting "hey, hey, hey." A drunk got so excited that he started climbing the length of the car on the standees' rings but missed a ring and fell on his face. The chanting was fun for a while. But then Eugene's stop came and he had to get off. This was, in a sense, a metaphor for his first stay in Japan: the journey was a kick, but there was nothing to be gained in going on.

Eugene was no longer thinking of Japan in terms of pleasure. Eugene wanted to know. Having looked to Japan and, like so many others, seen the future, Eugene wanted to acquire knowledge that would set him apart, apart from all the investment bankers who'd moved to Tokyo, the securities traders and stock analysts. He wanted to know Japan so well that he could offer explanations for hefty fees. This would truly make him stand apart, he believed, because Westerners who knew the Japanese intimately were rare.

But to do so would require a deep immersion. He would have to join a Japanese company and see not only how business was done but how the office worked, how conflict was addressed, how decisions were made, how the games were played.

Eugene had big plans. Perhaps he might be the president of his own company. Perhaps he might be a consultant to important people. Perhaps he might be president of the United States. Eugene liked entertaining that notion. His parents had both died and in the absence of a home, Eugene had found a close approximation in his lofty dreams. Eugene worked in Think Laboratory's two-man international sales division. His starting salary, $25,000 a year, represented a significant pay cut from that of his law firm. Eugene did not mind. He did mind the elephantine pace at which business in Japan proceeded—Eugene possessed a mind as restless as it was quick—and having to type his own letters.

Shigeta insisted upon it. Shigeta did his own copying and answered his own phone. Shigeta, who was forty-six, tall and rumpled, worked every day and late into the night and work was all he talked about. Think Laboratory made the cylinders that made the gravure printing system especially cheap and fast. Shigeta had cornered ninety-five percent of the Japanese market. He wanted more and he wanted Eugene to help him get it.

Shigeta had certain views on how to do this. Eugene had others. Their differences would be overlooked on the company trip. But they would not be overlooked much longer.

The company assembled on the bullet train platform at 8:15 A.M. The train departed twenty-seven minutes later. Then the drinking began. People ate their breakfasts and drank beer. It did not take long for people to get drunk. Eugene was not one for getting drunk before lunch. But he was told, "There are no days off at the company. You have to get drunk."

The first lottery had preceded the drinking. This was the lottery to determine seats on the train. Other lotteries followed, lotteries for dinner seats and room assignments at the hot spring inn, all of which were meant to force people into randomly selected friendships within the company. The thinking was explained to Eugene this way: "Everybody has to like everybody." Eugene did not protest, even when he found out that going away with the company meant staying with the company and setting aside selfish desires—such as the tour of the motorcycle racetrack Eugene hoped to make. Eugene did not go to the motorcycle racetrack. He played miniature golf with everyone else.

Teams were chosen by lottery. "I thought I was gonna kick ass," Eguene told me. "I got to the first hole and did this back shot. One of the girls said, 'You're really good at this.'" Meanwhile, his nemesis in the office, Nagase, the international sales manager in charge of everything but America—that was Eugene's—announced, "I am a golf man." Nagase was fifty-five and prone to declarations about his worldliness. He would say, "I am international man" and "I am outside Japanese mind." He would say to Eugene, "You do not know international way." On the first hole Nagase shot a 21. Then it began to rain.

At the hot spring inn, Eugene's name in the lottery came up with that of Yamaguchi, the plant manager. Yamaguchi was gruff and blunt and had been with Shigeta for the twenty years since Shigeta founded Think Laboratory. When they got to their rooms Eugene lay down and Yamaguchi said, "Are you sick? Tired? You didn't drink anything."

Eugene fell asleep. When he woke up people were standing in a circle around him, watching him sleep.

"Eugene," someone asked, "how big is your penis?"

Eugene did not answer.

"Eugene," asked another, "how long can you can have sex for?"

Eugene did not say.

He rose and announced that he was going to the hot spring. Everyone followed. A parade formed behind Eugene. More and more people joined when they heard that Eugene was going to the hot spring. Eugene would have to be naked at the hot spring and people wanted to see what he looked like naked.

By the time Eugene got to the hot spring, not only people from the company but other guests of the inn had crowded inside to watch. Even Shigeta came to see.

Eugene entered the changing area. He took off his robe.

"Ah ha!" said the people when they looked at Eugene.

Eugene sang after dinner. He came to the long banquet room where the low tables were set, and picked his number for the seating lottery. The people from the company wore cotton robes, except for two young men from the plant who dressed like the Blues Brothers in black porkpie hats and dark glasses. Eugene saw how excited people were about the banquet meal and understood that the men he worked with seldom ate so well. Hostesses poured their beer and *sake* and engaged them in idle banter. And though the men had hoped there would be geisha—"I want geisha," someone grumbled, "this is company trip; it wouldn't be company trip without geisha"—the hostesses were adept at flattery and the men were pleased. Eugene looked at the men and at the hostesses and at the four women from the company who were the only women there besides the hostesses. Everyone was happy. Even he and Nagase were getting along. When a hostess began telling Eugene how well he was doing with Japanese food and chopsticks, Nagase told her, "He can eat anything. He's not a normal foreigner."

When the time came to sing, Eugene thought of singing his favorite Japanese song, "Falling in Love." Shigeta liked the way Eugene sang "Falling in Love." He also liked the way Eugene sang "The Star Spangled Banner." Eugene knew how to sing for an audience.

He considered "Falling in Love," but wanted to sing "Amazing Grace," which was his mother's favorite song. The song was not on the music machine, which played the music for people to sing along with. Eugene came to the front of the room, took the microphone, and announced, "First I'm going to sing 'Amazing Grace,' which is an old church song." He sang *a capella*.

"It's quiet. Quiet," Eugene told me that night at the Rocking

Chair as he recounted the company trip. "No pins dropping. I'm into it. I'm in church. Hitting the high notes."

When he was done he sang another song. He sang a jazzy version of "The Star Bangled Banner." Eugene won the Company Trip Singing Award.

He woke up at four in the morning, when his roommates were sleeping. It had been a raucous night. After dinner the young men began complaining about there only being four women on the trip—and one of them was Mrs. Shigeta—because there was no chance for the traditional company trip frivolity. They danced in the disco for a while. Mrs. Shigeta, who kept the company books, danced too. Her husband declined. After eight dance songs, the singing resumed and with the singing, the drinking. When Eugene went to sleep, Yamaguchi the plant manager came into the room and woke him.

"This is company trip," he told Eugene.

"I'm asleep."

"You drank a lot during dinner," said Yamaguchi the plant manager, "so it's okay."

When Eugene woke, everyone was curled up on his futon, sleeping. Eugene felt a bond with the men in his room, an attachment almost as strong as the one he felt for Shigeta. It was Shigeta who had hired him when others might have balked at hiring a black man—let alone a foreigner—in a country that still looked upon blacks not as a people but as another species, a backward and frightening species. Eugene respected Shigeta for many reasons; but he respected him most because he, too, had had a big plan and had made his plan come alive in the company he created. Shigeta was a high school graduate; and in Japan high school graduates often end up making deliveries. Eugene had plans for Shigeta and his company. Shigeta had plans and dreams, too. Together they sat and drank and talked about their plans, both assuming they were dreamers of a common dream.

But as he looked about the room and watched his new friends sleep, Eugene was not thinking of the future.

"Everyone's lying there," he said, remembering the dawn of his first company trip. "And it's our group, our team."

✦ ✦ ✦ ✦ ✦ In Aizu-Takada, where Armin and Evelyn Kroehler lived, the rice fields were covered with flaky dirt that blew like dust when the wind picked up. The spring was the driest anyone could remember. It had been a mild winter with little snow and so the runoff from the mountains was meager. The farmers planted their seedlings and waited for the rain to come and help flood their rice fields. The skies threatened. Dark clouds came and, for a minute or two, a light rain fell. Then the skies cleared and the farmers were left waiting beside their dry fields. In the mornings a fine mist still covered the mountains. But the sun soon burned the mist away and made the mornings pleasant for the Kroehlers, who began each day with a walk.

They said hello to everyone they passed. The farm wives, in wide white bonnets and baggy pants, greeted them; but the school-children who did not know the Kroehlers, did not know that they had come to the town before they were born, and before their parents were born, huddled together and giggled. Armin and Evelyn smiled at them and, in English, gently said, "Good morning." The children who knew the Kroehlers from the church kindergarten, Sunday worship services, the town Christmas pageant, or English conversation classes offered tentative hellos before hurrying off to school.

The town was quiet in the morning, as it was most of the day. The main street, with its long row of single-story shops, was all but deserted. The only faces were those of the children or the elderly. It was rare to see a young adult's face in Aizu-Takada, now that the young people had decided that the future was no longer on the farms, but in the cities. Their parents and grandparents remained behind. The young people visited in the summer and winter, when the big companies closed down their factories for a week.

The Kroehlers walked along the main street, passing shops they had been passing for the thirty-seven years since they came to Aizu-Takada as United Church of Christ missionaries committed to life-times in Japan. Little had changed. The street was paved now. Some shops and homes had their wooden walls covered with aluminum siding and their thatched roofs with sheets of tin. The older shops were dark inside and their ceilings sagged. The Kroehlers left the commercial strip and passed narrow streets lined with small, wooden homes whose owners kept little flowerbeds near the doorways. Drainage ditches sluiced along the roadside. The Kroehlers reached a wooded grove and a path that led to the village shrine. A row of tall stone lanterns marked the way to the shrine.

It was an old shrine whose wooden buildings had faded to a dull, lifeless brown. During the war years, young men from town and from the nearby mountain villages came to the shrine before leaving for battle, and prayed to the emperor and the shrine gods. Though emperor worship had been abolished after the war and Shinto was no longer the state religion, the shrine retained a prominent position. The town chamber of commerce had built its headquarters on the shrine's grounds. Armin wondered whether this was a harbinger of the rise of the faith that had given Japan's nationalism its religious foundation.

Aizu-Takada had conservative roots. A hundred years before, the region had been one of feudalism's last ramparts. In nearby Aizu-Wakamatsu stood the remains of a fourteenth-century castle that had been the stronghold of the shogun's half brother. The castle fell in 1868, with the conquest of the shogun's defenders. Near its grounds were the graves of the nineteen teenagers of the White-Tiger Company, loyalists to the shogun who committed suicide when the castle was burned by the emperor's army—the army of the new order. Armin was not so sure that the spirit of the feudal era had been buried with those teenagers. When people from the Aizu district gathered for festivals they still performed the Dance of the White-Tiger Company.

In the morning, however, the shrine compound belonged to the roosters who might have woken the town's late sleepers had there not been the daily seven A.M. loudspeaker announcement from the police patrol car warning drivers to watch out for children on their jway to school. It was impossible to sleep late in Aizu-Takada.

The Kroehlers left the compound and, along the side of the road, passed a cluster of flowers, oranges, and packaged food left as an offering. There had been a fatal automobile accident on the site and the offering was consolation for the spirit of the deceased. The Kroehlers walked along the riverbank, which had been cleared, paved, and landscaped with shrubbery. There were stone animals for the children to sit on. Beer cans and food wrappers were tossed along the bank and sometimes the Kroehlers brought trash bags and cleared the litter. One morning they were stopped by a man who insisted upon apologizing on behalf of the town for the mess. The walkway was also sprinkled with white petals, blown from the cherry trees that had begun to bloom. With the blossoms came cherry blossom viewing parties, and with the parties came the litter, and with the litter came the drunks who sometimes, late at night, appeared at the Kroehlers' door.

The other night a drunken man stood at the door and asked to come in. He told Armin, "I want to talk to you about English." The man told Armin that he knew him and Armin invited him inside. Then he asked Armin if he could call him a cab. Armin asked the man where he lived. He got his keys, drove him home and invited him to come back and talk. The man never came back; but that was not surprising. Many people came to the Kroehlers in a moment of need but, once sober, dispensed with a return visit.

"We used to have more drunks come to the door,'" Evelyn said when I asked the Kroehlers about who sought them out.

"They don't come around anymore," said Armin. "It's people who have a feeling of being lost. They say they have *nayami*."

"Worries," Evelyn said. "Troubles."

"Sometimes it's a psychological thing and they're trying to find some kind of peace. I don't know. What do you think?" Armin asked Evelyn. "There're all kinds of motives. There have been people who've been emotionally unstable. Sometimes the young people are looking for something to give their life to. I think sometimes they're people who are lonely."

The Kroehlers listened as these people spoke of their problems. They did not preach. They did not press their faith. They listened and hoped that people might see that answers to their troubles might lie in Christianity. Some people came back and wanted to hear more, but most did not. Still, the Kroehlers worked at spreading their message by making friends. When they came to Aizu-Takada they asked the local pastor, a forceful man named Endo, what he wanted of them. "Stay for twenty-five years and you will have succeeded," Pastor Endo told them.

They stayed, reared five children, taught English, conducted Bible classes, took part in any number of church and community functions, and in all ways made themselves available. They listened as people came to them to carp about neighbors and friends, because the Kroehlers were close enough to confide in, but still remote enough as foreigners to be neutral confidants. A lot of what they heard had nothing to do with God and faith and conscience. Sometimes people just needed to talk. Sometimes the Kroehlers wondered whether they were making any difference at all.

They doubted not their faith but themselves. For a while they even considered going home. In the first years in Aizu-Takada, Armin contracted hepatitis and Evelyn had to care for him and their two eldest children, Ken and Kaye. Evelyn boiled their water and cooked their meals on a wood-burning stove in the kitchen of the first Western house ever seen in Aizu-Takada. Armin lay in bed, Evelyn fed her babies, and the neighborhood children gathered by the curtainless windows to watch. Evelyn moved to the next room and the children followed her. Women's groups conducted tours of the house and stood at the bathroom door to see the toilet flush. "Your house is not the zoo," Evelyn's mother wrote in a letter to her daughter. The Kroehlers hung curtains. The tours stopped.

The doubting and frustration did not, even though Evelyn was, in a sense, home. She had grown up in Japan, the daughter of missionaries. Her father had also been an amateur photographer, which was the pretext the secret police had used to accuse him of spying and imprison him for six months in solitary confinement just after Pearl Harbor. Evelyn, her mother, and her sister had been placed in detention and had not known if he was dead or alive. When her father returned—in time to be sent back to America with his wife and children—he worried only that his children might not believe he was an innocent man.

When the war ended, Evelyn's parents returned to Japan. Her father died in Japan. Her mother, at eighty-eight, still lived in the city of Morioka. Evelyn's parents had made friends. They believed that even those who were not friends and who had done cruel things were not inherently cruel men, but simply men following orders. They forgave. Evelyn, too, wanted to come back. The day she first saw Armin and learned that he was going to Japan as a missionary— he told the mission board he would go where he was needed; the board sent him to Japan—she came home and told her sister that she had met the man she was going to marry.

They remained a couple who held hands and kissed each other hello and good-bye. Evelyn made Armin laugh. Armin could be hard on himself, critical of all the ways he sensed he was failing at his work. He was a serious man who suffered from a nervous stom- ach. He was tall and rangy, with long arms and big hands. He was a full head taller than Evelyn, who was often bubbly and seldom tentative. In the mornings, they put on their sneakers and headed off for their walk. They walked close together, a couple unmistakable to everyone in town, except for children who did not know them and who pointed and said, "Foreigners."

Armin was sixty-five. He was ready to retire. He and Evelyn asked the United Church of Christ headquarters for replacements. No one volunteered. Missionaries wanted to go to poor places where the needs were urgent. Japan was unique among nations to which missionaries had come when times were hardest: in a single gen- eration the once poor had eclipsed those missionaries in income. The Kroehlers believed that while the needs in Japan were not dire, there was still important work to be done. Wealth made it important. Armin believed that if Japan could embrace a Christian ethic and come to see the world in universal rather than parochial terms, it could be a force for good. Japan could share its great wealth. When the United Church of Christ wanted to close its rural missions in Japan because, it believed, the work was done, Armin wrote a passionate letter, insisting that the work was not done.

"There is a struggle going on today for the soul of Japan," Armin wrote. "In which direction will the country go?"

The people of Aizu-Takada wanted the Kroehlers to stay. And when the church headquarters reduced their subsidy, the local churches made up the difference. The Kroehlers served a purpose beyond teaching and listening: they were a conduit to the world beyond Aizu-Takada, and the world beyond Japan. They introduced new ideas. They reported on what they had seen in America when they came back from their trips. Although some of the district's pastors were concerned only with the administration of their churches, others applied what they heard from the Kroehlers. They organized marches for peace. They conducted Bible classes in English. They joined clubs where books were discussed.

But now the Kroehlers worried that when they left Aizu-Takada, no one would come to take their place. Perhaps there might be an occasional English teacher on a short-term mission. But no families were offering to come to Aizu-Takada. Though he was quick to diminish the importance of his role—"Oh, they'll get along without me"—Armin wondered what would happen to the district if it were cut off from outside ideas.

The situation, he explained, was analogous to a principle of physics—to centrifugal forces pulling the flow away from the center, and centripetal forces directing everything inward. Experience had taught the Kroehlers that so much of what came into Japan did so centripetally. It was absorbed and it stayed and it was not shared.

The Kroehlers volunteered to stay on, hoping that someone new might be found.

✔ ➤ ✎ ❧ ➸   The photographers converged on Kathy Morikawa a block from the courthouse. They stood on stepladders to take her picture. They raced to her, pushing to get close. Kathy walked past them and into the courthouse. There were no empty seats in the small, steamy courtroom.

The photographers were waiting when Kathy emerged. There might have been a hundred of them. They clogged the doorway, blocking her path. They flashed their flashbulbs in her eyes. Kathy pushed past the photographers as reporters ran to the telephones and alerted their offices that the first American had been found guilty of violating the Alien Registration Law. If she did not pay her fine she would go to the workhouse.

The reporters asked Kathy, "What was your impression of today?"

Kathy said she was not surprised, but she was disappointed in the judge's ruling that foreigners and Japanese were different, and that it was therefore proper to require foreign residents to be fingerprinted periodically and carry alien registration booklets wherever they went.

Kathy had not been fingerprinted. She had gone to her city office on the appointed day and when the clerk asked for her fingerprint for her alien registration booklet, she had refused. The clerk had pleaded with her to give her fingerprint, but Kathy would not. Jun, her husband, was very proud of her.

He and Kathy had gone out for curry. When they finished their curry they went home to their house in the Tokyo suburbs, assuming they would resume their pleasant and not terribly exceptional life. Kathy would continue teaching English. Jun would return to the university where he taught international relations.

But that night the newspapers began calling for comment. In Pittsburgh, her hometown, the *Press* ran a front-page story under the headline: EX-PITTSBURGHER STIRS UP FUSS IN JAPAN. The story noted that Kathy had been a member of the Future Teachers of America and the Girls Athletic League and was remembered by one classmate as someone "who didn't have much to say." The same Kathy—now Morikawa, then Kunold—was now a subject of debate in a committee of the National Diet.

Still, the Morikawas had believed that Kathy's transgression would, at worst, mean a modest fine for Kathy and an admonition to Jun that he keep his wife in line. Kathy did not expect that she would be interrogated, indicted, tried, convicted, and subject to up to five days in the workhouse for what had seemed to her a simple statement about a law she regarded as foolish and unfair.

"We thought the government might respond in a reasonable way," Jun said.

"I didn't think anybody would care that much if I gave my fingerprint," said Kathy. "I wasn't out to change the world. I was kind of thrown into a role that I'm not the right type for."

She did seem an unlikely rebel. She smiled quickly, as if to please. She was prone to a nervous giggle. Her face was round, and her hair was red and curly. Kathy's voice was especially high-pitched, which made her sound, unintentionally, the way Japanese women did when they tried to sound their most feminine. She did not like speaking publicly. She liked to take her time and collect her thoughts, unlike Jun, whom she let do her talking for her early on in her case. Jun was the sort of teacher who scolded his students when they thought that being different meant wearing different kinds of clothing. He dreamed of establishing a seminar house in the country where people from different countries could come together and discuss the issues of the world. Jun collected brochures from architects on designs for such a seminar house. Jun dreamed, and then he began to plan.

It was Jun who exuded the passion and the sense of outrage. I made the mistake of confusing Kathy's strength with her girlish voice. Kathy's father had been a plumber on construction projects. He died at forty-five. Kathy's father wanted to be an officer in his local union because he did not think the local was doing what it should have done to protect its members. He was a shy man and so afraid of speaking before an audience that he took a public-speaking course. Kathy, shy like her father, liked to think she had some of his will in her. It took Kathy several months and speeches to dispense with using her husband as a substitute. She spoke for herself, in English and Japanese. The speeches took on an angry edge.

"I didn't have illusions about changing things," Kathy told me. "But changing the law was not the only reason for not going along with it. You may not change what's going on but you don't have to go along with it."

It was not the law, as such, that Kathy objected to, although that was how the government saw her action. It was the principle behind the law, the idea that there existed two sorts of people—the Japanese, and those who were not Japanese. Kathy believed that governments had a right to keep their borders secure. But she objected to the principle of exclusion that dictated that a person born in Japan, raised according to Japanese sensibilities, and educated in Japanese schools was still a foreigner if his parents were not Japanese.

Kathy's concern extended beyond her own case: there were those who had been in Japan long before she had ever considered coming to the country, especially Koreans, who, convinced that Japanese citizenship was not a passport to acceptability, did not become naturalized Japanese.

Many were children and grandchildren of the 700,000 Koreans brought to Japan to work as slave laborers during the thirty-five-year occupation of Korea. But the reason for their being in the country was peripheral. What mattered was their current nationality; if it was not Japanese the government wanted them fingerprinted periodically, just as the wartime rulers of Manchuria had required fingerprinting of the indigenous, non-Japanese population to check the spread of anti-Japanese dissidents and to keep enforced laborers from running away.

Jun drew this analogy for his students when he explained the government's thinking about inside and outside: there was a candy called Kintaro, named for a famous hero. The candy was made in a long roll, with Kintaro's face running all the way through. No matter where you cut the candy, you still had a piece with Kintaro's face on it. Every piece had the same face. That, insisted Jun, was what the government wanted to see when it looked at the nation: every face the same. Everyone playing by the same rules. The faces that were not the same, those suspected of playing by different rules, were to be separated out for special scrutiny.

"But it's kind of vague and amorphous," Kathy said of the discrimination that grew out of the legal distinction between Japanese and others. "It's hard to get a handle on it. People say, 'Oh, you're just making it up.' "

So amorphous, and so endemic, was that discrimination that it was difficult to find an issue suitable for protest. Fingerprinting became the issue. It was a difficult issue. Other countries fingerprinted. Governments had the right to know who lived within their borders. But in Japan, Kathy argued, fingerprinting was a tool for maintaining a parochial and, in many cases, cruel and arrogant distinction.

And so she did not give her fingerprint.

Kathy had been in Japan for nine years. She had come alone, at twenty-three, her parents dead and Pittsburgh holding nothing for her. She had worked on an Indian reservation in South Dakota, which had brought an unexpected benefit: when Kathy applied for enrollment at an international university in Denmark (she wanted to go someplace new; the school's tuition was modest and she had some inheritance money to spend) the admissions office mistook her for a Native American. They rushed along her application, and admitted her quickly, although others—her husband among them—had waited years to enter.

At the school she met Jun, and other Japanese who became her friends. She knew nothing of Japan. She had not thought of going there. But when the six-month semester ended, Kathy decided that with no place else beckoning, and with good feelings about the Japanese she had met in Denmark, she would go to Japan and learn the language.

Her Japanese friends took care of her. They barely let her out of their sight. They invited her to their parties. One neighbor even killed her cockroaches because he knew Kathy could not stand the sight of them. For a year Kathy enjoyed the uncomplicated pleasures

Japan extended to those who were innocent and vulnerable. Then, one day, a friend invited Kathy to her house.

"I'm happy you are my friend," she told Kathy, "because I can practice my English with you."

Kathy's feelings toward Japan grew more complicated. She wearied of the attention directed at her simply because she was a foreigner and therefore a curiosity. She had felt like a movie star; but she wanted the staring to stop.

Kathy saw the limitations of a foreigner's place. Luckily, Jun returned—after Denmark he had gone to Nigeria—and their relationship blossomed. Friends began drifting out of her life. She and Jun married and moved to the countryside. Kathy wrote and wove and Jun wrote his master's thesis. Kathy was happy in the countryside: if Japan was to be limited, then it would be limited to Jun, who did not see the world according to nationality.

Others had refused fingerprinting before Kathy. But almost all of those twenty-seven people were Korean; and Koreans, Kathy learned, were more easily overlooked than was a Westerner. Within a year of her conviction, ten thousand people had refused fingerprinting and the South Korean government was calling upon its one-time ruler to change.

The Japanese government considered change; but it also made it clear to Kathy that it cared little for criticism, especially from a guest. When she applied for a permit to enter the country after a trip abroad, Kathy was told that she could not have one because she had not been fingerprinted. She could leave Japan, but she might not be allowed back in.

That was when Kathy, who was seeing just how much her father's daughter she really was, sued the government of Japan.

Aware as she was of what was reasonable to expect from Japan, Kathy did not think it unreasonable to dissent. She believed in Thoreau's principle of a citizen's duty to disobey bad laws. Kathy was saying simply that if the government wanted to treat foreign residents of many years' standing in a way that it would not treat its own people, it would have to do so without her.

Later, Kathy would discover that it was not the government alone that wanted her to conform: even in dissent there was a way things were done. Those who wanted to be too different were chastised for their selfishness. In Japan protest was a group activity; the conscience of the group was a matter for debate and ballot, like the selections of group president and recording secretary.

That Kathy wanted none of this did not matter.

2

Matsue

*L*afcadio Hearn headed West, away from the cities, toward Matsue. He traveled with a Japanese friend. They left Yokohama by train and at the Inland Sea hired a ricksha for the journey through the mountains. They rode through valleys. Rice fields rose along the sides of the mountains. The terraced fields looked to Hearn like long, green flights of stairs. They rode ever higher. The air was warm and still. The distant view was covered with mist. They rode past thick columns of cedars and pine.

The villages grew smaller. In the hamlets along the way Hearn saw naked children and men wearing only white loincloths in the heat. People studied him. They stopped at a hot spring where the owner explained that he had seen only one other foreigner and could not tell whether it had been a man or a woman.

They passed Buddhist temples and as they rode deeper into the countryside, they stopped at a Shinto shrine dedicated to gods that watched over horses and cattle. When their drivers were too weary to go on, they stopped at an inn whose elderly owner insisted upon washing Hearn's back in the bath. Hearn stuffed himself on rice, eggs, and vegetables prepared by the innkeeper's wife who apologized for not serving him enough. He admired the gold-flowered lacquerware and the little *sake* cups decorated with figures of leaping shrimp.

The night in the inn fell during the Festival of the Dead. The innkeeper's young grandson led Hearn by the light of a crimson paper lantern to an open field. Against the moonlit sky Hearn saw the outline of a sloping temple roof. In the distance he saw the white lights of the cemetery and the profiles of tombs. A young girl beat a great, deep-voiced drum. The dancers assembled in a row and began to move in a slow procession.

"I am bewitched, bewitched by the ghostly weaving of hands, by the rhythmic gliding of feet, above all by the flitting of the marvelous sleeves—apparitional, soundless, velvety as a flitting of great tropical bats," he wrote. "No, nothing I ever dreamed of could be like this."

The pleasures of the trip did not end when his steamer docked at the foot of the Ohashi Bridge and deposited him in Matsue. The river was wide and emptied into a lake. Mountains ringed the lake, mountains whose shades of green were diffused by the sunlight. Hearn crossed the wooden footbridge and at the other end found a room at an inn. The inn looked out onto the lake and the mountains and the river. From his room, at dawn, he listened to the dull echo of a temple bell. He listened to the clopping of wooden sandals across the bridge, to the songs of the vegetable and kindling peddlers, to the clapping of hands as the townspeople signaled the attention of the gods. He opened his paper screen window, looked out onto the river and saw a single junk.

People were kind to him. On his first day at school the dean who would become a friend, Sentaro Nishida, escorted him about the new school buildings, explaining the guidelines for texts and schedules. English signs had been painted onto the doorways for Hearn's benefit, so that he would not get lost in a sea of ideograms. Nishida brought him to the teachers' room and introduced him about. Then he brought Hearn to his teenage students. The classroom was large and its walls were whitewashed. The students wore dark blue uniforms. One, with captain's stripes on his sleeve, barked

"Stand up!" The students snapped to attention. "Bow down!" commanded the captain, who spoke in English, just for Hearn. The students bowed in unison. The obliging Hearn bowed back.

"I think," he wrote within a month of his arrival, "I shall be very happy in Matsue . . . ."

The city's 35,000 inhabitants lived in ten thousand homes set along thirty-three streets which, in turn, lay across districts still divided by class. The largest district was the merchants' in the center of town, where all the buildings were two stories tall. There was the temple district. And there also remained the district of samurai homes, even though a generation earlier, the samurai had been forced to surrender their swords and status. The wooden, single-story samurai homes sat in a row alongside a moat. High atop the moat, on a hill that gave it both a commanding view and presence, sat the castle that had once been the stronghold of the feudal lords who ruled the province. The castle was built on a base of heavy stones. It ascended like a pagoda, growing ever narrower as it climbed toward the sky. Its black roof was topped with dragon's horns.

The castle's military usefulness was finished. But on its sizable grounds children could display what they learned in school. In the afternoons Hearn would cut through the castle grounds and watch a group of thirty little boys sing and march. "A pretty spectacle," he wrote. "While they sing they keep time with their little bare feet. If any mistakes are made, they have to sing the verse again." The curriculum at the Middle School included daily bayonet and shooting drills. Students were expected to salute when they passed a teacher. The students sat erect at backless desks that were too small to permit any leaning. When they came together for the prefectural field day, the students gathered on the castle grounds.

Hearn watched the races, drills, and tug-of-war with one hundred students to a side. He liked the dumb-bell exercises best: "Six thousand boys and girls, massed in ranks about 500 deep; six thousand pairs of arms rising and falling exactly together; six thousand pairs of sandaled feet advancing or retreating together . . . six thousand voices chanting at once . . ." At five o'clock, when the games were done, the students and their parents rose to sing the national anthem. They gave three cheers to the emperor.

All of it was evidence for Hearn that the coming of the West had not robbed Japan of what he perceived as its soul. It was a soul that lived, he believed, in the hearts of the young men he taught. Hearn saw nobility in their faces. Their facility at drawing, he concluded, was better by half than that of their Western counterparts. They had a bond with nature. Their compositions especially pleased him because no matter how prosaic the subject the writing always included a moral. The compositions displayed for Hearn not only proper values, but a devotion to tradition. Hearn's students knew that Mount Fuji was to be compared with a white, half-opened, inverted fan; the print of cat's feet with plum flowers; cherry blossoms with white clouds. Their fidelity to what Hearn regarded as the nation's better values was not limited to appropriate analogies: when he asked his seventy-two students to write about their ambitions, nine wrote that they hoped one day to die for the emperor.

"Isn't it grand and beautiful?" he wrote, "and do you wonder that I love it after that?"

Reading his letters, I realized how well I understood what he meant. Though moved by sensations far different than those that enraptured Hearn, I, too, had had moments when Japan transported me.

The pleasures changed with the seasons. In the spring Susan and I went with friends on a picnic to view cherry blossoms. We went to a cemetery and spread our blankets under the trees and alongside the tombs. Families gathered at the gravesites of relatives, opened beer and *sake* bottles, and got very silly. The Japanese did not believe in drawing too broad a distinction between the world of the living and the world of the dead. We drank red wine until the Japanese next to us insisted upon sharing their *sake* and keeping our cups filled. People invited us to dance folk dances. I stood by and watched as a friend joined the circle and tried to keep time with his hands and feet. Children ran under the cherry trees, trying to catch the falling blossoms. Groups of ten and twenty sat in circles and sang sentimental songs. A drunk woman pulled up her shirt as she danced, and everyone kept laughing and drinking and singing.

That summer we went, as Hearn had, to a Bon-Odori, a Dance of the Festival of the Dead. The dance was held in the plaza of the rail station in the Tokyo suburb of Kichijoji. A wooden dance floor was erected in the center of the plaza and on top of the dance floor sat a tower where young men beat a heavy drum. Men and women wore cotton summer kimonos. Their children, in pajamas, ran around in circles and tried to imitate the dance steps of the grown-ups.

In the fall, on National Health and Fitness Day, I watched teams of elderly Japanese in golf hats and matching windbreakers play croquet. They were teams from company "Old Boy Clubs." They went on day trips together and on weekend visits to hot springs. They played quietly, walking slowly from gate to gate, noting their scores. It was an uncluttered scene. And that, I discovered, was why I found such scenes so appealing. The components were plainly visible and remarkably simple—white cherry blossoms, an elemental dance step, silence broken by the tap of a mallet against a wooden ball. Yet set against a backdrop that was almost always neutral, they came at the senses in a burst—a whisper in a silent room, a red dot on a blank canvas.

Of all the seasonal pleasures, however, I liked winter's best.

Winter meant the end of the year, which in turn meant celebrations for forgetting the old year before celebrating the coming of the new. There was a lot of drinking in December in Japan, and late at night the rail terminals were jammed with men in business suits trying to walk without falling down. But after the drunkenness ended the cities grew quiet, an eerie quiet that comes when crowded places are emptying. I remembered a night two days before the end of the year when, at the end of a language lesson, my teacher—who was not supposed to speak to me in anything other than Japanese—leaned forward when I asked about the quiet and explained in whispered English that everyone was going home, to the countryside, to parents and grandparents and ancestral homes. In the coming days, he said, I would see many men and women in kimono. I could not wait.

On New Year's, at midnight, following the hollow ring of a heavy bell, Susan and I found our neighborhood shrine. The shrine was small, wooden, and undistinguished. It sat across the street from a grocery, on meager grounds that always needed tending. It was a bitterly cold night. In the temple courtyard wood fires burned in metal drums. The line to the altar stretched outside of the grounds and down the street. Families were together. One by one neighbors we had not met and whom we would not meet again stepped before the altar, rang the tinny chimes, closed their eyes, clapped their hands twice, and bowed. The bow completed their brief prayer, their call to the gods for protection in the coming year. They stepped down from the altar and took the cup of *sake* that was offered by smiling friends who stood and served at a long white table. Susan and I stood off to the side, reluctant to get in the way. A man asked if he could have his picture taken with us and we complied as others watched and giggled.

We stayed a little longer, and when the time came to leave, I turned to look back at the families on the long line, standing in the cold, their faces lit but barely warmed by the fires in the drums. I heard only the crackle of the burning wood, the rattle of the altar chimes, and the call of the temple bell, ringing 108 times, like all the other temple bells all over Japan, ringing as they had for a thousand years.

By nine-thirty Tatsuo Shigeta's eyes were closing and it was time to go. It was not a late night for Shigeta and Eugene. The night before had been a late night. The night before, they had run into each other in the parking lot of Eugene's sushi bar at two-thirty in the morning and Shigeta had decided he did not want the evening to end.

Eugene and Shigeta stayed at the snack bar till three-thirty. They were back at work the next morning in time for Shigeta's daily 8:05 speech on the terrible shape the company was in and the bleak future that lay before it. A long day followed. By nine-thirty that evening Eugene and Shigeta were sitting in Eugene's sushi bar and Shigeta's eyes were closing. That was when Eugene decided to run home and get his motorcycle so he could show it to Shigeta.

Eugene lived across the street from the sushi bar, in an apartment comprised of two small rooms stacked on top of two equally small rooms in a modified honeycomb arrangement. This did not leave the restless Eugene much pacing room. He slept upstairs, on a futon spread on tatami. The place was serviceable. Eugene slept there. Otherwise he was at work. And when he could find the time, he was on his new, red and shiny Honda 450-cc motorcycle, heading away from Kashiwa.

Kashiwa looked as if it had been built by committee. On the edges of town were rice fields and, next to them, wooden farm-houses with gray tile roofs and paper-screen windows. In the spring the rice planting began; and by the summer, when the air was heavy and still, each farmhouse stood apart, seemingly anchored in its own sea of flooded paddies that shimmered in the sun-light. There was a shopping center downtown and near the shop-ping center a long, covered walkway of rice-cracker shops, noodle shops, boutiques with windows filled with imported fashions, super-markets, stationery shops, coffee shops, and, at the end of the street, a Kentucky Fried Chicken and Baskin-Robbins ice cream stand where the portion sizes did not vary. Newer, taller buildings with stucco or brick fronts sat next to short, older buildings whose faces were wooden and fading to gray. The commercial district spilled into the district of two-story apartment complexes to such a degree that the notion of a district as a separate entity did not apply. You could go from end to end and side to side in Japan, get off at any railway stop, and step into a town that looked just like Kashiwa.

Eugene escaped when he could, which meant when Shigeta did not want to go out for dinner. When they were not working late, and Shigeta did not have dinner with a client, he would ask Eugene to join him. Now Shigeta sat at the sushi bar counter, chatting with the owner; "Miami Vice" in dubbed Japanese was on the TV, but no one was watching. Eugene, on his new motorcycle, came thundering up to the door. Shigeta and the shop owner came outside, and Eugene beamed as they looked his bike over. Eugene invited Shigeta to climb on and Shigeta grabbed the handlebars and gave them a twist back and forth, the way boys do behind the wheel of the family car. Eugene pointed out the bike's features and the two men did a lot of thoughtful nodding. But Shigeta was fading. The sushi bar owner went to get his keys because Shigeta had had a bit to drink and the owner was not going to let him drive.

They watched Eugene drive off. He put on his red helmet and gunned the engine. He sped down the street and the two men watched him lean into the turn. Eugene was still wearing his navy blue suit, and his red bow tie was still knotted at his throat. Had he not had to conduct a tour of the plant for a visiting customer, Eugene would not have worn a jacket and tie to work. He would have worn the royal blue Think Laboratory jacket and pants that all the men—including Shigeta—wore. The women wore smocks which, like the men's uniforms, had their names stitched next to the Think logo. The name Eugene, when sounded out in Japanese, left the bearer with a choice of ideogram: one meant friendly person; the other meant great person. A friend had suggested the latter. Eugene liked the suggestion. People advised Eugene to switch characters in the interest of international harmony and understanding. But Eugene kept the name.

Eugene spent his days in the middle of a row of small gray metal desks that faced another row of small gray metal desks. Four people shared a phone, which spun on its gray metal caddy. The room was lit by fluorescent bulbs. Were the ceiling lower, you could have heard their hum—because the business of Think was conducted in muted voices and with the relative minding of one's own business. Conversation was limited to work-related conversation, especially when Shigeta was in the office. Eugene had quickly sensed that the people of Think were terrified of Shigeta.

Only Shigeta sat alone. His desk sat at the front of the long linoleum-floored, clapboard-walled office whose black metal beams were left exposed. His desk was not walled off. It was distinct from the desks of his employees in that it had its own phone. In fact, Shigeta's desk might have looked like all the other desks were it not for its additions, additions that reminded me of the sort built onto traditional Japanese homes when an aging parent moved in. The additions—a tall safe, squat file cabinets—were covered with the primary feature of the president's desk, which was clutter. Shigeta sat in his Think standard-issue battleship-gray swivel chair, surrounded by stacks of magazines, calendars (at New Year's piles of them arrived at every Japanese office as gifts from other Japanese offices), videotapes, papers, catalogues, namecards, folders, assorted individual sheets of paper of varying shades of yellow, and a blue Think baseball hat.

The desk spoke volumes about the president: there was no aspect of Think's operation in which Shigeta was not intimately involved. Little, if anything, was delegated, not on the firm's technological side, and not in business. From his crowded desk, Shigeta ran his company in the manner he saw fit. Before him sat his wife, who had the only key to the safe and the only access to the bookkeeping computer—this in the tradition of the Japanese wife who handles the family finances. Like everyone at Think, she called her husband *shacho*, "president."

Eugene was hired on a Friday and started on Saturday because, Shigeta said, he had a lot to learn. Eugene learned that in the United States the printing of packaging is done in single impressions and high volume. Not so in Japan, where the volume for a particular run is low, but the turnover on impressions high—a phenomenon dictated by the market. Think's quickly manufactured cylinders had proved ideal in Japan where new products appeared with such frequency and in such eager pursuit of ever-wealthier buyers that exteriors had to be more than presentable: they had to be new. A new line of instant noodles was doomed to be remaindered if its packaging did not fairly grab the buyer by the collar and give a few shakes. The representation of the contents had to be vibrant, exciting, and too good to resist. If it was not, someone else's packaged noodles would be.

Fashion enjoyed a fleeting life in Japan. This was not restricted to consumables. In the course of three years, the frilled lizard was replaced by the koala bear which, in turn, was replaced by the panda as the animal Japan most wanted to hug—and place, as a stuffed replica, on its bedstand. Eugene had arrived at the height of the Koala Era, just as special zoo facilities were being opened in Tokyo and Nagoya for the koalas Australia was sending over. Stores stocked battery-operated koalas that made little purring sounds. For the price of one message unit you could call the Koala Hot Line and hear a chirpy-voiced woman making believe she was a koala who spoke Japanese. There were koala buttons, "Lovely Koala" stationery, koala sweatshirts, and little koalas that could be attached to the eraser end of a pencil. Adults bought these things for themselves, adults with families and responsibilities.

Then the koalas got boring. I had an image of their going the way of the mythical alligators brought back from Florida by vacationing grandparents and soon afterward flushed down the toilet, thereby doomed to lives as albino alligators lurking in the sewers of the Eastern seaboard. The koalas began disappearing from shelves and T-shirts and people's hearts. Actually, just as they were beginning to fall out of fashion, the live koalas quite literally began falling out of their trees, apparently succumbing to non-Australian air. The hue and cry was muted; the panda had already taken their place.

Tastes changed. New faces were forever in demand. And with that demand came the need for ways to print those faces at a reasonable cost. Shigeta, though hardly a slave to fashion in attire, was keenly aware of what his countrymen wanted when they were spending their money.

Eugene studied on Saturdays and Sundays in the office with Shigeta, and became a believer. He led customers through the Think complex past the rows of desks, the drafting tables, computer terminals, and design boards, to the factory where the cylinder-making machines were assembled—Shigeta called the machine Boomerang:

"Your money goes out," he would say, with a smile, "and then comes back." Eugene brought the customers to the display case where he showed them the end product of Think's cylinders—printed packages for Buttercream cheese biscuits, Blue Berry gum, Corn Potage, and Choco Flakes.

And as Eugene began believing in Shigeta, the sixty employees of the company began believing in Eugene. This did not come without some effort. There had been people in the company who would not talk to Eugene. Still, Eugene tried. Sometimes he was rewarded. When he saw the company painter outside the plant, Eugene asked him about his technique in painting the metal sections of Think's machines. The painter was only too happy to oblige. Later he bought Eugene a bean-paste cake. When one of the engineers in the experimental laser division was hospitalized, Eugene visited him. The engineer's mother owned a bakery. She gave Eugene a cheesecake. Sometimes, the overtures came to Eugene. One day, just before New Year's, Saitoh, the chief designer, approached him. Saitoh spoke to no one. He sat at his desk and thought and sometimes stared at the opaque windows. He was the one person in the company over whose shoulder Shigeta did not peer. They had been together for twenty years.

"Do you like to fish?" Saitoh asked Eugene.

"I can fish."

"You can fish?" asked Saitoh. "We're going fishing the day after tomorrow. Will you be up?"

"I'll be ready," Eugene said. "I'll be ready."

Eugene was asleep when Saitoh came to get him at five-thirty in the morning. He dressed in a hurry and went to the car. He drove with Saitoh and Yamaguchi the plant manager to a shack by the sea. They sat down with the shack's blustery proprietor and began drinking. They drank till lunchtime. They drank beer and *sake*. Eugene asked about fishing and was told, "We fish later." The men talked about the ocean, about Japan, and about women. Then they went to Saitoh's mother's house for lunch. The trip ended after lunch. No lines were cast.

Eugene was not only making friends; he was making deals. And the action of deal-making was something Eugene especially enjoyed. He had been with the company for just over a year when he brought it its biggest contract, worth over $2 million with one of America's largest printing companies, the Massachusetts firm of Dennison. The deal called both for a Boomerang machine and for seven thousand cylinders. But more significantly, it signaled a triumphant entry into the American market, the market that had thus far eluded Shigeta. Now Eugene had helped bring it to him. Dennison brought Eugene not only Shigeta's praise and admiration—suddenly, enemies became friends, and everyone had time for Eugene.

The first person to congratulate him when he returned from America with the Dennison contract was the salesman who had not talked to him for six months. Nagase, the international sales manager, took him out, asked him how he had done it, and wanted to know whether Eugene would take him to America. Secretaries who had ignored Eugene did his copying. The prettiest girl in the office admitted that she was always trying to catch his eye. And the young men in the cylinder-making plant, those who would benefit most by all the new orders that would come flooding in, told Eugene that they knew he wanted Shigeta to pave over the plant parking lot and build a basketball court, and that if forming a basketball team would help bring Eugene his court, they would play for him.

Eugene called the team the Think Lakers. They practiced on Tuesdays, after work. Eugene told me to bring my sneakers and come to practice. He could not be sure what time practice would begin, only that it would start after work. The time varied. The workday ended when Shigeta had nothing else for anyone to do.

The sports center was crowded and not heated. The team had to share a court with badminton players. This would have left things congested on the court had they played a game. The Think Lakers were not ready to play a game. But they were ready to practice. Thirteen men showed up, men from the machine-making plant, from the cylinder factory, and from the design division. They came for Eugene.

Eugene called for two lines, one for shooters, the other for rebounders. The shooters dribbled to the basket. When they got close they tossed the ball in the general direction of the hoop. A shot or two went in. Eugene had to remind the rebounders to get the ball and pass it to the next shooter. But everyone was having too much fun laughing at all the bad shots their friends took. Soon all the Lakers were on the shooters line, grabbing each other's crotches. Eugene said to me in a flat voice, "They like to grab each other's penises. They call it 'touchee.'" The grabbing was done without homocrotic overtones. It was simply something to do when overcome with the need to do something dumb. Eugene also explained that everyone's favorite part of last week's drill was practicing plays that made the other fellows look foolish.

There was no more point in drilling. The Lakers broke off into teams. My team lost to Eugene's team but my teammates had fun pushing each other and guarding Eugene by grabbing his penis. Their laughing did not stop when Shigeta arrived.

He stood on the sideline, his arms folded across his chest. He smiled an approving smile. And when the practice ended, he kept his distance as Eugene had the Lakers sit in a circle on the cold hardwood floor. Eugene admonished the smokers not to smoke. He told them they had to practice hard.

Shigeta said nothing until he heard that the court had been reserved for seven-thirty the following week. He asked Eugene whether that might cut the workday short.

After practice Eugene and Shigeta took me with them to Eugene's sushi bar—Eugene's because he had discovered it; but now Shigeta's too, because he had opened a company charge account. The owner was ready for us. He was a ruddy man with the short, permanently waved hairstyle that had become popular in Japan. Eugene was a favorite of the owner and his wife. When Eugene mentioned that he was making fried chicken for friends, the owner said that he would buy the chicken for him at his wholesaler. One night the owner told Eugene to come by the shop at midnight because he was taking him to the tradesmen's festival at the Asakusa Shrine in Tokyo. Eugene and the owner stayed out until three in the morning.

The owner brought warm *sake* for Eugene and Shigeta, and a beer for me. He wiped the glass counter clean. He started us with tuna sashimi. Shigeta turned the conversation toward work.

"I like the way Eugene targets a big company," he said, thinking not only of the Dennison deal but of a prospective joint venture with an Israeli company, Scitex. "These people all know each other. When something is good technically, word spreads."

"Now the top people at Dennison talk with Mr. Shigeta," Eugene said. "We have good feelings with Dennison."

Good feelings were important. Shigeta had spent twenty years cultivating good feelings among customers in Japan, knowing only too well that the surest route to failure in his country was an absence of good feelings. Shigeta spent a lot of time nurturing his business associates. Often this was done at dinner, over beer or *sake*. Sometimes, when they were visiting Kashiwa, Shigeta brought these associates to Eugene's sushi bar.

"We're using an American laser now," Shigeta said, referring to the next technological direction Think might take.

Eugene turned to me and said, "How does he know all this shit—printing, physics, metallurgy, ink, lasers, cylinder making? The dude is smart." He sipped his drink. "The dude is smart."

"I learn by watching videos," Shigeta said.

"He's got eight hundred videos," said Eugene.

"I've also learned a lot from contacting people. We'll do research for them and they do research for us. I learn it all on my own. I read every book on laser engineering. I didn't go to college."

"The dude is bad," said Eugene, who grew excited whenever Shigeta spoke about how he educated himself.

"I worked in the technical division of a printing company. I did two years of research on my own. I didn't make any money off it, but it was fun. I lived in a small apartment. I had a bed and machines and nothing else. My idea was about the future. I had ideas about electrical printing and the company didn't like them. They wouldn't listen to me. So I quit. I was twenty-six years old.

"From the beginning everybody laughed at me. When I started out DuPont was the most respected company I could think of. So

I wondered, 'How long will it take me to be as big as DuPont?' I thought forty years. We're only twenty years along and we're not even halfway there."

"There's no question; if he was in America he would have gone to Harvard," said Eugene. "The dude is too smart. He'd be a billionaire right now. I help him with his English. He's my friend."

"I know a lot from people," said Shigeta. "You've got to go to exhibitions and shows. That's where you learn."

"He goes to technical fairs that aren't even his technology. He's a self-made man."

"I go to thirty exhibitions a year. Two times a month. Electronics. Biotechnology. Plastics. Toys. You get good ideas from toys."

"They put a lot of good ideas into a small space."

"They dream," Shigeta said. "They dream."

"And he didn't go to fucking Harvard," Eugene cried out. He was howling and clapping his hands in excitement. He pounded my back.

"A lot of these things aren't necessarily practical," Shigeta said, continuing in his even-tempered way. "They're people's dreams. And machines that go beyond technology are dreams. The things kids like have to be good or they don't work. My customers used to be children."

We ate grilled sea bass, and tuna with scallions rolled in seaweed. We ordered more to drink. Eugene bummed a cigarette from the owner's wife who said she wanted to come see the Think Lakers play. Eugene said to Shigeta, "I met a lot of smart people. You're smart."

"I'm not that smart," Shigeta said.

Eugene turned to me and said, "Ask him what he thinks of me." I did.

"He's a good man," said Shigeta. "He's good in discussion and in focusing on a target. When we have free discussion it's good. When we find a target we go after it."

"With his technological expertise and my focus on marketing . . ." Eugene began saying, thinking of their future.

"My customers ask me in and ask my opinions," said Shigeta. "When it comes to people, I'm good."

"We come in on Sundays. We come in on off-days. We blow these guys away."

"In three years we are going to build our new plant in America," Shigeta said.

And Eugene turned from him to me and said, "If he's not pushed to do it sooner."

Later that night, after Shigeta promised to build a basketball court for Eugene; after Eugene said how happy Shigeta made him when a task came up and he told Eugene *"Yaro"*—"Get it done"; after Shigeta talked about the wisdom of joint ventures between two or even three countries—"Japanese people try to use the best from whatever source"; after the owner fed us to the bloating point, we walked outside. It was a chilly night. We stood in front of the sushi shop, on the dark, empty street. The street was quiet, except for the faint sound of drunken singing coming from the bar next door. Eugene and Shigeta smiled at each other, and I envied Eugene his friendship with Shigeta. I envied him even though that relationship came at a price—coming in the next morning at 8:05 for the daily doom-and-gloom speech; Sundays and holidays in the office; never knowing when the workday would end; seeing days stretch into evenings and the evenings into early mornings and the early mornings to yet another day at the office where English was never spoken and barely understood. I envied him even though I had seen how tightly wound Eugene was on Think's early nights when we met in Tokyo and he started talking to every woman he saw, just to talk, to flirt, to vent a week's worth of sublimated foolishness.

I thought at that moment that the price might be worth paying. I saw what Eugene got in return: Shigeta's admiration, which came in a form that transcended a handshake and compliment and became something closer to love. I never had a boss care for me the way Shigeta cared for Eugene. It never occurred to me that any boss would or could, or that any employee would want it. Yet as I watched I could see that, given the right situation, it might be a measure of approval worth the personal sacrifice. I had not seen this before. I had seen a lot of people give pieces of their hearts to the office, and get nothing of the office's heart in return.

Eugene sang before we left. He sang "The Star Spangled Banner" because he knew Shigeta liked it so much. Eugene sang in a soft voice. Shigeta looked at him and nodded. Eugene looked straight ahead. And as he reached the end of the anthem his voice grew with a slow crescendo. Eugene sang the last words very slowly. When he reached the word "free" he held it for a long time.

The shop owner's wife clapped her hands.

The owner said, "You're good."

Shigeta, now wistful, said, "Eugene."

✦ ✦ ✦ ✦ ✦ In the eight months since the first time I went to court with Kathy Morikawa, her infant daughter Julie had begun talking—a development, I discovered, that was infinitely faster than the workings of the Tokyo High Court. I had been to four hearings and witnessed four continuances. Documents were submitted, and the sessions were hastily adjourned. By the third hearing I was timing the proceedings with a stopwatch—could they break three minutes?—and calculated that the aggregate time the Morikawas had spent in court in the past eight months fell just below the 15-minute daily segment of the ongoing, six-month-long television series about the adolescence of a popular TV personality's mother. Kathy, now the television critic for one of the English-language dailies, gave the series a favorable notice.

One day, after yet another hearing, we went to the park across from the courthouse for a picnic. Kathy and Jun brought tuna sandwiches and egg sandwiches, and we spread the meal on a picnic table. At the next table, a drunk man slept. It was a good day to talk about innocent times, one of the balmy days in the weeks before the rainy season when the sky is clear, the trees are green, and there is a hint of a breeze. It was warm, but not yet stifling. In Tokyo I lived for spring and fall—seasons of joy between the oppressive summer and the dank, bleak winter.

Salary men in white shirts spilled out of their offices and came to the park with their baseball mitts. They paired off and played catch, though they did not loosen their ties. Couples strolled and took each other's pictures seated on park benches. A mother and her baby daughter made their own picnic under a tree. The little girl, like all little girls on sunny days in Japan, wore a straw hat tied tightly under her chin. The park was still but for the smack of baseballs against mitts, an occasional crow squawk, and, in the distance, the faint crackle of the loudspeakers on the rightists' sound trucks as they drove to Ginza for their noontime rally. The martial music and calls for spiritual renewal felt far away as Kathy and Jun told me about Chino. Life had never been better for Kathy Morikawa than it was when she was with Jun in Chino.

They had wanted to live away from the city. Kathy was weary of Tokyo, and Jun needed a quiet place to finish his thesis. They had nowhere in particular in mind, only the idea of someplace inexpensive and far away. So upon the advice of a friend they settled on Chino, a city of 38,000 set between mountains and a lake.

Chino was noted for its *sake*, soy sauce, fermented bean paste, camera parts, watches, and musical boxes. Money was scarce for Kathy and Jun. Yet now, eight years later, they remembered Chino as a time when the dearth of cash offered curiosities rather than causing any real privation.

"I only used to shop at this one supermarket, and the owner used to give me old stuff for free," Kathy said.

"We were fighting for survival," said Jun. "We had lots of ideas and lots of friends and no money."

The mornings in Chino began at six o'clock, heralded by the town's public address system. Dawn brought the day's announcements: "Mama-san volleyball today . . ." "Swimming pool cleaning day begins . . ." "Exercise classes at . . ." "Early morning baseball practice . . ." The baseball field was next to Kathy's and Jun's apartment, alongside a mulberry field. When there was no early morning practice, Kathy and Jun went to the field and played.

"Softball in a big stadium," Kathy said. "Just the two of us."

"It was ideal," said Jun. "Early in the morning, in summer, just playing by ourselves."

"In touch with nature," Kathy said. She laughed her high-pitched laugh. When she spoke about Chino it was mostly about the pleasure and humor in seemingly inconsequential things: being first in line for the supermarket's pre-renovation half-price day; the fiasco of Jun's attempt at making pickled radishes.

"How idiotic we were," Kathy said. "They're very famous for pickles there. But we didn't know what we were doing."

"No one thought of hanging them to dry with clothespins," Jun said of his jerry-built drying technique.

"One little girl came by and said, 'Your radishes are outside,' " Kathy said.

"I said, 'I know, I'm making pickles,' " said Jun. "And she said, 'But it's raining.' "

Jun studied; Kathy wove him a blanket. In the mornings, she rode her bicycle down from their apartment; and on the way home from shopping, her bicycle loaded down, Kathy would pass the truckers from the local bean-paste factory. The truckers always waved.

"If the same thing happened in Tokyo it would get you really mad," Kathy said. "But you're the local foreigner, going up the hill. And he's the local truck driver. It didn't bother me. I was always the outsider anyway. You had a town drunk. You had a town foreigner."

Chino had precious little else. There was one dentist in town and he was booked for the year. Kathy had to travel fifty miles to the prefectural dental college and let the students practice on her teeth. Chino offered little, if anything, that could attract a crowd— that is, except for the day someone drove a dead whale on a flatbed truck down the main street and the townspeople decided to hold a parade.

"Did we tell you about the *yakuza* next door?" Kathy asked. The *yakuza* were the gangsters of Japan's underworld. "One morning this man comes to our apartment in pajamas and sandals. It was snowing. He was looking for a place to live."

"He was actually a student of the *yakuza*," said Jun.

"It seemed like his assignment was to set up a bar in Chino," Kathy said. "This was not exactly the kind of place to set up a bar and make a fortune."

"They were a young couple," Jun said of the tyro gangster and his wife. "And they fought."

"One day she locked him out, went upstairs, and started throwing her high heels on his head."

"Was it the same time they started throwing their photo album?"

"She set it on fire. It was pretty windy. Our eggplant crop almost went."

Entertainment, luckily, was free of charge, because when their savings began to vanish, Kathy and Jun found themselves with little means of support.

"At one time we had five thousand yen in the bank," Kathy said.

"Two hundred dollars," said Jun.

"Two hundred?" Kathy said. "More like twenty."

But they had their school.

The school was not a cram school. Kathy and Jun made no promises of improved scores on high school and college entrance examinations. Millions of children all over Japan attended after-school cram schools—*juku*, they were called—in the hope that they might better their scores in the highly competitive entrance examinations. There were tests for college entrance, high school entrance, even kindergarten entrance. It was crucial to score well at an early age to ensure a place on the track to the best schools— and, by extension, the better government and corporate jobs. *Juku* were so widespread that it became all but essential to attend one, if only because the competition did. In *juku* the students wore headbands emblazoned with the word *Persevere*.

"I wanted to do something else," Jun said. "So I told the students, 'If you want to come here to get good test results, I can't assure you of that. But if you want to study, you are welcome.' Happily, the parents were patient and tried to understand our policy. Perhaps they thought, 'They're so young; let them try.'"

And so Kathy and Jun established the International Terakoya

School. It was both an after-school academy for teenagers and an adult education course for those anxious to practice their English. The *terakoya* in the name was based on the idea of a Buddhist temple school. It was Jun's idea to add the "international" concept, a concept that stood at the heart of the way Jun saw the world, a concept that seldom left him at one with his countrymen.

Kathy had been on her way to Japan when she stopped in Denmark at the international university where she and Jun had met. They had become friends during the six months Kathy studied at the school. Jun had stayed on, waiting for a visa to Nigeria. In a wooded, secluded spot on the grounds was a cottage where students met for symposia, or just to talk. Jun was the cottage overseer. He cleaned it, made coffee, served the fresh strawberries he picked, and took part in the discussions. It was the talk that most appealed to Jun, talk about ideas. He had studied international relations at Meiji University and was anxious to go to Africa. When he was a freshman in college, however, Jun had contracted tuberculosis—a disease thought to have been exacerbated by all the hours he'd spent preparing for his college entrance exams. (The Japanese have a saying about those tests: Sleep five hours, fail; sleep four, pass.)

Jun spent a year and a half in a sanatorium. He was told that if he spent another year resting, he would recover most of his strength and could certainly look forward to a life of limited stress, perhaps as a postal clerk. Jun said that he was going to Africa. His doctors assured him that Africa was out of the question—that is, unless he took the risk, and endured the pain, of an operation that would remove a section of his diseased lung.

When Kathy stopped in Denmark on her way to Japan she learned that Jun had a scar that ran from his rib cage to his back. They spent a month together that summer. Their relationship deepened. But Jun was on his way to Africa, and Kathy was going to Japan to study Japanese. Jun took Kathy to the airport. He returned to the cottage and waited for his student visa. And when he got tired of waiting for a student visa he flew to Nigeria on a tourist visa, assuming he could change his status at a later date.

A year passed. Kathy got a letter from Jun asking if she would meet him at the airport.

Between her arrival at Haneda Airport the year before and her trip to Haneda to meet Jun, Kathy had learned not only a passable level of Japanese, but had graduated from helplessness to an appropriate application of local rules and standards.

The initial phase began at the airport, where friends from Denmark met her. They assisted her with the sleeping bag and banjo she had lugged from Pittsburgh. Kathy's friends took her to her tiny apartment, then to Sophia University and showed her how to enroll for her language courses. When she was done enrolling they took her home.

She was put under the care of a friend's sister, who took Kathy to the neighborhood bath house and showed her how to wash herself before soaking in the communal tub. The woman took her ice skating and to her family's home at New Year's. Kathy had been in Japan for three months but had not been given the chance to test her commuter skills. On the day she was to meet this woman and head north for the family weekend, another friend dropped her at the vast and mazelike Shinjuku rail station—a million commuters passed through it every day. Because he was rushing to work, Kathy's friend told her just where she was to meet the woman. Not wishing to be a bother, Kathy nodded, said she understood, and proceeded to walk around the station for forty-five minutes. When she reached the place where she had begun, Kathy decided that if she did not get on a train and head home—the only direction she was sure of—she might be lost forever.

Sensing something was amiss, the woman telephoned the man who'd dropped Kathy off. He telephoned and found Kathy at home. He took the hour's train trip from his office to her apartment and escorted her to the right place, as if he were passing a baton in a relay race.

That weekend, Kathy wore a kimono for the first time. She joined the woman's family when they went to the local shrine at midnight. An old woman sitting alongside the road looked up, saw the blond woman in a red kimono, and laughed herself silly.

"At that point you realize what a nuisance you are," Kathy said. "Then I got into my *on* and *giri* period."

Kathy began to read. *On* and *giri*, she learned, were obligations. Of the two, *on* was the greater, primarily because it never went away. But *giri* could be more taxing: it demanded payment in kind for services rendered. *On* was the sort of debt a child owed his parents or a student his teachers. No matter what he did he could never repay it. *Giri* was a debt of the quid pro quo variety. It was the social constraint that held Japan together: being a Japanese meant recognizing that every favor extended meant a reciprocal favor, whether you liked it or not.

In Japan you owed. You owed everyone who ever did anything for you and they, in turn, owed you. And unlike bookmakers and numbers runners who recorded their debts in little books, Kathy learned that Japanese were adept at cataloguing these debts in their heads, the same way they remembered how to walk and breathe.

Kathy also read books on Japanese psychology, in particular *The Anatomy of Dependence*, a widely read treatise whose author, the psychologist Takeo Doi, argued that the quality that set Japanese psychology apart was the elevation and celebration of the universal need to be indulged. Kathy read that while Westerners might regard the need for indulgence pejoratively, the Japanese sought it continuously. Kindness was extended because then kindness would be returned. Every introduction came with the request, "Please be kind to me." Moods should be sensed, needs anticipated. Words were not necessary. A good friend was the friend who extended kindness or who indulged another without having to be asked. To have to be asked was to be insensitive; friendships ended when silent calls for kindness went unheeded. Kathy read these books and learned the concepts, then structured her life in her new home accordingly.

People, after all, had been kind to her—in good measure because she was their responsibility, or rather she was a friend of friends to whom responsibilities were owed. When she moved into her apartment, one friend lugged a bulky futon back from Shinjuku on the subway. Another helped her buy a table and got her a discount on a lamp. On her birthday, a friend brought her a cake. People extended themselves for the sake of her comfort, treating her as if they were overprotective parents waiting for their toddler to take a spill on the nose. So Kathy decided, "I have to do that for someone else."

Edie of Eagle Butte was an early recipient of Kathy's *giri* and indulgence. The *giri*, the debt, was to a friend from South Dakota who wrote to tell Kathy that a woman named Edie was coming through Tokyo. The friend wondered whether Kathy could put her up. Kathy decided that her obligation to her distant friend extended beyond accommodations alone.

She headed out to Haneda with a sign in hand. The sign read EAGLE BUTTE EDIE. Having no idea what this friend of a friend looked like, and knowing only her first name and hometown, Kathy took the chance that only one Edie from Eagle Butte was taking that flight.

Edie spotted the sign. Kathy took her home. She offered Edie a modest serving of thin yogurt because that was the sort of snack that people, extending kindness, had served her. Sensitivity dictated that one did not ask a guest what he or she wanted because that meant burdening the guest with decision-making. One simply served. If unsure of the guest's preference, several items could be served, one right after the other. Edie, ignoring the little spoon Kathy gave her, swallowed the yogurt in a gulp. Kathy looked at the meager meal and the little spoon and said to herself, "Maybe I'm getting too Japanese."

The "*on* and *giri* period" was followed by the "Japanese friends only period," which coincided with the return of Jun. It was not an aloof Kathy that Jun found upon his return, but one who sought the company of Japanese friends whom she'd met through friends of friends from Denmark. Kathy was not trying to be exclusive. Rather, in a very Japanese way, she had focused her attention and affection upon those in her group. Among the lessons that Kathy had learned was that kindness and obligation were too important to be spent on the less than intimate. Strangers pushed, jostled and threw elbows in crowded places; teenagers seldom surrendered their subway seats to the elderly—even when they were sitting in the designated senior citizens seats; folks at the ballpark did not strike up those very American instant friendships that lasted only until the last out in the ninth inning. It was hard enough satisfying the needs of those who mattered without cluttering the network of social obligations with gratuitous kindness to strangers.

The *on* and *giri* Kathy had learned and honed in her previous period was now applied to that small circle of intimates. In this regard, Kathy demonstrated that she had not only learned the rules for suitable behavior, but was applying them correctly.

"I could see why people get so fanatically attached to their group," Kathy said. She explained that you did not have to be funny to be included in the group. You did not have to be a good talker. You simply had to be a kind and considerate member and the other members of the group would be kind and considerate to you. You did not have to "bring" anything, Kathy explained, only a good heart. There was a large place in Kathy's heart for her group. "Before you realize you can never belong," she said, "you try to belong."

Jun, who insisted upon a macroscopic world view, played by different rules. Not only did he ask Kathy to meet him at the airport; he asked his parents. Jun wanted to make a statement—one he later described as a "Pearl Harbor attack"—for the benefit of his parents, to whom he wished to introduce his Western girlfriend in a way that would represent a fait accompli.

Kathy rode to the airport with a friend. On the way to the airport they wondered whether Jun's parents would be there. Kathy thought he wouldn't have arranged so awkward a scene. Her friend was not so sure. They waited by the customs gate, in a crowd that included Jun's parents and brother. Jun's family had not seen him in three years.

"I just wanted to give my parents a demonstration," Jun said.

"Shock treatment," said Kathy.

"Certainly it was effective."

The customs door opened and Jun walked out. He waved to his parents.

He walked to Kathy. He hugged her.

It is customary in Japan upon greeting a loved one to bow and simply say, "Welcome back." Hugging is not done. Kissing is uncalled for. Hugging one's girlfriend before greeting one's parents represents a gross violation of *on* laws.

Jun's mother, upon seeing these goings-on, retired to a public rest room, where she remained for quite some time. Jun's mother had assumed that her wayward son would return home, marry, and move into the second-floor apartment in the family home. His wife would work in the cosmetics shop she owned—a life that, in other circumstances and with a different mother, might have condemned his wife to perhaps the heaviest *giri* of all, the *giri* a daughter-in-law owes her in-laws, a *giri* that can mean a life of cleaning and serving in endless repayment for having been taken into a new family and given a home. And while Jun by no means saw his mother in so Draconian a light, he had other plans. Jun said, "I didn't like the whole idea."

June no more liked that idea than Kathy liked the idea of his airport "demonstration," even if it was a statement about his affection for her. The encounter had made the formality of spoken introductions redundant. Jun followed his parents and brother out of the terminal, and rode home with them. In the car he talked with his brother. Their parents did not speak.

Jun waited a year before his next salvo. He and Kathy had been dating, and he had been living at home. They had spent time with the circle of friends from Denmark, going to parties, coffee houses and picnics. Jun's parents said nothing about his foreign girlfriend. Jun assumed that they had decided to wait him out, hoping that in time they might break up. He spoke with them about Kathy. He explained why he had chosen her. This had less to do with Kathy's foreignness, than with Jun's idea of internationalism: he did not wish to impose boundaries on whom he might choose as a spouse.

It did not matter to Jun whether his wife was Japanese or Western. But if she were Japanese, she could not display the behavior that Japanese women affected in the hope of attracting a man. She could not giggle; she could not feign a little girl's voice. Twentieth-century Japanese femininity had evolved into the socially acceptable feigning of adolescence. Japanese men, it seemed, liked their women young and accessible, so much so that an entire industry had evolved for dressing and accessorizing Japanese women keen on preserving a teenage demeanor. While most were content keeping their voices high-pitched and their wardrobes several years too young (pink ribbons on top of their hair; plastic heartshaped earrings), there were those who took the charade to nearly burlesque proportions. They were the *burikko*. *Burikko* means "little pretender." They were the Japanese equivalent of California's Valley Girls. Their speech was filled with such expressions as *"eh?"*—"whaaaat . . . ?"; *"honto?"*—"really" (as in, "Really, he didn't . . ."), and *"iyada,"* or, "ugh." A true *burikko* wore tartan miniskirts, knee socks, silly hats, hoop earrings, rhinestone rings, high-topped Converse sneakers (with untied laces), and a large crucifix in the spirit of Madonna, the singer. The *burikko* may have represented something close to parody, but they were simply taking a social phenomenon to its logical extreme. Perhaps these men liked vapid women. God knows the women would have stopped immediately if they did not. Marriage was too crucial a rite in Japan to be jeopardized by counterproductive behavior. Of course, all the foolish talk and adolescent charm ended after the wedding, when the husband brought home his first paycheck and handed it to his new and suddenly grown-up wife.

Jun wanted none of this. "I couldn't help but compare her with Japanese girls," he said of Kathy when he explained why he fell in love. "I don't like the shallowness. I wanted something substantial. When I met Kathy her parents were dead. So in a way she was all alone. But instead of trying to be cute, she was trying to create something, face hardships, make new horizons by going to Denmark and South Dakota and helping Indian children. I felt she was very rich in terms of mind."

And so Jun, who'd seen little point in further attempts at explanation, came to his parents and announced, "I'm going to move out tomorrow."

A year later he and Kathy married.

. . .

Slowly, Kathy found that her Japan was shrinking. From her early attempts at extending *giri* to the unknown Eagle Butte Edie, to the more concentrated attention directed toward her group of friends, Kathy's view of Japan was narrowing like a contracting camera lens.

She was weary of the sometimes stifling atmosphere of the group. "In the very beginning," she explained, "there is a certain attractiveness—to know you know five or ten people. You never have to do anything by yourself. The group plans things to do. It's very secure, being in a group of people who are thinking about you. But if you're really in a group it's a little oppressive." Being in the group meant assuming group responsibilities. It meant forever being attentive to others' needs. It allowed little if any latitude for such selfish behavior as doing that which had not been agreed upon by everyone else.

There was no falling out with her friends; but there was the growing sense that, at best, their friendship would always be defined by nationality. Having passed from helplessness to independence without losing all of her innocence, Kathy one day opened her mail to find the magazine the group had put together about itself. The cover showed each member portrayed in caricature. One was a musician. Jun was a student. Kathy was labeled "foreigner."

For all the *giri* and *on* Kathy had learned and displayed, for all the time spent together with these friends, and for all the affection that had grown between them, Kathy saw that, in the end, she was still the "foreigner."

She said nothing of her hurt feelings to her friends. Kathy simply closed her lens that much more, until her Japan was embodied by a single, thin face with long hair and penetrating eyes.

They were married on Albert Schweitzer's birthday, which was both of their birthdays, too. Neither wanted an elaborate wedding. Jun, in particular, did not want to contribute their limited funds to what he called "the marriage industry," which would have meant a wedding in a wedding hall, which, in turn, would have meant the seldom-varying standard Japanese wedding: four changes of clothes by the bride (white wedding kimono, red after-ceremony kimono, white Western-style wedding dress with requisite puffy sleeves and crinoline, satin and lace cocktail dress, preferably purple or blue); two changes by the groom (black and gray kimono to vanilla tuxedo); the candle-lighting-in-the-cloud-of-dry-ice ceremony; gifts for all guests; beer for all guests; speech by the company president; flowers presented by the bride and groom to their respective parents, with attendant tears. The ceremony could be Shinto (joint sipping of rice wine), or "Christian" (clergyman provided by the caterer) if the bride, who did not have to be an actual Christian, wanted to be married in a white gown.

"We didn't want to do anything," said Kathy.

Still, a professor of Jun's who'd been the official go-between in fifty marriages insisted upon a party. Kathy and Jun first stopped at the American embassy where Kathy was given a marriage form and a typewriter upon which to complete it.

Jun's parents came to the party, as did friends. Each guest paid the equivalent of twenty dollars for food and drink—more reasonable than the fifty- or one-hundred-dollar cash gift (the only correct gift) generally expected of wedding guests. A buffet was arranged.

"This is my memory of my wedding," Kathy said. "Everybody had to give a speech or do some kind of a trick. One guy cut a pair of chopsticks with a piece of paper. That was the highlight of my wedding."

Another friend insisted upon performing a Shinto marriage rite because his father was a priest and he felt the ceremony was necessary. Jun's parents wanted to take the new couple out for sushi. But the professor whisked them off and took them to their apartment. Jun's friends stopped by.

Jun and his friends talked and ate noodles. Kathy went to the public bath.

A year later, they moved to Chino where Kathy, though no longer an innocent, could take pleasure in the innocence she still saw around her.

. . .

The biggest mistake Kathy and Jun made in running the International Terakoya School was delegating the finances to Jun. Jun did not want to advertise. Jun wanted to keep enrollment limited to four students in a class.

"We had twenty students and they each paid ten dollars a month," said Kathy. "It was extremely high for the area. We got lots of presents."

"Celery. Vegetables," said Jun. "In the winter we got a blanket."

"Jun got long underwear from one of his private students."

"It was the extra-warm kind. We had no central heating in our apartment. It was so cold, I used to wear a long coat in the house."

Classes ran from four to eight in the evening. Most of the students were in high school and junior high. The adults were, for the most part, engineers who wanted to sharpen their conversational English before overseas assignments. Jun and Kathy did not restrict themselves to conventional teaching methods. And because the parents had already taken the bold step of sending their children to the non-cram school, they did not resist an unorthodox approach.

"One girl in the high school class liked the Beatles," said Jun. "Everyone thought she wasn't serious enough. She just talked about the Beatles. I told her, 'Why don't you study more—not just books about the Beatles in translation.' I had a John Lennon book and said, 'Why don't you study this.' "

"She translated the whole thing," said Kathy.

The school's reputation grew. A local public school asked Kathy to teach an English course, and the district newspaper ran an article about Kathy and Jun. It was headlined, THE CHARM OF RAW ENGLISH, and ran under an advertisement seeking an arranged marriage for a woman who wanted a tall man.

Jun continued writing his thesis—the topic was economic and human rights developments in Uganda as addressed through the question of Asian exploitation of Africa. When its completion was in sight, Kathy and Jun decided it was time to return to the city.

It was December, and on the night before they left a Christmas party was held in their honor. Students and parents came and the parents brought gifts. One brought a bag of rice, another a Christmas tree. The next morning, one of the adult students came to help load the mover's truck. Kathy and Jun gave him their Christmas tree. When the truck was loaded, Kathy and Jun climbed into the cab with the mover, and drove away from Chino.

Jun finished his thesis and got his degree. Kathy took a job teaching English at a Tokyo university. Their students kept in touch. The girl who loved the Beatles went to a music college. Another student wrote to say he was going to medical school. And one day in class, Kathy looked at her new students and saw the face of one of her Chino students who had done well on his examinations and had come to the city for college.

They found a home in the Tokyo suburb of Minami-Rinkan. The house sat in the flight path of the Yokosuka Air Force Base and often, at night, the house shook during touch-and-go drills. Still, Minami-Rinkan was a pleasant place. There was a garden outside their house and from their living room they could look out at the trees, shrubs, and stone lantern. In the living room Kathy hung a corkboard and covered it with pictures of friends and postcards of Pittsburgh. Their dog, Hana, lived in the doghouse at the edge of the garden. Still, the summers in Minami-Rinkan were steamy. In August, when her mood turned sour, Kathy longed for the breeze of the mountains near Chino.

On the day of our picnic we moved from the table to a grove of trees. We sat on a long, flat stone, watching the joggers and the tennis players. Office ladies in matching jumpers opened their boxed lunches and ate their rice and fish with little bites. Elderly women held umbrellas to shield themselves from the sun. Their daughter Julie sat in Jun's lap and slept. Kathy said, "If we had always stayed in Chino I wouldn't have refused fingerprinting. You were accepted in a small community. You wouldn't want to disturb anybody."

"You were still concerned about the Koreans," said Jun.

"I was interested in the issue. But there's something different in being a Western foreigner in the countryside. Even if there are ten thousand people, they all see you eventually. I wouldn't have wanted to make trouble. People were trying to be nice to me. You don't want to make a fuss."

◢ ◆ ◢ ◣ ◣ ◢ In the teacher's room of the Matsue Middle School, Lafcadio Hearn sat next to Nishida, his friend. Nishida spoke English and sometimes, during their breaks, they chatted. Nishida was twenty-nine years old. He looked after Hearn, who was eleven years his senior. He invited Hearn to his home. He introduced Hearn to his wife, who was the first Japanese woman Hearn came to know. Nishida was the one person in Matsue with whom Hearn could share the events of his new life. When the governor's daughter sent Hearn the gift of a bird, Hearn sent a note to Nishida, telling him all about the bird and its Buddhist legend.

"My dear Mr. Nishida," Hearn would write. "You are really too kind and good! Now I trust you will find time to dine with me some day, with any friend you like . . ." Or, "Dear Mr. Nishida: . . . You have taken a great deal of trouble on my account today . . ." Or, "Many, many thanks for your visits. You know they are always good medicine,—even if they are short." Hearn signed his early letters, "Very gratefully." In time he concluded with, "Ever your friend."

In class Hearn's students asked about love. They asked about marriage and about the relationship in the West between husband and wife. The students amused Hearn with their questions.

"Teacher," he was asked, "I have been told that if a European and his father and his wife were all to fall into the sea together, and that he only could swim, he would try to save his wife first. Would he really?"

"Probably," Hearn replied.

"But why?"

"One reason is that Europeans consider it a man's duty to help the weaker first—especially women and children."

"And does a European love his wife more than his father and mother?"

gardless of the work they did. The club read about the Burakumin
The River Without Bridges, and only when they saw the English
rsion did they learn that the Japanese translation had been sani-
ed of critical passages. Companies kept lists of Burakumin names
that no Burakumin might be hired accidentally. Detectives were
red to check family birth records before marriages to ensure that
ospective in-laws were not Burakumin. It was a rare Japanese who
knowledged familiarity with the word Burakumin. It was as if by
noring the discrimination against the descendants of butchers and
nners, people might forget that it existed.

"The younger women thought that there wasn't a problem,"
rmin told me one morning, before we left for the monthly club
eeting. "But the older ones said, 'When it comes to marriage it
ways comes up.' "

The issue was, in a sense, an appropriate one for the Books and
ea Club, whose members shared the misfortune of living on the
illy social periphery of Aizu-Takada.

"Most of them are outsiders," Armin said.

"They're not Aizu born and bred," said Evelyn.

"I don't know how much they're accepted," Armin said.

Each month Armin and Evelyn penciled the Books and Tea Club
nto their calendar, as they did for adult English conversation class,
fter-school English class for children, Sunday worship services in
ny one—and sometimes several—of the nearby churches, English-
nguage Bible class, and the seemingly never-ending series of meet-
ngs with district pastors, district leaders, and anyone else who
anted the perspective of long-term foreign residents of the Aizu
egion. The calendar sat under the phone. The phone rang a lot.
here were calls asking if Armin or Evelyn could come around the
orner to the church and assist at the kindergarten; calls asking
velyn to bake a pie because the woman who was going to bake
he pie couldn't and the church meeting needed a pie; calls for
rmin to come to the district tourist association's meeting and ex-
lain what foreign visitors to the Aizu region might need in the way
f assistance. (Armin suggested English signs at the train stations.
he suggestion was ignored. *Sake* factory tours were arranged in-

"Not always—but generally, perhaps he does."

"Why, Teacher, according to our ideas that is very immoral."

Instead of love, as he knew it, Hearn found obligation. Relationships were not predicated on something as ethereal as a feeling.
They were built upon need. Hearn did not try convincing his students of the glory of romance. Rather, he sought conversion for
himself.

"Much of what is called personality and individuality is intensely
repellent, and makes the principal misery of Occidental life," he
wrote to his friend, the British Japanologist Basil Hall Chamberlain.

Nishida may well have liked Hearn, but he was also responsible
for him. As dean of the Middle School, the younger Nishida was
Hearn's superior. Hearn was his charge. When Hearn needed a
letter of introduction to visit the Kizuki shrine, Nishida wrote it for
him. When Hearn was sick, Nishida looked in on him. And when
he grew increasingly incapable of caring for himself, Nishida found
him a wife. The marriage was not at all what Hearn had had in
mind. Hearn had longed for explosive passion. What he got was
something quite different. He got a friend.

Hearn's women had embodied perfection. He had had few intimate
relationships. He was ill at ease. As a schoolboy he had lost his left
eye in a game. The left eye was covered with scar tissue, and his
right eye bulged. Ashamed of his disfigurement, he tried keeping a
hand over his missing eye when he spoke. Women eluded him. In
Cincinnati, however, he had briefly found a wife.

She was the black cook in his boarding house. She was kind to
him. She talked to him. He wanted to marry her. The State of
Ohio, however, prohibited marriage between the races. Still, Hearn
married her and kept the marriage secret. When word of it spread,
he lost his job and tried to kill himself. The marriage disintegrated,
and Hearn's wife slipped out of his life.

Later, in New Orleans, Hearn pined for the young French
woman who cleaned his rooms. He longed for a love that could
equal his dreams—"Let me be the last of your idol worshippers, O
Golden Venus . . ."

Instead he married Setsu Koizumi. Their union had less to do with passion than with the weather.

The winter of 1890 was an especially cold and snowy one in Matsue. The snow piled five feet outside Hearn's house. He spent weeks in bed. Nishida visited; but then Nishida too got sick, and Hearn was left in the occasional care of the elderly woman who cleaned his house. He could not teach. He could barely breathe. He promised Nishida he would not be sick anymore. He promised to come to school. Then his fever returned and he was left in bed, in his house, where all he had were his books, a suit of clothes, a table, a chair, and a kimono. Nishida decided he needed a wife.

He found the twenty-two-year-old daughter of an impoverished samurai family. Her marriage prospects were, at best, limited. It was said that she had married, but was then abandoned. She was a plump woman with a broad, flat face. Hearn accepted Nishida's proposition. He and Setsu Koizumi were married in January. She spoke no English. He barely spoke Japanese.

Yet order began appearing in a life once ruled by domestic chaos. Setsu assumed control of her husband's muddy finances, as was her responsibility. She even managed to converse with him in a combination of infant Japanese and simple English. Setsu provided Hearn with more than a companion and caretaker; she brought with her a family. Hearn was especially fond of his wife's grandfather who, in feudal times, had been a tutor at a noble court.

Curiously, he wrote nothing of his marriage to his friends, nothing until the summer after his wedding, and even then, as a passing reference to his "little wife." He still wrote about women, but with an altogether different appreciation.

"But how sweet the Japanese woman is!" he wrote to Chamberlain. "All the possibilities of the race for goodness seem to be concentrated in her. . . . Which is the highest being—the childish, confiding, sweet Japanese girl—or the superb, calculating, penetrating Occidental Cerce of our more artificial society . . . ?"

When he spent money on his wife, she thought him extravagant. When he argued with townspeople, she was embarrassed. When he

turned pale from sitting and writing too long at
that he might be mad. Really, she did not u
But she tended to his needs.

"One cannot dream or desire anything m
friend in America, "after love is transmuted in
marriage."

The Books and Tea Club wa
idea. Once, on a furlough visit to Pennsylvani
of women who gathered to drink coffee and o
had all read. Evelyn liked the idea of a group
about books and ideas and decided to introduce t
Takada. She substituted tea for coffee.

Pastor Endo liked the idea. He liked it so m
to join the group. Men, however, were allowed
ings only if their wives brought them. The Book
to be a setting for women to talk with impuni
places to do this—bars, mostly. Mrs. Endo did
the meetings, so her husband could not join.

Armin went because Evelyn took him. He j
wives, several schoolteachers, and the wife of P
the nearby Hongo church. Each month they me
house.

They had been meeting like this for a doz
years they had not only read but had acted up
read. When the group read *The People's Earth*, the
money to replace trees in the denuded forests o
They did not shrink from subjects that those arou
ignore, such as the fate of Southeast Asian fisherm
fishing waters by fleets of Japanese fishing compa

They even read about the Burakumin. The Bu
scendants of butchers and tanners. Their forebea
casts because their work violated the Buddhist pr
handling carcasses and skins. Now, centuries lat
dants—numbering as many as three million—w

stead, thereby leaving any non-Japanese reading visitors to fend for themselves. Armin smiled the knowing smile of a man who had seen it all before.)

I never heard the Kroehlers say no. In a sense, they were in no position to say no, because that would have meant jeopardizing the relationships they had spent a generation cultivating. Without those relationships they would lose whatever chance they had for their isolated and often modest successes. So the Kroehlers answered the phone whenever it rang; and I would sit and listen and, in my faulty Japanese, still understand what was happening. Always it was one word that I heard Armin and Evelyn repeat. And that word was *yes*.

Books and Tea was different, in that Books and Tea represented ongoing success. If the Kroehlers' work was an attempt to imbue the people of Aizu-Takada with a Christian world view—one that eclipsed the immediate and particular—then Books and Tea embodied both dream and realization. The club had grown to include a dozen women. Half were Christians. Religious affiliation was not a requirement. Books and Tea offered a way of seeing the world that existed beyond the mountains that ringed Aizu-Takada. Sometimes the conversation could get overly specific—"My son . . ." "My husband . . ." "I heard the other day . . ." Armin and Evelyn let it run whatever course it followed.

"In the group," Armin said, "they can say what they want and won't be held responsible for it."

This month's book was *The Diary of Anne Frank*. Topics for discussion would include the Holocaust and anti-Semitism. Curiously, the latter had become an issue in Japan even though there were hardly any Jews in the country. Two books blaming the Jews for the rise of the yen and the strain on the economy had sold 650,000 copies. Masami Uno, author of *If You Understand Judea You Can Understand the World*, argued that the Jews were planning to make Japan their "sacrificial lamb" when the world economy collapsed. Only two years before, my Japanese teacher had looked at me as if I were talking pig latin when I mentioned that I was a Jew. The concept had eluded him. Now the newspapers were filled with stories about the Jews and ads for books on how the Jews ran the world. *Judenrein* was scrawled on the old Kobe synagogue's wall. Swastikas were pasted on lampposts in Ginza.

Jews had become an issue not only because exports were down and companies were hurting, but because there was the growing belief that you could get rich by following the Jewish lead in the stock market. A different sort of "Jewish" book offered financial advice based on "the secrets of the Jews." People who were not quite sure what a Jew was or what one actually looked like were increasingly fascinated by them—as they were with other foreign concepts that were either threatening or useful. Talk of the Jews was so topical that one of the big Tokyo department stores even presented a photographic exhibit on the life of Anne Frank. Armin and Evelyn brought the show catalogue with them to the club meeting. They also brought me, the first Jew the members of the Books and Tea Club would meet. Armin could not be sure where the discussion might lead.

Before the meeting we talked about the price the Kroehlers had paid for a modicum of success. That they had succeeded at all, that they had been a factor in people's lives, had come only because Armin and Evelyn understood—and were comfortable with—the idea of passive persuasion.

A team of young evangelists once spent the summer in the towns near Aizu-Takada. Armin had warned them about the futility and foolishness of preaching, and advised them simply to make friends with the Japanese they met. The students ignored Armin's advice. At one meeting they looked out at the thirty faces in the audience and decided to move away from the singing that had gone over so well and engage in some passionate testimony. At the emotional apogee of the prayer meeting, when the students were expecting to see a line to the altar forming and tears streaming down the beatific faces of the faithful, they saw instead the same pleased but placid looks they had seen during the singing. The smiles, Armin explained to me, had less to do with proximity to faith than with proximity to native English speakers with whom the attendees were looking forward to practicing language skills. "Turkeys," said one of the evangelists, close enough for the bemused Armin to hear.

The Kroehlers laughed, remembering the more peculiar people who had come to their door. Some of them had terrified their children, like the elderly alcoholic who lived along the river and who had a plan for a five-story building with a helicopter pad. One night he came to the house when only Kaye, the eldest daughter, was home. He was drunk. He banged on the door and Kaye did her best to hide and make no noise so that he might go away. When the demands upon them began extending into family time, Armin and Evelyn packed the kids in their Willys Jeep station wagon— they drove the car for nine years; it was the best transportation for the gravel mountain roads—and headed for a hot spring.

At the end of the weekend they returned home and resumed their listening. They listened no matter how familiar the complaint about a neighbor or a child. They did not make many converts; but then, that was not their only intention. If the people of Aizu-Takada were going to embrace their faith—and its attendant world view— the Kroehlers were going to have to convey their message through means other than words. It took a long time for the Kroehlers to see evidence that this approach was working.

One day, twenty-five years after they came to Aizu-Takada, the Kroehlers discovered that their long years spent listening and hoping were not all in vain. That was the day that Rikie Yamauchi came to unburden the long-buried weight in his heart.

They had known Yamauchi for years. He was a member of the church and often came by the house to grouse about people and goings-on that displeased him. Yamauchi was a farmer and a veteran of the Imperial Army. As a farmer he organized the local dairy cooperative. Of his wartime experiences the Kroehlers knew nothing. In the thirty-three years since his repatriation from the Philippines, Yamauchi had told no one, not his wife or children or friends, what he had seen in the jungles of Luzon. Then he came to the Kroehlers and said that he had a story to tell.

At the age of thirty, and in the final year of the war, Yamauchi was conscripted into the Aizu-Wakamatsu Eastern 24th Corps. Four months later he arrived in the Philippines, where he was assigned to the communications unit of the Hashimoto Artillery Corps. The war was going badly for Japan and the army was in retreat. "I did not have to carry a gun. I was in headquarters, doing decoding. I did not hurt anyone. I feel that maybe God put me there so I wouldn't have to do those terrible things," Yamauchi said when he recounted for me what he had seen. "The Japanese soldiers killed many civilians because they were afraid they would pass along information. They bayoneted civilians in the heart. Officers had swords and cut off the Filipinos' heads. Those who they claimed were spies or guerrillas were executed. Soldiers were dying of starvation and malaria. The soldiers would march and collapse. They didn't have the strength to chase the flies away from their faces. Some of the soldiers got the idea that with all the dead soldiers around they could pick up a bayonet or a gun, so they would leave their gun and helmet behind and pick up another as they went along."

The soldiers slept among the dead and one night Yamauchi used a dead man's legs for a pillow. The soldiers ate insects when food ran out. When there were no insects they ate the remains of the dead men. Years after he came home—he was hospitalized for three years, suffering from malaria and malnutrition—Yamauchi had this dream: "I see people weak and lying by the roadside and others who have gone crazy. Our battalion was moving at nighttime and we took a short rest. I doze off and when I wake up everybody else is gone and I'm alone. I go off in the direction I think they've gone. But I realize I've left my helmet behind. I can't go back. I can't take from the dead soldiers."

He did not tell the Kroehlers everything at once. He came back again and again and told more stories about what he had seen his friends do. He told them that the Japanese had killed a million Filipinos, even though the government had insisted that the figure was far lower. That he told them anything at all was remarkable in itself because hardly anyone spoke about what Japan had done in the war. When the war was spoken of, and that was rare, it was of Japan not as the victimizer, but as the victim—the victim of the

Tokyo firebombings, the victim of Hiroshima and Nagasaki. Few mentioned the Rape of Nanking—where Japanese soldiers raped, mutilated, and systematically executed 100,000 Chinese civilians in six weeks; or the destruction of Manila, when Japanese troops rampaged through the city in the closing days of the war, raping, gouging out the eyes of children, setting hospitals on fire, and, in the end, leaving 100,000 Filipinos dead.

When the worst of what Japan had done was spoken of a generation after the surrender, it was often by scholars who insisted that they had evidence proving that "the so-called Nanking Incident" was not quite as bad as people said. Talk of the prison camps, or bayonet practice with Indonesian children, was generally confined to journalists, scholars (scholars of a different political persuasion), and foreign governments that had found their own evidence proving just how brutal things had been. In Japan, I learned, the war was a bad memory. And unlike their wartime allies, the Germans, whose questions of guilt and responsibility remained part of a national debate, most in Japan found it easiest to subscribe to the Buddhist notion of letting bad memories float away like the tide.

Yamauchi had tried, but could not let go of the war or the lasting image of his nation's dark side. "That extreme patriotism," he said one afternoon in the Kroehlers' living room, when he tried to explain why Japan could have acted as it had. "The feeling that the Japanese are a special people. What does that give you license to do to other people? I wonder what outsiders think of Japan. One aspect is very frightening. In the time of the samurai human life was not highly valued. There is a barbaric streak, savage, cruel. Within Japan there were wars where the strongest would consolidate as large an area as they could. Later that was applied internationally—to move into Manchuria, Korea, China. They had the idea of the superiority of the Japanese race and the mythology of the Japanese gods who protected only the Japanese."

After he told the Kroehlers about what he had seen, Yamauchi decided to go back to the Philippines. He learned that members of his unit were planning to return to the places where they had fought and Yamauchi decided to join them. "I couldn't get these people out of my mind. I remembered them and wanted to do something concrete. I wanted to console the war dead. We have to make amends to the Filipinos. For all the bad things that we did I want to say, 'I'm sorry, please forgive us.' "

So with his comrades, Rikie Yamauchi had gone back and stood in the places where others had died. He had called out to friends who had fallen, "I am here. We have not forgotten you." He went again the following year, and had returned every year since. "I feel as though those who died are crying out to me. Each time I break down and cry. I say, 'This time I'm not going to cry.' But I break down. I can't hold it in." The unit erected a plaque commemorating the American, Filipino, and Japanese war dead. They collected food and clothing and brought that with them. They bought the Filipinos 144 reed organs and a piano.

Yamauchi was seventy-five years old. He was short and wiry and his long gray hair was parted in the middle. Like many elderly Japanese men he said what he wanted to say regardless of what he was asked. It was one of the perquisites that came with age. He talked a good deal about the horror of war, about the need for peace. He talked about the Bible. Yamauchi had been a Christian when he went to war, and when he chose to unburden himself, it was to a clergyman. Yet the decision had less to do with faith than with a feeling toward the Kroehlers, a feeling built upon years of coming and talking to the Kroehlers about everything but that which he could not bring himself to talk about.

"There is a level of friendship that I experienced here," he said that afternoon, sitting in the Kroehler home, "that I did not have with Japanese as a whole."

It had been almost ten years since the first time Rikie Yamauchi had told him about the war, and in all that time, Armin could remember no time when he had felt more deeply that after so many years of patience, he had made a difference.

There were other moments, other successes, all of which came as a result of decades spent letting feelings evolve. For years Armin taught a monthly English-language Bible class in the distant mountain village of Tajima. The drive took him over steep, unpaved roads so narrow, only one car could pass at a time. Trucks used the mountain road and Evelyn worried until Armin got home at night. Sometimes he drove the narrow roads for over an hour to find that only a single student had come to class. Yet each month he went; and each month, even when the others were absent, that same student was there. His name was Ryuzo Ishida and he was a high school student whose father, an unusual man, thought the study of Christianity might be an interesting idea. Ishida came to Armin's Bible class for three years and then moved to Tokyo where he was baptized. Later, he entered the seminary and became a minister.

Now Ishida was the pastor of the ten-member Tajima church. Although he and Armin seldom saw each other, there remained a bond between them. It struck me, when I first saw them together, as a curious bond: their relationship seemed frozen in time. Ishida was now forty years old and married and the pastor of his own church. He had been a pastor in Hokkaido, which had been a trying experience—his salary had been small and his congregation had objected to his part-time teaching—and then had a crisis of faith that led to his leaving the ministry for several years. In all that time, and through all that ordeal, Ishida did not come to Armin for counsel or comfort. Their relationship had not moved to what I thought of as the next logical step—a progression to words. Yet when I asked him why he had chosen the life he had, Ishida said that it was Armin who had inspired him. Armin embodied a feeling; and whatever guidance Ishida might have sought from him would not have come in advice, but in the memory of what had moved him to come to Bible classes every month.

"I remember him talking about the fishermen—the first disciples of Jesus," Ishida said of the classes. "I remember him talking about Luke 10—the parable of the Good Samaritan. He brought books with pictures of Israel, of Galilee, and Jerusalem. I didn't understand much of Jesus's personality. But the fact that he would come, the thought that there must be some driving force that brought him. . . . Reverend Kroehler was rather gentle. I was influenced by his presence."

. . .

The Books and Tea Club was meeting at the home of Mr. and Mrs. Itoh. Mr. Itoh was a retired high school teacher. He was teaching himself Korean. Mrs. Itoh took yoga lessons and Mr. Itoh went with her. They rode together on one bicycle. Armin and Evelyn told me that the Itohs had an unusual marriage in that they had married for love and had placed that marriage at the center of their lives.

The Itohs lived in a modern house surrounded by rice fields. Armin and Evelyn picked up Mrs. Kikuchi on the way. Some of the women would not be able to attend. It was planting season and there was work to do on the farms. Even if it were not planting season, the farm wives would still have been busy. Because they had married into their husbands' families, the housework was theirs to do. Their mothers-in-law supervised.

"We've talked about education and the role of women—the role of the bride in the house," Evelyn said. "One was married into a farm family and wasn't permitted to eat with the family."

The seven attending members of the club took their places around the long table in the tatami-mat room which, like all the rooms in the Itoh home, overlooked the rock garden in the center of the house. The Itohs had built their house around the garden. In the center of the garden was a plum tree, and in the late morning, a pale light shone on the tree.

Everyone congratulated Mrs. Kamita on her son's acceptance to Aizu-Wakamatsu High School. It was the best high school in the district and admission was competitive. Mrs. Kamita's son had moved to a higher educational plane than his friends, who had to go to high school in Aizu-Takada. Admission to Aizu-Wakamatsu High School could mean admission to a good university. Mrs. Kamita was very excited for her son.

Evelyn joked about the problem of the chairman. The club had never chosen a chairman, thereby leaving a void in which conversation rambled. Someone suggested that the host chair the meeting. But the host, said another, was always so busy cooking and serving that she didn't have time to chair. Mrs. Itoh, at this point, was in the kitchen. Another woman suggested that perhaps the person who had hosted the previous meeting should chair. The discussion went on a while longer, until Armin and Evelyn took out the catalogue from the department store exhibit on the life of Anne Frank. Everyone nodded when they saw the book.

"Even if she hadn't had that experience, she'd probably still be very sensitive," Mrs. Kamita said of Anne Frank. "She was so grown-up in so many ways."

"I was interested in her love of Peter," said a second Mrs. Itoh. The hostess served a special tea brewed with seaweed. She returned to the kitchen to get cookies and rice crackers.

"She had the ability to stand outside herself and look at herself," said Mrs. Torii, a teacher.

"I have a twelve-year-old daughter who's just entering that stage," said Mrs. Kayaki. "She criticizes her mother. All the young people go through that period."

"I feel that Anne was expressing what they feel," said Mrs. Kamita. "Others may not be able to express it."

"This kind of student would probably be very difficult for a teacher to have in class," said Mrs. Torii.

All this talk about adolescent girls left Mrs. Kamita wishing that she had a daughter. Her son was her only child and Mrs. Kamita said she was lonely for a daughter. The women, who liked to play off each other, teased Mrs. Kamita about her tall son and how hard it was for her to look up at him when she scolded him. The women talked about being short. Mrs. Itoh said that women were generally small and had to look up at people. She said that when she talked to Armin she got "an awful inferiority feeling" because he was so tall.

No one mentioned the Holocaust until Mrs. Itoh said, "If this book had not been set down it would have been easy to forget this kind of thing." Mr. Itoh, the host, told about a similar diary of a girl who lived in Stalingrad during the long siege. The women talked about those who helped the Dutch Jews survive, even at the risk of their own lives.

"Even before they went into hiding there were all kinds of re-
strictions against the Jews," Mrs. Kayaki said. "They couldn't go out
at night. They had to wear the yellow star."

Mrs. Kamita asked, "Why are the Jews disliked?"

"The Jews tend to be very wealthy and they have an ability to
succeed at business," said Mrs. Itoh.

"There are a lot of books in Japan about the power of the Jews,"
Mr. Itoh said. "The rise of the yen is being blamed on the Jews.
Prime Minister Nakasone is saying that the Japanese are superior
and it looks as if, if that spirit goes any further, Japan will be like
Nazi Germany—the feeling that the Japanese are a master race and
look down on other people."

"The fact that Japan is so dependent on Arab oil tends to make
them friendly with the Arabs," said Armin.

"I feel there may be an attempt to deflect anti-American feeling
with anti-Jewish feeling," said Mr. Itoh.

Mrs. Kikuchi turned to me and asked, "Are there Jewish faces?"

Her candor surprised me. The meeting was surprising me. The
discussion touched upon Japan; but it had not yet taken what I
assumed would be the inexorable slide toward parochialism. Questioning of foreigners by Japanese was common. What was rare was
the question that did not seek a comparison as its answer—"Are
Jews like Japanese, and if so, how?" Prepared to be annoyed by
having to play the role of subject, I hesitated before answering, not
wanting to reply in the offhand way I found effective for deflecting
questions about, say, my fondness for fermented bean paste. I
wanted to answer carefully, seriously, in keeping with the tone of
the conversation. I replied that there were certain facial characteristics found in the gene pool of Eastern European Jews. I said that
all Jews do not look alike, that Jews do not all have long noses and
curly hair, even if I had a long nose and curly hair.

I was asked, "Do Jews all live together?" "Are all Jews religious?"
I replied that not all Jews are religious but that the most religious
live close together to be near synagogues, schools, and kosher butchers. I explained, briefly, the key points of Jewish dietary law. The
members of the club nodded thoughtfully.

And because I, too, wanted to know, I asked, "Were you aware of the Holocaust before you read this book?"

Mrs. Kamita said, "We were aware of it historically." She added that it was not until she read this book that she could identify with what was done to the Jews because she had a daughter who was Anne Frank's age.

"When I read this I was reminded of Japanese history," Mrs. Kikuchi said. "What the Japanese leaders did. No freedom, the secret police, people put in prison because of their beliefs. My father was a pastor. He was sent to prison for two weeks, twice." Then she said, "We knew nothing about the outside world during the war."

I waited for the talk to swing toward Japan, or at least toward the acquisition of such useful information as my positions, as a Jew, on Pacific Basin investment and the price of gold. Yet each time I was prepared to discount the meeting as another forum for assessing the Japanese experience, the talk would again swing away from Japan, so that it could encompass more than what was immediately applicable to the members' lives.

"What made this come about?" Mrs. Torii asked, thinking of war and suffering. "What causes pain? We have to learn from history."

"When the Russians came into Manchuria my family had to flee," said Mrs. Itoh, the hostess. "When war comes people lose their humanity."

"There's something in human nature that says that when we can't get along we find a scapegoat," said Mrs. Kamita.

Mrs. Kayaki told of a book she had read about the Jews. "In this book it says that they were the chosen people and that Gentiles felt rejected and were jealous. It says that the Jews put Jesus on the cross and that they are behind the scenes, controlling the world."

"The first thing I heard about Jews was *The Merchant of Venice*, so that was my view," said Mrs. Kamita.

"But in the case of *The Merchant of Venice*, moneylending was the only work available to Shylock," said Mrs. Itoh, the hostess.

Mrs. Itoh, the guest, said, "Just because someone is a Jew doesn't mean they should be persecuted. Jesus was a Jew."

"It's like in America—the poor whites take it out on the blacks," Mrs. Kayaki said.

"It's like with the Burakumin," said Mrs. Kikuchi.

The longer I knew the Kroehlers the more the club stood apart: its members had asked me about what it meant to be a Jew and had asked for no reason other than wanting to know. I knew other Japanese with whom conversation was all I could want it to be. But they were unusual. Mostly I was asked how it was possible for me to display the dexterity needed for eating with chopsticks.

I had attributed the limits of conversation to my inability to speak intelligible Japanese. Yet after thirty-seven years, after gaining fluency and establishing relationships, the Kroehlers' experience with serious talk was not that much greater than mine. I could see why they enjoyed the meetings: even if the conversation ran far afield of the subject of the month, the talk was still filled with thoughts that began, "I read . . ."

There was a lot of laughing during the meeting of the Books and Tea Club. The meeting was not rushed; it lasted all morning. Mrs. Itoh served ice cream, cake, and crêpes filled with vegetables and beef. The women passed the plates, helping themselves to the crepes.

But then the time came to go home. The women lingered at the doorway, chatting, as they slipped on their shoes. They had lunches to prepare. There was the laundry. There was the shopping for dinner.

Leon Lee could sing two Japanese songs. The team interpreter had written out the lyrics on cards. Leon carried the cards with him so that he could sing with his teammates when they took him out.

One was an old song about a famous street in the city of Sendai. The other was a sentimental song about a man leaving his home for the last time. For a long time Leon had sung only the one or two English songs played by the music machine—it was called *karaoke*,

"empty orchestra"; all that was missing were the vocals, which patrons provided. Leon practiced the lyrics until he could sing the
songs when it was his turn to take the microphone. Soon he did
not need the cards anymore.

It took two years for the Whales to make Leon feel like part of
their team. At the end of his second season they invited him on the
team golf outing. Afterward they went to an expensive Japanese
restaurant where geishas poured their drinks. Leon enjoyed himself
that day, but not as much as he did the second time his teammates
invited him out to play golf and then took him with them to eat
Korean barbecue.

The Whales ate grilled meat and asked Leon questions about
life in America. Some of the players could speak English and Leon
could speak a little Japanese. They helped each other when they
did not know the right words, patching together conversation until
it was time to sing.

For his first five years in Japan, Leon's contact on the team had
been limited to one player, and that was his brother, Leron. Leron,
who had played for four major league teams, came over in 1977 to
play for the Lotte Orions. He was the best hitter in the Pacific
League that year. Leron finished first in home runs and first in runs
batted in. He was among the leaders in batting, too. When the
Orions came close but did not win the league championship, the
manager told Leron that they would have won if he had only won
the batting championship. The statement, absurd as it was, was only
the clincher to a very long season that ended with Leron sitting in
front of his locker, crying. He cried because he was happy—happy
that the season was over—but also because he was drained, more
emotionally than physically. Leron went back to Sacramento, a city
he had left at eighteen for a life in baseball. He had bounced from
St. Louis to San Diego, to Cleveland, to Los Angeles, to Mexico,
to the Dominican Republic, to Tulsa, to Little Rock, and now to
Japan. He came home filled with stories that he sensed no one much
wanted to hear, stories about all the strange things that had happened to him in Japan. For two weeks he rested and then he tried
remembering what it was that had left him crying in front of his

locker. And in the way that the particular sensation of pain cannot be recalled, Leron could remember the events but not the hurt. In the spring he returned to Japan and brought Leon with him.

Leon had not followed his brother to the major leagues. He had reached the top levels of the St. Louis Cardinals minor league organization and sensed that he would go no further. Leon could hit but he could not run very fast. Every so often, Leon would lament his decision not to become a catcher, because if he had converted to a slow man's position, perhaps he might have played in the major leagues. Instead, he played the outfield and felt opportunity slipping past him. Roommates and friends were already in the major leagues. Leon was twenty-five years old, and Japan was offering to quintuple his salary. His wife Pam, reluctant to see her husband abandon his major league dream, wanted him to stay. But that spring, Leon went to Japan with his older brother; and, as happened to almost all of the 286 Americans who had gone off to play in Japan, Leon, in a baseball sense, disappeared from the face of the earth.

He joined the Orions, Leron's team. The Orions played in Kawasaki—Gary, Indiana in a Japanese context. Even on sunny days Kawasaki was industrial gray. Its stadium was the sorriest in the league. Though old, it lacked the charm that can come with age. Its bleacher seats were worn and cracked and painted a queasy green. The infield was a large expanse of dark brown dirt ringed by an outfield so pitted that its grass was not green, but something closer to tan. In the rainy season the field became a bog.

The Orions were not a draw. This was not their fault; the Orions were a good team. The Orions, however, played in the Pacific League. Tokyo's Yomiuri Giants played in the rival Central League. Because they never played the Giants, the team Japan wanted to see, the Orions had a modest following, as did all the teams in their league. The Giants, meanwhile, sold out not only at home but on the road. People came to see the Giants, the team that won the Japan Series for nine consecutive seasons. Because the Giants had triumphed in the late 1960s and early 1970s, when the nation was rising in wealth and confidence, the team came to embody the new Japan. They were the team of Sadaharu Oh, the home run champion of the world, and Shigeo Nagashima, who was to Japan of the 1960s the incandescent sports personality that Babe Ruth was to America of the 1920s. The Orions had the Lee brothers. All the Lee brothers had was each other.

That was how things were arranged. At least that was how they were arranged by Masaichi Kaneda, the manager of the Orions. Kaneda, who had been one of Japan's best pitchers—he had won over four hundred games, an incomparable feat—aided, it was said, by his penchant in his later, managing years, to insert himself into the lineup late in the game and pick up a win. Kaneda was blunt. Just how blunt Leon learned the first time he watched Kaneda beat up an umpire. Leon had seen arguments and watched American managers bump umpires with their chests when they wanted to press a point. But he had never seen a manager beat up an umpire. His brother had told him he would see peculiar things in Japan but Leon thought he had to be exaggerating: baseball was baseball and beyond extensive remodeling.

Kaneda, however, routinely beat up umpires. He would kick the umpires, karate-style, until the coaches restrained him. After the coaches assumed he'd calmed down enough to be released, Kaneda would kick the umpire some more. Kaneda kicked umpires when he thought their judgment faulty. The first time Leon saw Kaneda do this he said to himself, "This is it. He's out of baseball," because such a beating would not be tolerated at home. But Kaneda was not even thrown out of the game. All the umpires, it seemed, were afraid of him, so afraid that once, as Leon watched, a first-base umpire called one of the Orions out on a close play, but, upon seeing Kaneda emerge from the dugout, quickly changed the call to safe. The first time Leon saw him beat up an umpire, Kaneda returned to the dugout and said to him, "That's Japanese baseball. A foreigner cannot do that."

On the road, the Orions stayed in roach-infested hotels—all the Orions except the Lee brothers, who, in Osaka, stayed at the Royal. That was Kaneda's idea: he did not think it seemly for the Americans to stay where the Japanese stayed. The Lee brothers saw where their teammates had to stay and did not protest. Their teammates, in turn, would marvel at the Lees' rooms. The brothers did not spend much time with their teammates. They were seldom invited along. The one time they were, the brothers were so much the focus of attention of all the people clamoring for their autographs that their teammates did not ask them out anymore.

Leon soon discovered that in Japan he would have to abandon the concept of baseball as he knew it. Though the sport would be the same, the game, his brother warned, was different. The new game was "Japanese baseball." The distinction, Leon learned, was not merely one of semantics. It was Japanese baseball because American baseball could not be what it had to be in Japan. It was Japanese baseball because it celebrated—as every society's games do—the qualities the nation admired in itself.

Baseball was simply another in a very long line of attractive things from other places that, before being given a place in the nation's life, were redesigned for local consumption. I was a doubter in the early phase of the education Leon provided for me in the ways of Japanese baseball. The rules of play were the same, as were the distances between bases. The winner still scored the most runs. Even the uniforms looked the same. The Giants' looked like their namesakes from San Francisco. The Hiroshima Carp's looked like the Cincinnati Reds. The team names were written in Roman lettering, as were the players' names across their backs. Leon explained that the surface did not matter. I was dubious. It took a while for me to appreciate how truly impressive a job the nation had done in taking a sport quintessentially American and making it Japan's own.

Leon, too, needed time to adjust. He came to Japan wanting only to play ball. But in Japan, he learned, sport and play had nothing to do with each other.

Baseball was introduced to Japan in the late nineteenth century. No one is sure whether it was brought over by an American mathematics teacher or by a Japanese railway engineer who came back from a trip to America with a bat and three balls. By the 1930s, such American stars as Babe Ruth were coming to Japan for exhibition games and beating the locals by embarrassing scores. By the time the Lee brothers came to Japan, the American major leaguers were still beating the Japanese. But the Japanese were taking an occasional game and showing that, even if they could not beat the bigger, stronger Americans, they could play with them. Every so often there was talk about trying to arrange a "real World Series" between the best of Japan and America. The talk originated in Japan, for the Americans had nothing to prove. Their stars would come over after the long season, complain about the food, flirt with waitresses, hit some very long home runs, and leave a few thousand dollars richer.

When the Baltimore Orioles came over after Leon's second season with the Whales, an old friend and star with the Orioles, Eddie Murray, said to Leon, "You're a king here." Leon smiled. While the compliment pleased him, it was doubtful that Murray had any idea what it had taken for Leon to become the king he seemed to be.

He had made mistakes. Early on Leon fell in love with the fences. He had never seen such inviting ones. The outfield fences in Kawasaki Stadium—and in the stadiums all over Japan—were twenty or thirty feet closer to home plate than they were at home. Leon thought of all the fly balls that in the States might have dropped into outfielders' mitts but in Japan would be home runs. He could not wait to take a shot at the fences, even though he had never been much of a home run hitter. Maybe he would hit thirty. The end of Leon's love affair with the fences coincided with his discovery of the Floating Strike Zone. In order to hit those thirty home runs Leon would need pitches to hit. Fastballs would be nice. Fastballs over the plate would be even better. Leon did not see many fastballs. He did not see many pitches over the plate. Instead he saw balls called strikes, balls that a catcher might nearly dislocate a shoulder trying to reach. Balls would drop in the dirt and be called strikes. His brother had warned him about this. He kept tapes of his funniest balls-as-strikes. His best was a ball that hit him on the back of the leg which the umpire called a strike just the same.

Leon, sensing that something was very wrong, asked an umpire about the Floating Strike Zone. The umpire told him, "You are a foreigner and so strong and the Japanese pitchers need assistance against you." Leon had grown up believing that baseball was a game in which the ethics were not situational. A ball was a ball and a strike was a strike and these absolutes were not determined by the nationality of the man at bat.

Then came practice. At home Leon had practiced hard in the spring. When the season began, however, the practice schedule had been reduced to batting and fielding drills before a game, just to get tuned up. Leon arrived in Japan in the spring and began running. He had never run so much or so often in his life. The Orions, like all Japanese teams, ran all the time. Leon's teammates had an advantage in that they'd been running since the fall, during postseason practice, and in the winter, during pre-spring training.

Kaneda told him, "We're going to make your body strong." For the first ten days of spring training, Leon did not swing a bat. All he did was run. "I thought I was going to die," Leon said, remembering that spring. He ran and did not complain. When the exhibition season began—by then Leon was allowed to swing a bat— the team practiced in the morning and played in the afternoon. One day, after a game, Leon sat down on the team bus and passed out. His head dropped back like a lead weight and, for a moment, looked to his brother as if it had fallen off.

Leon lost fifteen pounds in three weeks that spring. When he sagged with exhaustion Kaneda told him, "This is business. Make money. Just keep pushing yourself. You're going to play first base every day. I don't care if you hit .200. You're going to play for me. You're a gentleman. I like you."

Kaneda liked Leon because Leon drove himself. He sought out drills he could have avoided, drills like the dreaded Thousand Ground Ball drill. The drill called for one man to stand in the infield and catch ground balls without pause for an hour. Every day during spring training another player was selected for the drill. Several required oxygen. When they collapsed in the middle of the drill, Leon saw how proficient the coaches were at aiming batted balls at the fallen men. And still Leon decided that he would show them he could do it.

The coaches told Leon, "Twenty minutes."

Leon said, "Thirty."

After half an hour Leon said, "More."

In those last thirty minutes, Leon prayed, "God, let me die."

His teammates cheered him on. And on that day Leon moved closer to them. As he lay on the ground for ten minutes trying to recover from the hour's ordeal, Leon's teammates saw that he was willing to endure what they had to endure. That he did so without a murmur made him all the more worthy of their respect.

It had not mattered how many ground balls Leon caught during the Thousand Ground Ball drill. What mattered was survival, for this was a drill for honing a quality never called for at home. This was a "Fighting Spirit" drill. Batting and catching mattered in the Japanese definition of the game; but in a sense they were only means for achieving a greater end. That end, contrary to everything Leon had been taught and grown up believing, was not victory. Victory was all well and good but unless it came suitably, its value was cheapened. If victory meant triumph, then it was not so much triumph over the day's opponent but over the weakness that existed in men's hearts. Victory came through will. Winning teams were determined teams, teams with "guts," with *"fighto,"* with Fighting Spirit.

Fighting Spirit meant dirty uniforms. It meant playing through pain because pain could be overcome through determination. But because baseball is, by and large, a contactless game, it became necessary to find ways in which so crucial an element could be displayed. Gestures helped. Two years before Leon arrived in Japan, the Giants, preparing for the Japan Series, insisted upon practicing in a downpour to display their Fighting Spirit to the gaggle of photographers who'd come to see them. Davey Johnson, later the manager of the New York Mets but then second to Sadaharu Oh as the team power hitter, got the flu. The Giants lost the series in seven games.

When the Baltimore Orioles came to Japan after Leon's second season with the Whales, he went to see them play. The Orioles were playing an exhibition in Yokohama and before the game Leon stopped by the cafeteria under the stadium and sat down with Tim Ireland, who had never quite learned the essential point of Fighting Spirit. Ireland, the Hiroshima Carp's second baseman, envied Leon his statistics—he had batted .321 that year and hit twenty-one home runs—because he knew that after his own mediocre season, he was finished in Japan. "Leon's got the big numbers," Ireland would say, wishing that he too had big numbers so that he could stay in Japan. Ireland had thought that if he offered a lusty brand of play—one that displayed a healthy measure of Fighting Spirit—his employers would overlook his meager home run production and keep him around. Ireland would slide head first. He even broke his collarbone, trying to score from third base by slamming into the catcher. He succeeded only in keeping himself out of the Japan Series.

All the Fighting Spirit in the world was not going to keep Tim Ireland in Japan. Foreigners were brought over to hit the long ball. Ireland never could hit the long ball. Still, he thought that he was giving the Japanese what they wanted. But Ireland had not learned what Leon knew only too well—that "guts" in Japanese baseball were a curious quality. People were forever talking about them, but avoiding situations in which they could be tested.

Leon had watched for seven years as infielders dove for ground balls, but often when the balls were past them, thereby getting enough dirt on their uniforms to indicate Fighting Spirit but avoiding the risk of flubbing the play. He had endured seven years of infrequent fastballs because pitchers were taught not to challenge a strong batter with a hard pitch, but instead to change speeds and try to slip a good pitch over the outside corner. Leon had mastered what Ireland recognized but could not manage to apply: the *idea* of Fighting Spirit sounded terrific, and that was generally enough to keep everyone happy.

Leon could appreciate the logic, even if it altered his perception of his game. In a nation covered for the most part by uninhabitable mountains, and where fully ten percent of the population lived in one city, Tokyo, accommodations had to be made if people were going to avoid tearing each other to bits. You could not very well have folks going around throwing baseballs at each others' heads or sliding, spikes flashing, into second base. It was one thing for American kids to play baseball with that sort of aggressive abandon, because even if tempers flared and hands balled into fists, the combatants could, at the end of their tussle, retreat in opposite directions and avoid each other for as long as it took for passions to cool. Japan did not offer that option; there wasn't room. You could not fight and expect to avoid the unpleasant aftermath. You were bound to run into each other. The terrain did not allow for long, solitary walks to the far sides of an endless field.

The Japanese were hardly immune from the inclination toward aggression. But rather than keep it shut away—a futile effort that would only make it that much more enticing, like admonitions on a newsstand not to flip through the pages of the racy magazines— it was first neutered and then raised to a level of significance. That meant being encouraged to slide hard, but avoiding upsetting the man applying the tag. This way both men seemed to be playing hard and neither went home with his feelings hurt.

Leon and Ireland sat in the cafeteria and talked about Fighting Spirit. Leon said, "You added three hours to our meetings. You took our third baseman out with a slide. He said, 'I'm a nice guy. How come he did that to me?' I told him, 'That's baseball.' We had to go over every game. We had to discuss every play we made. And you took the extra base on us religiously. The first time you did that we had the longest meeting in the world. We were told, 'When Ireland gets a hit, take one step and throw to second.' They were trying so hard they overthrew the base."

Ireland laughed. "It's just a state of mind," he said. "Aggressiveness."

Sadly, for Ireland, it was the wrong state of mind. Ireland could not overcome the inclination to keep word and deed consistent. He understood but had difficulty absorbing the variable concepts of truth in Japan: *tatemae*, truth that was stated; and *honne*, truth that was meant. For Ireland, baseball was a difficult game that a man with limited skills could master through grit, both spoken and displayed. But that succeeded only in making him suspect. He could not be counted upon to behave consistently. He argued with umpires. He kicked dirt when he was angry. It was one thing for Kaneda to argue with an umpire, and even to inflict harm, because he was Kaneda, a hero, and people expected that sort of behavior from him. Ireland tried to accommodate. He tried too hard. Ireland taught himself passable Japanese. He learned rules and customs. Then he invited his teammates to his house. But no one came.

Leon had the counsel of his older brother. More important, he had the use of his own better instincts. Argument and confrontation did not come naturally to him. He spoke in a quiet voice. That was why people told Leon he had an "Asian heart." It did not matter what he was thinking. What mattered was that he kept these feelings to himself, and displayed only an easy smile and agreeable manner. Leon did not have to be taught the most important lesson of Japanese baseball. It was instinctual for Leon to help preserve that most essential quality, the team's *wa*, the harmony.

Leon understood that harmony extended beyond friendship. It meant recognizing one's role. When Leon came to Japan he was struck by every team's insistence upon bunting whenever a runner reached first base. By bunting a runner to second, that runner had a better chance of scoring. But because the bunt was an intentional sacrifice, the tactic also meant that the team was an out closer to the end of the inning. Sacrificing improved the odds of scoring a single run but diminished the chances of scoring a lot more, of putting a game out of reach. But, as Leon told me, explaining what he learned, if one team changed strategies and did not bunt— thereby going for broke—everyone else would be caught by surprise and the equation for happiness would be skewed: while one team would win, all the others, in a sense, would lose. That would not do. By bunting, by taking the expected route, each team could rely upon all the others to behave as they should; and baseball could proceed at its predictable pace.

Harmony also meant consistency. And consistency eliminated mistakes. That it also worked to eliminate risk was a lesser consideration. On the day the Orioles played in Yokohama, I sat with

Leon in the stands and watched the Americans build a lead. Late in the game, with the Carp in the field, one of the Orioles hit a sharp bouncing ball to first. For a moment, a brief moment, the first baseman froze. Leon recognized that the Carp first baseman was trying to remember what he'd been instructed to do—and what he'd practiced for hours every day, hours that did not end when the season ended but that extended into the fall and winter and then into spring—when faced with just such a sharp bouncing ball. The problem was that the ball was bouncing in an unusual way, one for which he could not have prepared. Really, it was inevitable in a game with a round ball, a cylindrical bat, and a slightly uneven playing surface. Leon explained to me that the first baseman was afraid to commit himself to instinct. He did not want to make a mistake. Instead of risking an error by attacking the ball, he waited for the ball to come to him, as if it might assume a more familiar trajectory by the time it reached his mitt.

The first baseman bobbled the ball. Because the batter was a speedy runner, he reached first base by the time the first baseman had the ball in his mitt. He hadn't dropped the ball, and so he hadn't made a mistake. He simply hadn't made the play. This did not represent failure. Rather, it represented success in not having failed. Leon had seen this happen for seven years and could still not quite understand the reluctance to take the risk. But he knew well enough not to ask. If that was how the game was to be played, then he was not going to tell people that he knew a better way.

"It is to be admired," Leon would say, "if you can get so far away from the game and still have an image of the game for the people."

Venting to his brother or Ireland or the other twenty-three foreign players was one thing. That was like going out drinking with the boss, berating him to his face and feeling no shame the next morning because in Japan alcohol entitles a man to say what he wants to say without fear of the consequences. In time, as his Japanese improved and his teammates felt more at ease with him, Leon even complained to them and saw that they often felt the same way. Like his teammates, Leon did not tell his managers when he was upset. He did not tell his coaches. He smiled and nodded and did not let them think he disapproved. If their game was less fun than his, that was their business. If Fighting Spirit was, in American eyes, a hollow concept, that was a reality he would accept. Confrontation might have seemed noble. But Leon had learned enough to know that in Japan his suggestions for change would lead nowhere but to the exit.

"They don't want to make a mistake," Leon said to Tim Ireland as they groused a bit before the game. "I've seen guys who've made some mistakes on the field. They'll have those guys out for an hour taking fly balls and then send them down to the farm team."

Leon had hoped to play in the Orioles' exhibition series, but the people who ran baseball in Japan decided that only Japanese players would face the Orioles. This upset Leon and it was on his mind the day I met him for the first time in the hotel coffee shop in Yokohama. I asked whether he'd push to play.

Leon smiled.

"I wouldn't fight it," he said. "I've been here a long time and know to keep the pressure off the Japanese. It makes things a lot easier for a foreigner. I don't ask a lot of questions."

Leon was true to his word, until the following season. Then he started asking many questions about how the Whales could do to him what they did.

Hearn found in Matsue what he had never really looked for: contentment. He was content with his wife and his job. He was content with his home until it got too cramped and he decided to move. Hearn and his wife moved to the street behind the castle where the samurai once lived. The house had fourteen rooms and looked out onto three gardens. At home, after school, he put on a kimono and sat in the shade of the veranda, looking out at his gardens, listening to the birds and the occasional splash of a frog.

His new address was once that of significant men, and that made it an appropriate home for Hearn, who had become a prominent man in Matsue. When he lectured before the local education association on "The Value of Imagination as a Factor in Education," the governor ordered the lecture translated and printed. He joined the society for the preservation of Kizuki shrine buildings. He was popular with his students, who visited him in his new house.

They would sit with him and avoid asking too many questions, because that would have been an imposition. They tried instead to speak of things that they hoped might interest him. Sometimes they would sit happily in silence, enjoying each others' company. Hearn would break the silence. He spoke slowly, in English, so the students could understand him. They used a dictionary when they did not know the words.

The students brought him flowers. They brought pictures and heirlooms and books to show him. They looked at his books. One invited him to his house during festival time when the student's father and brothers played the flute and drums at the temple. The students lingered at Hearn's home, looked at his gardens.

He, too, contemplated the gardens, especially one that seemed to him a world in miniature—"a miniature lake fringed with rare plants, and contained a tiny island, with tiny mountains and dwarf peach-trees and pines and azaleas some of which are more than a century old, though scarcely a foot high. . . . From a certain angle of the guest-room looking out upon it, the appearance is that of a real lake shore with a real island beyond it, a stone's throw away."

In the late spring, when the country was at its most pleasant, Hearn began detecting flaws. He did not want to see them and when he did, he did his best to dismiss them. He wrote to friends about his bouts of ambivalence. His writing for publication reflected little but rapture.

"Perhaps it will interest you to know the effect of Japanese life upon your little friend after the experiences of a year and a half," he wrote to Chamberlain. "At first the sense of existence here is like that of escaping from an almost unbearable atmospheric pressure into a rarefied, highly oxygenated medium. . . . But on the other hand, how much one loses! Never a fine inspiration, a deep emotion, a profound joy or profound pain—never a thrill . . ."

He traveled. During the summer recess, he and his wife jour-neyed to distant temples and shrines. He went back to the great Kizuki shrine and saw a special dance with three hundred dancers that lasted until two o'clock in the morning. During the Festival of the Dead he watched the launching of the Ships of Souls, small paper vessels each with lanterns to light the way for the spirits returning home.

Yet when he read Chamberlain's critique of Japanese poetry he wrote to his friend saying how difficult it was for him to read criticism he knew to be true: "Depth, I have long suspected, does not exist in the Japanese soul-stream."

He thought of leaving, of returning to New Orleans to write. But that seemed impossible. He felt bound to Japan because he knew that leaving would make his wife unhappy.

But he was not only staying for her; he was staying for himself. He wanted to stay even though he was seeing so much that was alien to what he had once defined as happiness.

"The oscillation of one's thoughts concerning the Japanese—the swaying you describe—is and has for some time been mine also," he wrote to Chamberlain. "There are times when they seem so small! And then again, although they never seem large, there is a vastness behind them—a past of definite complexity and marvel—an amaz-ing power of absorbing and assimilating—which forces one to sus-pect some power in the race so different from our own that one cannot understand that power."

Faced with ambivalence and unpleasantness, he rationalized. When he and his wife stopped in their travels in the village of Otsuka, the townspeople ceased their dancing and came to the inn where he was staying. They surrounded the inn and threw sand and pebbles at him. But Hearn was not upset.

"The hostility of the Otsuka folk was really very childish," he wrote to Nishida, "not worth making a fuss about;—a Western crowd would have thrown stones and eggs."

He still had his home and his gardens where he could see a world where only beauty existed. He could seclude himself from disappointment. But now even his gardens did not feel secluded enough.

"Already a multitude of gardens, more spacious and beautiful than mine, have been converted into rice-fields or bamboo groves," he wrote. "Not from here alone, but from all the land the ancient peace and the ancient charm seem doomed to pass away."

He left Matsue in the fall. Another winter aproached and, remembering the gloom and illness of the previous winter, Hearn wanted to move south. His wife felt no bond to Matsue, where her family had fallen from grace into hard times. Chamberlain helped find him a teaching position at a government college in Kumamoto, a city on the southernmost island of Kyushu. His salary would double. Hearn now had his wife's family to support.

His colleagues sent him a farewell gift of a pair of tall vases decorated with birds and flowered trees. The students of the Middle School bought him a samurai's sword. The crimson lacquer sheath was decorated with golden-eyed lions.

"We have no words to express our feeling at this moment of farewell," said the students' representative. "We sent you a Japanese sword as a memory of us. It was only a poor ugly thing."

The Normal School students gave him a banquet. Each class captain rose and read a speech that he had written himself in English. When the banquet was done, the two hundred students sang a Japanese farewell song to the tune of "Auld Lang Syne." Then, marching, they escorted him home. At his gate they shouted, "*Ban-zai,*"—ten thousand years to you. They told him they would come back to escort him when the time came for him to leave.

He left four days later; but before he did, the town was struck by cholera. Students and teachers died. Hearn told his students not to see him off because he did not want them going near the river when they were sick. Yet, on the November morning when he was to go, two hundred students appeared at his gate and escorted him to the dock by the bridge, where he had arrived a year and a half before.

He saw people he barely knew, parents and students' relatives, people who had worked for him and from whom he had bought things, people for whom he had once done small favors. They smiled at him.

Hearn stood on the steamer deck and looked out at the bridge, the homes, the sails, and the mountains. Mist hung over the city. Matsue was chilly; Hearn felt winter aproaching. The whistle blew and the steamer pulled away from the dock. The students waved their caps. Hearn ran to the roof of the deck cabin, waved his hat and called out, "Goodbye, goodbye."

Faintly, he heard the people call out to him, *"Banzai, banzai."*

"The packet glides out of the river-mouth," he wrote, "shoots into the blue lake, turns a pine-shadowed point; and the faces, and the voices, and the wharves, and the long white bridge have become memories."

3

Kumamoto

A cemetery sat on a hill above the Fifth Government College of Kumamoto. The cemetery was abandoned and filled with weeds. Its stone memorials were cracked and moss-encrusted. In the cemetery sat a stone Buddha. He sat in a lotus position and looked down through half-closed eyes on the modern buildings of the government college. At noon, between classes, the new English and Latin teacher, Lafcadio Hearn, left the college and followed the path to the cemetery. When the path ended he cut through the brush, past snakes and grasshoppers, until he reached the broken steps of the cemetery. There he sat and ate his lunch. He sat next to the Buddha and shared the Buddha's view of the buildings below. The buildings, he thought, could have been the buildings of Kent or Auckland or New Hampshire.

He was miserable. He did not like Kumamoto. He did not like his colleagues and they did not seem to like him. So, at lunchtime, he retreated to the cemetery and looked out over the rice fields spread over the plain below. He liked the view because there were no shadows. Every place else he looked, Hearn saw shadows, and his heart sank.

"A vast, straggling, dull, unsightly town is Kumamoto," he wrote.

"There are no quaint, pretty streets, no great temples, no wonderful gardens."

Kumamoto had been a castle town, a feudal stronghold. But now the castle was in ruins, and the city that had been destroyed in feudalism's last gasp had been rebuilt along more Western lines. Its long avenues were lined with bland little homes. Hearn found a house two miles from the city. The house was large, he wrote to his friend Nishida, but its garden was ugly. Kumamoto, he lamented in his letters, offered him nothing. "There is no religion here, no poetry,—no courtesy,—no myths,—no traditions,—no superstitions. Beastly modernization!"

Even his students disappointed him. They were nothing like his Matsue students, who had come to his house and had looked at his books. The new students were men in their early twenties, some of whom had been dispatched to Kumamoto by fathers anxious that they be infused with "Kyushu spirit." Hearn was not quite sure what "Kyushu spirit" meant, but sensed that it was a vestige of the spirit of the samurai. Curiously, it did not please him. For all his longing for the unsullied "soul" of Japan, and for all his loathing of what he saw as its corruption by the West, the Kyushu spirit lacked the innocence that Hearn had loved so much about Matsue.

"The class I am not in contact with have no brains," he wrote to Chamberlain; ". . . their brains seemed to have shriveled up like kernels in roasted nuts. When they talk there is only a dry rattle. Perpetual questions about things that a new-born babe ought to know; and withal a conceit as high as the moon; —an ineradicable belief that they have mastered all the knowledge of the nineteenth century,—and that a foreigner is a sort of stupid servant to be used, but never to be treated as a real human being."

What he revered his students dismissed. The college's aging Chinese teacher, once a samurai, talked to the students about the importance of loyalty, honor, and ancient ways. One day, after such a speech, one of Hearn's better students approached him.

"Sir!" said the student. "What was your opinion of the old-fashioned Japanese when you first came to Japan? Please be quite frank with me."

"You mean old men like Akizuki-san?" Hearn asked, referring to the Chinese teacher.

"Yes."

"Why, I thought them divine . . . and I think them more divine now that I have seen the new generation."

"Akizuki is a type of the ideal old samurai. But as a foreigner you must have perceived faults."

"How, faults?"

"From your Western standpoint."

"My Western standpoint is philosophical and ethical. A people's perfection means their perfect fitness for the particular society in which they belong. Judging from such a standpoint the man of the Akizuki type was more perfect than any Western type I have ever met. Ethically, I could say the same."

"But in a society of the Western type, could such a man play a part?"

"By their unaided exertions?"

"Yes."

"No: they have no business capacity, and no faculty for certain combinations."

"That is true. And in what did their goodness seem to consist to you?"

"In honour, loyalty, courtesy, —in supreme self-control, —in unselfishness, —in consideration of the rights of others, —in readiness to sacrifice self."

"That is also true. But in Western life are these qualities sufficient to command success?"

"No."

Then the student asked, "And Japan, in order to keep her place among nations, must do business and carry on industry in the Western manner?"

"Perhaps," said Hearn.

"I do not think there is a perhaps," said the student. "There is only a must. We must have manufacturers, commerce, banks, stock-companies—we must do things in the Western way, since our future must be industrial and commercial. If we should try to do things in the old way, we should always remain poor and feeble. We should also get the worst in every commercial transaction."

The old way, the student argued, did not apply in the new order: the new order meant hurting people in the interest of profit, seizing advantages regardless of damaged feelings, competing only to win.

The student asked, "Is Western competition based upon love of one's fellow man?" And Hearn, who could not argue with his students's logic, replied, "No."

Longing for the past, Hearn saw only a bleak future. His despondence transcended the sight of Japanese in Western clothing and a campus built of stone and red brick. Hearn saw the nation's heart disappearing, and in its place one all too reminiscent of the world he had tried leaving behind.

I could sympathize, to a point. I would read letter after letter, written week after week—sometimes day after day—and try to imagine Chamberlain's reaction to yet another sad letter from his brokenhearted correspondent. Did he roll his eyes and shake his head and mutter to himself about the poor man expecting more than was reasonable? Years after Hearn's death, Chamberlain did reflect upon him. The thoughts were not kind. Hearn, he wrote, "saw details very distinctly while incapable of understanding them as a whole." Hearn was missing the point: Japan no longer lived apart from the world. It wisely recognized the wisdom of playing by new rules. Hearn understood that but did not want to see it.

We parted here. My happy illusions were minimal. I had come with few; and while I had experienced some of Japan's innocent pleasures, my view had long before been formed by darker impressions. It was one thing to wax poetic about good times with Japan, but I could not share Hearn's pain. I did not care whether Japan kept smiling at me.

At least that was what I thought. But if I did not care, why did Japan upset me? Why did television shows in which Japanese starlets visited the huts of African tribes and laughed at their customs—as the studio audience chuckled along in the background—move me to condemn the Japanese as a small-minded, childish, and foolish people? I took that episode as evidence of flaws more profound than insensitive programming. I could not limit my anger to the moment or impression alone. It all seemed to point to an ugliness that existed someplace in Japan, someplace beyond my view. All I could see were hints. And these I could not dismiss. These I did not choose to dismiss.

My view had been formed by harsh impressions—impressions I found myself trying to confirm. I was born into a world that still aired World War II movies in which the Japanese were the cruel people who robbed Farley Granger of his voice and Richard Conte of his hands in *The Purple Heart*. They were the madmen who charged, bayonets fixed, from the jungles of Guadalcanal. And if afterward they had to support themselves by making cheap transistor radios and toys, it surely served them right for all the bad things they had done in the name of the emperor.

Unable to dismiss those long-held images as an aberration, I noted each suggestion of that darker side. I wanted a link between the Japan I saw around me each day and the Japan that I thought of when I thought of the Rape of Nanking. It was a link, I soon discovered, that seldom appeared—which explained why I leaped to broad conclusions when I saw examples of less significant un-pleasantness.

Then I found the link that I sought. And what I found, beyond the link, was how much it pleased me to learn that my impressions were not wrong.

The link was established through a death, the death of a freshman member of the Takashoku University karate club. His name was Tatsuya Mori and he was nineteen years old. His teammates beat him to death. Another freshman member of the club had forgotten to return the uniform of a senior member that he'd been ordered to wash. All the freshman members of the team were ordered to squat on the training-room floor. The sophomores berated them for the failure to return the uniform. Then they began to beat them. They kicked the freshmen in the stomach. The hardest kicks went to those who did not keep their backs straight during the beating. Mori keeled over. A third-year student ordered the beating stopped. Mori was taken to the hospital. He died that night of shock.

He was not the only one hurt. His teammate, Sadayuki Ichihara, was unconscious and bleeding internally. He spent ten days in the hospital. It took two months for his injuries to heal.

Eight months later Ichihara explained to me that beatings were justified. "They had the right to administer the beating," he said. "Yes, the right."

The sophomores had that right, he explained, because they were the freshmen's elders—their *sempai*—and were only trying to instill the proper spirit in their juniors—their *kohai*. Everyone in Japan, team member or not, had a *sempai* who watched over him; and everyone, in turn, was a *kohai*. The *kohai*, Ichihara explained, were always grateful to the *sempai* for their care and attention. Their relationships lasted a lifetime and extended beyond school and into the workplace. *Sempai* never stopped caring for their *kohai*, and *kohai* never stopped seeking the counsel and approval of their *sempai*. Ichihara explained that even when his *sempai* administered *shogiki*— hard training; literally, "squeezing water from a towel"—he, as a *kohai*, understood that this was being done to make him a better person.

"The *sempai* have the right to beat the *kohai*," he said. "If no beating existed then *sempai* and *kohai* would be equal. They are not supposed to be equal. The last incident went too far. But that type of attitude is necessary for a winning team."

The attitude was so necessary that Ichihara said that if he had *kohai* he might have to beat them. "Bodily punishment is more effective if the oral reprimand does not work," he said. But because the university had disbanded the karate club after his friend's death, Ichihara had no *sempai* or *kohai*. This saddened him. He and some freshmen practiced together and Ichihara said that "after a certain period of time we have to establish the *sempai-kohai* relationship. I think I have to establish the *sempai-kohai* relationship."

Ichihara was nineteen years old. He wore his hair in a crew cut. He had a wisp of mustache. He was soft-spoken and polite and I found him terrifying. I saw in his gentle eyes the eyes of one who would do what he was told to do without deliberation. His friend's death and his own pain had not moved him to question or doubt. They had changed nothing for him. The world he saw was still defined along clear and immutable lines. When he was a *kohai* he was subservient; when he was a *sempai* he ruled. Of course, he would always be someone's *kohai* as well as someone's *sempai*, and so he played both roles, as circumstances dictated. Equality was an inapplicable concept—yet one that I, as an increasingly enraged Westerner, could not help but apply.

At one point I told Ichihara that if recounting the night of Mori's death were too painful, I would stop the questioning. The dean of students, who sat in, insisted that I could ask anything I liked, because he had already asked Ichihara the same questions. The dean, too, saw Mori's death as an unfortunate application of a fine principle. The school, he explained, had been founded at the turn of the century as a training academy for the rulers of Japan's colonies. Its name meant "Reclaim the Land." Although Japan no longer had its colonies, the dean said that the school still offered many exchange programs. "Japan is the leader of the Asian countries," he explained, "so we are supposed to fulfill that obligation toward the developing countries in Asia." I wondered why he didn't just call it Greater East-Asian Co-Prosperity Sphere II. The euphemism had worked well in wartime, a generation before.

My interpreter, Seinosuke Nakakita, who at seventy had lived through the war as an adult, was upset when he came out of the room. Couldn't the dean see, he asked, how that kind of thinking had been Japan's ruin?

But I could not forget the gentle eyes and pleasant voice of Sadayuki Ichihara. I asked Mr. Nakakita, "You could have told him to do anything and he would have done it, wouldn't he?"

Mr. Nakakita did not disagree. And as we drove off I felt a peculiar satisfaction in finding justification for my antagonism.

I read and reread the letters Hearn wrote from hot and ugly Kumamoto. Though I sensed that he had brought it all upon himself through his fanciful expectations, I felt sorry for him in his sadness and rejection, sorry that after fifteen months of pleasure in Matsue, he had not only seen but felt Japan's harsh side. And as I read, and thought of Sadayuki Ichihara, I grew angry with Japan. Beyond the reasonable outrage in response to unreasonable cruelty, why did I feel this anger? Why did I, who so fancied himself the contented outsider, feel as the overly involved Hearn did when, at the end of a long and especially painful letter, he wrote, "For the first time I feel like saying, 'D—n Japan [*sic*]."

But what then of the other, happier impressions? Were they real, or were they simply my projecting innocence where it did not apply? At the times when my disappointment with Japan was keenest, when I swore that I had had my fill of the place, I sought justification for my anger in the letter Hearn wrote when he discovered that even the pleasure of happy times was built, in part, upon illusion.

He recounted for Chamberlain a conversation with a friend, presumably a Japanese friend, because he had no Western friends in Kumamoto.

"You think you were treated very kindly in Izumo?" asked the friend.

"Oh, yes!" Hearn replied.

"And that you have not been kindly treated in Kumamoto. Very well, —that is natural. But do you know why you were kindly treated in Izumo?"

"Well, I should like to get your opinion."

"Simply because you were a new thing, —therefore a wonderful and a strange thing. Everybody wanted to see you; you were a curiosity; —so they invited you everywhere, tried to please you, showed you everything. That was their way of gratifying their curiosity. They did it as politely as they could, so as to leave a pleasant impression. Also, they are very simple people there, and thought you much wiser and greater than you really are. So they asked your opinions about things, and published your opinions in the paper, — didn't they?"

"Yes."

"Well, that was all simply because you seemed to them a wonderful and curious person. But in Kumamoto you are not a wonderful or curious person. The public is accustomed to foreigners of various kinds, and the Kumamoto folk live in the routes of travel."

Other teachers, the friend explained, were familiar enough with foreigners in Tokyo to see nothing new or interesting in him. The people of Kyushu did not think it seemly to fawn over him as did the people of Izumo.

"In a place like Izumo, out of line of railroads, you are interesting to the innocent folk because you are a foreigner. . . . But in other parts of Japan you are uninteresting for the same reason. To educated Japanese you cannot be interesting. You cannot talk to them; you don't understand their ways,—don't belong to their life. You are not a show, or a novelty; you are a teacher,—with nothing re-markable to recommend you to strangers."

"But why didn't you tell me all this before?" asked Hearn.

"Simply because I did not want to spoil your pleasure. You were happy, weren't you?"

Hearn went back and reread what he had written about Japan when his view was limited to life in Matsue.

"I find I described horrible places as gardens or paradise, and horrid people as angels and divinities," he wrote to Chamberlain. "How happy I must have been without knowing it! There are all my illusions facing me,—on faded yellow paper."

⟨ornament⟩ Later, after he berated himself for having believing he was truly wanted, Leon Lee thought of the accident and wondered whether it was then that things began falling apart.

It did not matter that the accident was not as calamitous as it was portrayed to be. What mattered was that after the accident events began spiraling. The accident happened in June, during the rainy season, when each day brings rain and its attendant misery. With the rainy season comes the dank smell of mold, as well as its green residue on bathroom walls and unworn shoes. Even if there is no rain in the morning there will be rain by the afternoon. Only the rice farmers smile during the rainy season. Its coming means the end of the balmy spring. Even when the skies clear and the rains end, in their place comes the baking heat of summer. The rainy season is a time for frowns and irritability and furtive looks from under black umbrellas at the ever-gray sky. The accident happened on a rainy day.

It was a travel date for the Whales, who were flying south to Hiroshima to play the Carp. Leon was driving to the stadium, where he would leave his car. He came to an intersection and signaled for a left turn. At the intersection was a concrete support for an overpass. Behind the support stood a woman about to cross. Leon, his view blurred by the rain, slowly inched ahead. A car cut in front of him. Leon turned to look at the driver of the other car.

He did not see the woman until she was in front of his car. By then it was too late. He struck her on the hip and she fell. But because the car was going so slowly, she sustained only a bruise on her side and a scrape on her knee. The policeman on the scene told Leon that there was no need for him to stay, even though Japanese policemen were infamous for their interminable questioning. The policeman did not even insist upon the usual procedure of Leon's filling out a formal apology. He told Leon that he was free to go to the ballpark. Unfortunately for Leon, among the passersby was a reporter who, upon seeing who was involved in the accident, rushed to his office.

By the time Leon got to the ballpark, his teammates were sure the woman was in critical condition. "They made it sound like I tried to kill her," Leon said of the TV bulletin. He told his teammates that she was barely hurt. But Kondo, the manager, was upset about the accident's reflection upon the team. He told Leon that he was being fined $750 and suspended for a day.

"We have to show our good face to the public," Kondo told him.

"But what does this have to do with the team?" asked Leon, who understood that the way things seemed were often more important than the way they were. The accident called for contrition and punishment, which meant that Leon would pay and sit out a day.

But first it rained for ten days. When the rain stopped Leon endured his brief suspension. By the time he played again, Leon had been out for eleven days.

It took time to readjust. He did not hit well. After seven poor games, the team interpreter was sent to Leon with a message from Kondo: "If you do not start hitting you are out of the lineup."

Leon told the interpreter, "If he wants to take me out of the lineup, why wait?"

He was not taken out of the lineup; but he was questioned.

"You know they're going to throw you outside sliders," Kondo said. "Why don't you hit them?"

"But if it's not a strike, it's not a strike," replied Leon, who knew better.

"You should take up a longer bat," said Kondo. Leon did not know if he meant a broomstick, because that would have been the appropriate length.

Kondo was in his first year with the Whales, having replaced a manager Leon liked, Sekine. Sekine always seemed to be smiling. In the spring, Leon's teammates warned him about Kondo. They said he was a hard manager. But Kondo's reputation did not worry Leon.

Yet by July he was wondering whether playing in Japan was worth all the trouble. It was not his hitting that troubled Leon as much as what he sensed was Kondo's reaction to his hitting, and to the accident. He felt alone. He felt that Kondo and the Whales' management did not care about him or respect him and that their response to the accident—punishing him when even the police had sent him on his way—showed less concern for him than for appearances.

Though the season ended triumphantly for Leon—he batted .303, hit thirty-one home runs, and drove in 110 runs, numbers worthy of a raise—it did not end happily. The team had begun the season as a contender, but finished among the also-rans. Still, Leon had proven himself; he finished strong. Though he nursed the residual bruise of a punishment he believed did not fit the crime, he came to the general manager at the end of the season confident of his place.

The general manager set him straight.

"You didn't seem to be playing with as much enthusiasm," he said to Leon.

"I played the same as I always played," said Leon, who had assumed that the numbers themselves were eloquent testimony.

But the general manager said, "Even though you had good statistics this year, it didn't seem like it mattered to you as much. In the past it seemed like you wanted to help the team."

The general manager produced the charts. Leon had known about the charts the Japanese teams kept of their players. Each man was evaluated in every conceivable way after every game. The teams, all owned by large companies, had applied a tool of Japanese management to baseball—compiling charts and graphs to measure productivity. The graphs, however, measured more than numbers alone; they measured attitude. In the endless quest for self-improvement, Japanese baseball players knew that to impress their managers and coaches they had to display more than skill: they had to care.

Leon, chagrined, looked at his charts. The general manager wanted to talk about enthusiasm, a quality measured on a scale of ten. Leon had begun the season with a steady display of sevens and eights in enthusiasm. But by the end of the season his scores dropped to ones and twos. The downward slide, he noted, began after a rainy day in June, just before a trip to Hiroshima.

"It seems like you don't want to play for the team anymore," said the general manager.

"You guys know the kind of person I am," Leon said, sensing that he was still being punished for the embarrassment of the accident. "I was treated like a criminal. No one protected me. How about showing some respect for me?"

Enthusiasm was tabled. The general manager moved on to production level.

"You had a very low average with men on third base with less than two out," he said.

"How many chances did I have in that situation all season?"

"Only fifteen, so we'll overlook it."

"How do you get around just looking at the numbers, after all the years I've been here?"

"It's the context of your season we're concerned about," said the general manager.

Leon went home and told Pam that he had a bad feeling about the coming year. A few days later, at the team party, the Whales' publicist, usually a friend, did not meet his eye. Leon told his teammates about what had happened.

"No," they said, "we're in trouble. But not you. You're the only power hitter we have."

Leon was home in California, when he saw the telegram from the Whales. He punched a wall, got into his car, and drove for a long time. When he got home he said to Pam, "All the years, just getting stepped on like a bug."

That night he called the team interpreter and told him he was coming to Yokohama.

"No, you don't have to come over," said the interpreter. "We'll send your stuff back."

"Don't you touch any of my stuff," Leon said.

Leon's father tried, with Pam, to comfort him. They reminded him that even if he was finished as a baseball player there were many other things he could do.

Leron Lee was sure his mother was wrong about the telegram: baseball teams did not release players like his brother Leon, the best hitter on the team.

Leron had been rejected by enough teams to know that this was a release that made no sense. But then so much of what he had seen of baseball in Japan did not make sense. When he and Leon had played together for the Orions they had carried the team and, in Leon's third season in Japan, almost took the Orions to the Japan Series. That season the brothers took turns leading the league in batting—Leron won the title; Leon finished close behind and hit forty-one home runs. But when Kaneda, their fiery booster, was discharged as manager, his replacement announced that he was going to "control the Lee brothers" because the team had too much of a "Lee brothers image." Both brothers thought that Leron, the protective older brother, would be the one to go. Instead, Leon was traded to the Whales.

Leron remained in Kawasaki and did not seek the company of his teammates. He made few demands and asked few questions. Yet one crucial answer still eluded him. Leron could not understand why Japan wanted foreign players. "Deep down," he would say, "they don't want us to succeed here."

They could succeed, to a point. Foreigners had roles to play and qualities to be admired. They were displayed on posters and commercials and their lives in far-off countries were filled with buoyant, handsome people who represented the good life. If they made shoddy cars and had crime in their streets and lower test scores, they still had blond women, rugged men, and terrific surfing beaches suitable for group honeymoons.

Foreigners embodied myths. The mythic character embraced by the nation's youth, for instance, was James Dean. His face was on T-shirts and billboards. Always, it was a sad face, the face of the young and misunderstood. So popular was his legend that there was even a brand of cigarettes called *Dean*. Tom Cruise also had a run at mythology in Japan, especially after *Top Gun* opened and thousands of young Japanese men rushed out to buy U.S. Air Force flight jackets. (The appropriate patches were available at the theaters where the movie played.) Then Cruise played a pool shark in *The Color of Money* and "pool bars" opened across Japan. Young men who had never shot a rack bought cue sticks. They went to pool bars wearing white T-shirts and blue jeans because that was what Cruise wore. They shot nine-ball, Cruise's game. Tom Cruise, like James Dean, was an ideal, a figure suitable for admiration.

But foreign baseball players were not heroes. They were not major leaguers, whom the Japanese flocked to see when they flew over for exhibition series. They were foreigners of lesser value. Hitting a lot of home runs made them worthy of admiration in the way that the boy with the biggest biceps in grade school is admired by classmates: he may be strong but everyone knows the high school boys are stronger.

Playing in Japan diminished them. So too, it seemed, did being subject to orders from Japanese superiors. The foreign players were applauded when the team won and ridiculed when it lost, just like everyone else. But unlike everyone else, foreigners sometimes threatened the prevailing order by exceeding expectations. In Leon's last season with the Whales, Randy Bass, a friend of the Lees, was poised to break the single-season home run record of the revered Sadaharu Oh. Bass's team, the Tigers, were playing the Giants—now managed by Oh himself. Oh, it was later said, ordered his pitchers to pitch to Bass—to give him a chance at the record. Bass came to bat five times. He was walked four times. He managed to hit a single on a pitch well out of the strike zone.

Leon ignored the advice of the Whales' interpreter and flew to Tokyo. He went to Yokohama, to the Whales' office. When he opened the door, people looked down at their desks. The office was suddenly quiet. Leon announced that he wanted to see the president and the general manager.

"Do you have an appointment?" he was asked.

Leon said he did not.

"They're busy."

"I'll wait. Get me a cup of coffee. I'll wait. It's early. I'll wait all day if I have to. I have nothing to do."

The team statistician came out of his office and called out Leon's name to greet him. Everyone else kept their eyes on their work.

The interpreter came out and Leon told him he wanted to see the president.

"He's really busy right now," said the interpreter, whose face, Leon noticed, was turning red.

Leon waited a while longer, and then was brought before the president. The general manager was there, too.

Leon asked why he had been released.

Kondo, he was told, decided that he had not hit in the clutch.

Leon wondered how it was possible for a man to drive in 110 runs in 130 games and not hit in the clutch.

He was told that his productivity was down, that the team wanted new players, fast players.

The general manager questioned his enthusiasm.

The president raised the question of the accident. He told Leon that when he slumped after the accident, the team slumped, too. He told Leon that if he had been hitting the team might have won and remained a contender.

"We would have won if you'd driven in more runs," said the president.

"If I had hit .420 and driven in two hundred runs you wouldn't have wanted me to do that. Can you imagine what you would have had to pay me? You don't understand anything about baseball."

The interpreter hesitated.

"Tell them," barked Leon.

Leon told the interpreter to ask who had decided to release him.

"Don't ask," he said to Leon. "This happens."

"Tell them!" Leon snapped. "Tell them!"

The interpreter told them what Leon said.

"Don't ask for a reason," the president said. "Go on with your life."

✐ ✐ ✐ ✐ ✐ "Why don't you give your fingerprint?" Mr. Yamada said to Kathy Morikawa. Mr. Yamada, young, thin, and nervous, supervised the international division of the Yamato City office. Kathy would always feel a little sorry for Mr. Yamada. "If you don't, things will happen."

Kathy had just refused the division clerk's request that she affix her fingerprint to the designated place in her new alien registration booklet. The clerk called his supervisor, Mr. Yamada.

"You'll have a lot to put up with," Mr. Yamada told Kathy. He said that she could face legal action.

Kathy told him that the government could do whatever it liked, but she was not giving her fingerprint.

Mr. Yamada said that he had not been involved in this sort of thing before. He asked Kathy if she could just leave her fingerprint and then protest.

Kathy still refused. Mr. Yamada went to the phone and called the prefectural office for instructions. He was told to determine her nationality and to learn the reasons for her refusal. Mr. Yamada was told that if he could not persuade Kathy to change her mind, he should turn the matter over to the police.

A dismayed Mr. Yamada returned to Kathy and asked her why she refused to be fingerprinted. Kathy began explaining her reasons.

She had made up her mind only a few weeks before, having considered the act for months. Still weighing the risks and rewards of refusal, Kathy and Jun went on a trip to the northern island of Hokkaido. They followed the tourist route that led to a lake set in the mountains. Near the lake was a sulfur mine, a site where the tourist buses did not stop. But Kathy and Jun went to the mine. They got close but could go no further for the stench and choking air. During the war, Korean laborers were forced to work in the mine. Those laborers who stayed in Japan after the war were now parents and grandparents whose progeny still had to be fingerprinted. The trip to the mine convinced Kathy that she would not be fingerprinted again.

Jun had hoped Kathy would refuse, but said nothing because it was her decision to make. Fingerprinting, he believed, was an insidious means to a darker end. "Unity through diversity is very threatening here," Jun would say. He characterized the government's thinking this way: "In order to play a larger role in the world community, Japan should reestablish its identity. The great Japan belongs to the Japanese nation. All foreign elements should be minimized. The foreign element is untrustworthy because it is not Japanese. Very simple."

The Koreans who had been in Japan for generations were, according to Jun's interpretation of the government's attitude, untrustworthy. They could make themselves trustworthy by becoming naturalized Japanese. The government still wanted them to take

Japanese names—the requirement was softened to an "urging" in 1985—a step that came with painful memories. During their occupation of Korea the Japanese had ordered all Koreans to stop speaking Korean, learn Japanese, abandon their Korean names, and take Japanese names. Koreans went to the graves of their ancestors and begged forgiveness for forsaking their names.

The government did not require naturalization. A fifth of the 680,000 Koreans living in Japan, however, did become naturalized. There was, as is so often the case among new citizens, a desire to "pass"—a desire that sometimes ended with children crossing the street when they saw their parents because they did not want to be identified as Korean.

Naturalization did not necessarily mean assimilation, although assimilation—in name and tongue—was what the government sought and what previous governments had sought when they ruled Japan's empire. Municipal registries still kept family histories, which were consulted by companies that did not wish to hire Koreans and by detectives hired by prospective in-laws to ensure that their children married Japanese. For all their attempts at fitting in, many Koreans still found themselves living in the Korean enclaves of Tokyo, Kawasaki, and especially, Osaka. Work for Koreans was often restricted to subcontracting—a social station that brought none of the security, benefits, and comfort of being part of a company. The Korean subcontractors did business with the companies, producing parts cheaply. But they were not *of* the companies. Naturalization could mean access to loans from Japanese banks, and perhaps more business contacts, but in the end, the Koreans would tell of the futility of their name change and other attempts at becoming Japanese. In the eyes of those around them, they were still Koreans, assimilated in all ways but the one that most mattered.

The great center of Korean life in Japan was Ikuno Ward in Osaka, which felt like an undivided Korea in miniature. There were Koreans from the north and Koreans from the south and each group had their own schools, clubs, community bulletin boards, and banks for securing loans Japanese banks did not always extend. The alleys of Ikuno Ward were lined with Korean restaurants where the foods were kimchee and barbecued beef, and the colors bright red and royal blue—bold colors that contrasted sharply with the pastels of Japan. Small South Korean flags hung in the corners. The streets were lined with two-story homes—living quarters upstairs, a factory below. The sounds of Ikuno Ward were of the punch presses and motors that crowded the small factories. The district's smell was of the glue that held together the shoes and sandals the women made. When work was plentiful, Ikuno Ward was a noisy place. Work was contingent on contracts; and contracts came from the big companies where Koreans knew they "need not apply."

After she explained to Mr. Yamada why she refused to be finger-printed—reminding him that even Japanese criminal suspects could not be fingerprinted until they gave their permission—Kathy and Jun went outside and Jun shook her hand.

Two months passed. Nothing happened. Jun stopped by the Yamato city office to check on the status of Kathy's case. Mr. Yamada's supervisors told him that they did not plan to prosecute his wife.

Two days later Mr. Yamada's supervisors called. They said that the justice ministry had ordered papers prepared for prosecution.

"How far has the paperwork gone?" asked Jun.

"It's finished," said the supervisor.

Jun discovered that Kathy's name had come up at a Diet com-mittee debate on fingerprint refusers. He went back to the Yamato city office and berated the officials who had told him that Kathy would not be prosecuted.

The police called later that day. They wanted Kathy to come in for interrogation. Kathy refused. The police interpreter got on the phone.

"I understand you are refusing to come in for questioning," he said.

Kathy said that was correct.

"If you don't come in voluntarily I'm supposed to tell you that we will forcibly make you come in."

Kathy asked how the police would do that.

"We will issue a warrant for your arrest."

Kathy demurred.

"Why don't you come in today? It only takes an hour or so."

"That's not what I heard," said Kathy. "I heard you keep people there all day long."

"Why," he said, "have you been here before?"

She went in the next Monday. Sergeant Uchida of the security police led her to the interrogation room. Jun tried following. Sergeant Uchida told him that only "suspects" were allowed in the room.

Kathy shoved her hands in her jacket pockets, threw back her shoulders, and tried to look mean.

The room was a gray closet with barely enough room for a desk and file cabinet. The interpreter had no room to move his legs without banging them into the desk. The interpreter brought a dictionary, which he consulted frequently.

Sergeant Uchida ran Kathy through the preliminary questions. He asked about her birthplace, parents' names, siblings, and education.

"BA, University of Pittsburgh," said Kathy.

"Pittsburgh, University of America?" asked the interpreter.

"Yes," said Kathy, who liked the way it sounded.

Sergeant Uchida wanted to know when she came to Japan, why she came to Japan, and what she did after she arrived in Japan.

Kathy said she went to graduate school. The interpreter consulted his dictionary. He looked for five minutes but could not find the Japanese word for graduate school.

"Major?" asked Sergeant Uchida.

"Japanese art."

Kathy took notes. Sergeant Uchida did not want her taking notes.

"Tell her not to take notes."

"Why?" Kathy asked.

"No why. Just don't," Sergeant Uchida said, in English.

"All right. I have a good memory."

"How many times have you extended your alien registration?"

"Three."

Sergeant Uchida asked whether she had indeed refused to be fingerprinted.

Kathy said she had.

"And you were accused by the city office?"

The interpreter asked, "How do you spell accuse?"

Kathy spelled it for him.

The interpreter asked, "What's the difference between accuse and prosecute?"

"You're the interpreter," snapped Kathy.

"What were your reasons for refusing?" asked Sergeant Uchida.

"I considered it an infringement of my rights under the UN Covenants on Civil and Political Rights," Kathy said, referring to the 1979 covenants calling for equal rights for aliens and nationals. Japan had signed the covenants.

The interpreter asked, "What's the difference between infringement and violation?"

Kathy got angry. She wanted to know how she was supposed to get a fair hearing if the interpreter could not interpret. She looked toward the door and noticed other detectives looking through the peephole.

Sergeant Uchida calmed her down. He asked, "Have you changed your mind about refusing?"

"No. You can take it to the supreme court for all I care."

"It will never get to the supreme court," Sergeant Uchida said, under his breath.

Then he said, "You said there are twenty-eight refusers nationwide. How do you know?"

"I saw it in the newspaper."

"Do you have contact with any of the others?"

"That's none of your business."

"Where are those refusers from?"

"Various countries. I don't have to tell you."

Sergeant Uchida wanted to know whether she had talked with Jun about refusing, whether he agreed with her action and whether he was willing to support her.

"Did he tell you to refuse?" asked Sergeant Uchida.

Kathy said he did not.

Jun was waiting in the corridor. He was worried. Kathy had been in the interrogation room for two and a half hours. Sergeant Uchida presented him with a document in which Jun would promise not to go back to the Yamato city office and that Kathy would not leave the country. He told Jun that unless he signed the paper, Kathy might have to be interrogated some more.

Jun signed. Sergeant Uchida advised him that if he tried organizing support for his wife, he would be indicted.

Jun said that the sergeant could have him indicted if he liked.

Kathy and Jun went out for supper, but Kathy could not eat. She sipped a soda and tried to remember everything that had happened.

Kathy needed a lawyer. She called a human rights group but was told that it did not involve itself in "movements." She called the National Council of Churches. The council recommended Shunsuke Nomoto, a young lawyer with a confident air. Nomoto heard Kathy's story and said he would represent her. Kathy and Jun said that money might be a problem.

"Don't worry about it," Nomoto said, offering his services gratis. "Just one condition: Don't give up in the middle."

Nomoto was chairman of the Tokyo Bar Association's Human Rights Committee and a member of Amnesty International. He had publicly rebuked the government for having signed and then ignored essential tenets of the covenants on civil and political rights. Nomoto and his associate Aizo Murakami had worked on human and civil rights cases—disparate cases that all involved the same fundamental issue: the price paid for being different in a place where people were supposed to fit in.

For all the boasting about homogeneity, there were many in Japan who did not fit in. Burakumin did not fit. The Ainu, whose aboriginal ancestors populated Hokkaido before settlers from the southern islands of Japan arrived, were different because their ancestors were hairy, which meant that they too were regarded as hairy people who did not look like Japanese. The Burakumin and Ainu were considered minorities even though Prime Minister Yasuhiro Nakasone said there were no minorities in racially pure Japan. When he tried easing himself away from his statement, Nakasone noted that he probably had some Ainu blood in him, considering the thickness of his eyebrows and beard.

Children who had lived abroad were different. When they came back to Japan, teachers criticized them, and other children teased them, for picking up such foreign habits as asking questions in class and volunteering answers. It was bad enough living among Westerners, but it was worse still living among other Asians. Despite the country's Pacific locale, many Japanese did not consider themselves Asian: they were Japanese. Children who had lived among Thais, Malays, or Filipinos were told that they were now "Asian-looking," and that they now smelled like Asians. Teachers informed their parents that the children had become "slow" and "unpunctual."

Blind people were different. So too were the physically handicapped, mentally retarded, and mentally ill. Japanese cities went to considerable lengths to make life easy for the handicapped. Ramps were installed. Traffic signals sounded tones, letting the blind know when to cross. There was only one problem: the blind and handicapped were seldom seen in public. They went to special schools or they were kept at home. When thirteen wheelchair-bound people tried to enter the Supreme Court for a hearing on a handicapped man's lawsuit, they were told that only two could enter in the interests of courtroom safety and order.

The handicapped were an embarrassment, like the mentally ill, whose families were conditioned to believe that it was best to keep them quiet, so as not to bother the neighbors. There were 300,000 beds in the mental hospitals of Japan, institutions that were for the most part private and therefore not subject to government inspection. In 1985 the International Commission of Jurists cited Japanese mental health facilities for conditions bordering on "a serious human rights violation." The commission specified one patient "lynching," physical abuse, and curtailment of visits from and communication with families. One Japanese newspaper reported that patients were controlled with stun guns.

Westerners may have been different; but their differences were often acceptable, at least when compared to those of Asians, almost all of whose countries had been conquered and colonized by Japan during the war. I learned about Japanese attitudes toward Asians from a taxi driver talking about his vacation. He talked very quickly and I could not follow. I asked my wife what he was saying.

"Hold on," she said. "You're not going to believe this."

The driver told her how he arranged his vacations according to whores. The best whores in Asia, he said, were in Taiwan and Hong Kong. He also liked the whores in South Korea.

Others went to Bangkok, where the neon signs in the Patpong brothel district were covered with Japanese lettering. The over-whelming majority of Japanese tourists in Thailand were men. Many traveled together on sex tours, hopping from brothel to brothel. The sex tours also went to Korea, where in the midst of one violent antigovernment demonstration a tear gas cannister exploded in the middle of a party of Japanese men and their Korean hostesses. The Japanese men filed a complaint.

When the world was looking for refuge for the "boat people" of Indochina, Japan refused them entry. After considerable international pressure, Japan relented: first it granted residence to a family of three; then it agreed to let in 500. By that point, in 1980, the United States had taken in 388,000, France 66,000, Canada 60,000, and Australia 39,000. Three years later Japan agreed to let in 5,000.

When Koreans asked to be allowed to place a memorial in the Hiroshima Peace Park to the 2,318 Korean victims of the atomic bombing, they were told there was no more room in the park and that the memorial cenotaph was dedicated to all people—this despite the presence in the park of several other memorials to victims of the bombing. The Korean memorial was erected outside the vast, tree-lined Peace Park, across the Motoyasu River, a monument to the myth of assimilation. The Koreans could be forced to come to

Japan, work as slave laborers, and die in the atomic bombing, but their memorial was to be kept separate.

The government insisted that the fingerprinting was necessary because it was the best way of identifying resident aliens. Names could be changed and photographs doctored, but fingerprints were beyond alteration. The government also pointed to the twenty-four other countries that fingerprinted foreign residents, including the United States. But the United States, which had porous borders and millions of illegal aliens, had stopped fingerprinting immigrants except in the case of refugees. The Japanese government insisted that it too still had a problem with illegal aliens. Five hundred Koreans, it claimed, were caught each year trying to sneak into the country.

The government did not want them. "We do not accept any immigrants as a matter of principle," said Shunji Kobayashi, chief of the immigration bureau. Kobayashi explained that in Japan there was an "absence of demand." Despite that absence of demand, however, the underworld brought in Filipino and Thai women on tourist visas and put them to work as strippers, prostitutes, and cocktail hostesses. Thousands of men from Pakistan and Bangladesh still worked as day laborers and dishwashers, doing jobs that many Japanese no longer wished to do.

Those caught overstaying their visas were deported. Those with long-term visas could stay but had to be fingerprinted, as did those born in the country and educated in Japanese schools, but who were Korean only in heritage. They could try to become Japanese. They could even pass—that is, so long as people did not know who they were.

Faced with discrimination rooted in a celebrated ideal—the "uniqueness" of the Japanese people—the Koreans seized upon fingerprinting as a vehicle for campaigning against their consignment to unacceptability.

Kathy's lawyer, Nomoto, thought she would be convicted of violating the alien registration law, a conviction that brought a maximum sentence of a year in prison at hard labor and the equivalent of a two-hundred-dollar fine. But he did think she could win a suit. Nomoto advised Kathy to sue the government if indeed it was not issuing to fingerprint refusers the permits necessary for reentry to Japan. Christmas was approaching. Kathy applied for a permit. She thought she might go to Seoul.

The clerk at the Yokohama immigration office leafed through Kathy's application and passport. He verified her valid visa. He checked her fingerprintless alien registration card.

"She's here," he said excitedly. "She's here."

He rushed to his supervisor, seeking instructions.

The clerk and his supervisor checked through a pile of directives and looked at her application, frowning.

The clerk returned and said that her application would have to be checked.

Kathy asked why it was being checked.

The clerk did not answer.

Kathy asked how long the check would take.

A week to ten days, said the clerk.

"That long? I have to make preparations."

"Well, maybe you don't," said the clerk. He fumbled for words. Then he said, "One week probably."

The clerk checked back with his supervisor.

"Yes. A week or ten days," he said. "You'll get a postcard."

Two weeks passed. Jun called the immigration office. The papers, he was told, had been sent to the justice ministry.

Five weeks passed. Kathy called the ministry.

"I'm sorry to tell you your request has been refused," said a man speaking English.

"Why?" Kathy asked.

"Just because you refused to be fingerprinted, I suppose."

"That has nothing to do with it."

"Well, it has something to do with it."

"Then I can't go out?"

"Yes, you can go out."

"But I can't come back in."

"You can apply for another visa."

At New Year's Kathy and Jun had gone to a temple at Kamakura. Kathy wanted to see what the New Year held for her. She bought a fortune stick from a priest with *sake* on his breath. Kathy pulled the stick from the cluster he held. The priest checked the number on the stick and chose the corresponding fortune. He unfurled the paper, read the characters, and offered his regrets.

"A very bad year," said the priest.

Interrogated, indicted, and barred from re-entry—Kathy had not imagined that the government would so zealously pursue its case against her. Still, she had seen little anger. With the exception of Sergeant Uchida, she had experienced no hostility—that is, until she went to Kobe, to a meeting of supporters for Ron Fujiyoshi, an American missionary of Japanese descent who also had refused fingerprinting.

Fujiyoshi lived in Ikuno Ward and worked in a rubber factory. He had refused fingerprinting, he was quick to say, not because he was a missionary working with Koreans for whom he felt responsibility and solidarity. Rather, he argued, the requirement was nothing less than a principle of exclusion rooted in the traditional belief of Japan as a family with the emperor at its center—a system abolished during the American occupation, but which Fujiyoshi argued remained at the heart of the government's quest for homogeneity. Fujiyoshi had eight lawyers and three support groups. Kathy had two lawyers and Jun, and that seemed sufficient.

Others thought not. Soon after her case became public, Kathy began receiving calls asking when she was establishing a support group. Kathy said she did not plan to form a support group. One caller said, "You're going to ruin the whole cause if you don't have a support group."

"Why don't you form a support group?" a professor asked Jun. "It's not only good for your wife, but those involved will learn a lot of things."

When Jun explained that they did not wish to form a group, the professor said, "It's okay for you, but you have to educate the public."

"We want to break the routine where you get a support group and a chairman and treasurer are elected," Jun told the professor. "People think it has to be formal. But can we stand on our own two feet?"

Kathy and Jun had been to a meeting of other fingerprint refusers in Kawasaki. It was a somber affair. One by one people rose and told their stories. They passed a resolution, and the meeting was adjourned. Only afterward, in a coffee shop, did people break away from the strict formality of the meeting and begin to talk.

It was much the same in Kobe, at the meeting of Ron Fujiyoshi's supporters. First Fujiyoshi spoke, offering the keynote speech. Then Kathy spoke about her case and the need for working together despite differences.

In the middle of her speech a Korean pastor hurried into the room. When Kathy was finished, he rose to talk. He reminded Kathy of a speaker at a revival meeting.

"This is not Kathleen Morikawa's problem," said the pastor. "Her face is white."

Having refused fingerprinting, in part, to protest discrimination against Koreans, Kathy now heard that she was peripheral to the cause. She did not dispute the pastor's point about the target of the most palpable discrimination. But she did not agree that discrimination was exclusive to Koreans. She did not agree with Ron Fujiyoshi's attempt to link fingerprinting to the emperor. She did not agree with those who insisted she needed a group.

Kathy had acted alone against a system that celebrated conformity. She would support other attempts to change the law. But she would do so on her terms.

She would not be pressured into going along. She would be different.

Home, fortunately, was a warm place. In the morning Hearn's wife woke him and the servants came in and bowed. He rose and smoked his pipe as the servants prepared the small offerings for the spirits of the ancestors. After breakfast his wife helped dress him. Hearn had resisted the practice, but now he accepted each article of clothing as she handed it to him. He would have liked her to breakfast with him, but understood that she was obliged to eat with the other members of the family. She did sit with him and nibble.

The servants followed him to the door. They bowed and waved good-bye as he rode off in his ricksha, and when he came home from school, they were at the door to greet him.

In the evening, after dinner, the newspaper was read out loud and games were played. Everyone laughed. Some nights the servant girls went out for walks and stopped to buy trinkets. They were home in time to bow low and bid him good night. Hearn read or wrote in bed. His wife apologized if she fell asleep before him. He wrote, "I wonder whether Japanese life has spoiled me for any other. . . ."

But still the place eluded him. He would look at the smiling faces of the eleven people in his household and assume that their smiles meant happiness. Then, by chance, through a hole in a paper screen wall, he spotted the young cook in a solitary moment. He saw a different face. It was an old man's face, drawn, haggard, and deathly.

At school his students, who could sound so cold and harsh, could also surprise him with the sentiments they expressed on paper. They wrote about the day their mother or father died, about crying on their first day of school but coming home to fruits and cakes. Though the writing touched him, he felt distant from his students.

"Each new generation of students seems to me a little harder-featured, more unsmiling, more sullen, more lacking in spontaneity, and less courteous, than the preceding," he wrote to Chamberlain. "I don't love them much."

Yet he wrote like a man who wanted very much to be in love. He was happy and comfortable and occasionally moved not only by ingenuousness, but by rowdy, patriotic celebrations in honor of the imperial family. But he could not seem to locate a place for himself in people's hearts—"It is so difficult to reach the people."

He tried. He had the college's aging professor of Chinese to his home. The professor, whom his students scorned as a relic, brought a miniature plum tree and two scrolls bearing poems he had written himself. Hearn would remember the visit less for the details than for the feeling the professor brought to his home, a feeling that endured long after the plum tree lost its blossoms.

"Perhaps only the memory of that divine old man;—perhaps a spirit ancestral, some Lady of the Past, who followed his steps all viewlessly to our threshold that day, and lingers with me awhile, just because he loved me."

But that was a love of which he could not be sure. And because he was unsure, Hearn tried to seize and hold onto whatever held the promise of love. On a summer trip to the distant island of Oki, he and his wife stopped at a hotel where the young scion of a now-poor samurai family worked as a servant. Hearn pitied the boy. And from the pity came a plan: Hearn told the boy to come away with him and his wife.

They returned, together, to Kumamoto. The boy entered school and Hearn cared for him as an adopted son. But when he wanted to show the boy how much he cared, when he wanted to pet his head or stroke his hair, the boy withdrew. The boy became a problem. He ran away. He did not listen. The boy returned none of the affection Hearn tried heaping upon him.

Finally, Hearn let him go home.

"I know more about the Japanese than I did a year ago," he wrote to Chamberlain; "and still I am far from understanding them well."

His students asked him about romantic Western literature. "Teacher, please tell us why there is so much about love and marrying in English novels," said his students; "it seems to us very, very strange." He told them the story of Sir Bor, who, in *La Morte d'Arthur*, forsakes his dying brother to save a damsel's life.

"The story certainly is immoral," said one student.

"We think it is a very bad sentiment," said another.

"It is a horrible story," said a third. "The man who could abandon his own brother to death merely to save a strange woman was a wicked man. Perhaps he was influenced by passion."

But Sir Bor, said Hearn, behaved as brave and noble men of the West will behave.

He was told, "We would rather hear another story about another form of society."

He told them about Hercules but found that physical strength did not impress his students.

He told them the myth of Alcestis and Admetus—how Alcestis was willing to die in place of her husband Admetus, King of Thessaly.

One student thought Admetus's subjects should have been ashamed of themselves for not having begged for the honor of dying in his place. Another thought Admetus was a coward for being afraid to die. Still another said that perhaps Admetus was simply trying to be a good son who knew that if he died, his father would be left alone. Admetus, he said, should have told his wife, "If you love me, please die in my place"—thereby ensuring, said yet another, that her spirit would live on for thousands upon thousands of years because "it is the Formless who teach us more kindly than our own kindest living teachers . . . ."

Much that he once considered divine they dismissed as foolish. When he read a Tennyson ballad to his students—"She is more beautiful than the day"—they could not understand how a woman could be compared to the day. The day was part of nature; comparison to a woman was inapplicable. Romantic talk, romantic words like darling and adore did not exist for his students. They loved. They loved their mothers and fathers and siblings and grandparents. And they lusted. But lust was a function of passion; and passion was not love.

Hearn tried not to resist. Perhaps, he sensed, his view was too narrow. He began believing that the beauty Japan saw was beauty to which the West had blinded itself. The Western definition of natural beauty, he wrote, was too often embodied in a feminine form. In Japan, nature was neuter and its appreciation was without limitations.

He tried looking at the world through new eyes, Japanese eyes. He extolled the beauty of simple Japanese poetry, of Japanese art and dance. He contemplated the rocks in his garden. He listened to the sound of insects.

He wondered whether he was fooling himself. It was as if he were spinning around and around, trying to rid himself of ideas that had formed him, trying to redefine himself through all that was around him, and then returning to the starting point only to find the man he always was. Though he understood the limits of change, Hearn bristled at the indifference to his attempt.

"Again the foreign teacher is trusted only as an intellectual machine," he wrote to Chamberlain. "His moral notions, his sympathies, his intuitions, his educational ideas are not trusted at all;—a Japanese teacher is always consulted by preference. There seems to be the set conviction in every official mind that a foreigner *cannot* understand Japanese students."

It was as if his appreciation meant nothing. It was as if he could not really appreciate because he was still a foreigner and therefore unequal to the task. A foreigner could never know, could never feel, could never appreciate as could a Japanese.

✦ ✦ ✦ ✦ ✦ "*Laserstream* is interesting," Eugene Matthews told Tatsuo Shigeta. They were searching for a name.

"What is *stream*?" Shigeta asked.

"Stream. Whoosh," Eugene said, drawing an imaginary line across the air.

Eugene wanted a name from Shigeta this morning. His voice was weary. It was 10:30, and Eugene was spent. It was Tuesday and on Saturday Eugene and Shigeta would fly to Israel to sign the contract for the joint venture that would keep Think Laboratory just ahead of its competitors. The laser-operated cylinder-etching machine that resulted from this venture did not yet have a name. For days Eugene had been trying to get Shigeta's attention long enough for him to decide on a name because there were many important things to do before Saturday. But when the telephone rang, Shigeta jumped to answer it and when someone in the plant had a question, he rushed off for half an hour to see what needed to be done. Now Eugene had Shigeta seated on the soft leather couch by the gauzy hospital-bed screen where the customers were seated. He stood at a display board, writing down names.

"*Laserator?*" asked Shigeta.

"Ah, like *generator,*" said Eugene.

"*Laserator,*" Shigeta said again.

"*Laserstream,*" said Eugene.

"*Boomerang,*" Shigeta said, suggesting the name of the company's flagship machine.

Eugene did not want *Boomerang. Boomerang* was already a name. Eugene wanted a new name. He liked the *stream* idea.

"*Laserator,*" Shigeta said.

"*Laser beam,*" said Eugene. "*Laserstream* is close to it. *Laserstream.* Smooth." His hand glided along. "*Laserstream.*"

Shigeta sat with his arms folded. He set his jaw and looked down.

"Okay," Shigeta said.

"All right," said Eugene, sounding like he had just run five miles and was happy with his time.

Eugene smiled. I had not seen him smile in a while. On Saturday when we were on the subway, Eugene started talking about work and Japan, and his voice got loud. The more he talked about how angry he was about work and with Japan, the louder his voice got. People looked over their shoulders at Eugene and when he saw them looking at him he barked at them in English, "Isn't that right?" The people turned away and made believe that Eugene was not there.

Eugene worked the same endless hours; but now he came into town swearing that he was through with Japan and with Think and with Shigeta. Things were not proceeding as Eugene wanted them to proceed. The days would disappear under a flood of petty tasks: typing letters because he did not have a secretary; retyping the letter the temporary secretary had typed—he had pushed Shigeta to get her for a day—because she did not understand English and Eugene's words came out reading, "This commitment is facemast"; making travel plans; changing travel plans when Shigeta wanted his plans altered; all the while trying to prepare the documents for the joint venture and a speech he was to give at a printers' convention in

Chicago. Shigeta had not yet decided who would accompany Eugene to Chicago. Eugene wanted an English speaker to accompany him to America. Shigeta took this under advisement. When he could not bear to be at his desk, Eugene retreated to the company cafeteria, where he hid and drank Coca-Colas.

Eugene called me two or three times a week. The animation gone from his voice, Eugene would say that he could not work like this. He had not come to Japan to type and book flights. Nor did he think Shigeta should be answering phones left unanswered and seeing to deliveries. That was the way little companies operated; and Eugene wanted Think to become a big company. He wanted changes. Really, he wanted one change, a change in the way Shigeta ran his company, which meant a change in Shigeta.

Eugene and Shigeta would sit in the sushi bar and talk and plan and dream out loud of Think Laboratory in America. And then Eugene would ask, "When?"

"Soon," Shigeta would say. "A year, two years. Three years."

Eugene did not think this was soon; he thought it was a very long time. Eugene decided that he had two options: either he was going to make Shigeta define "soon" as he did, or he was going home.

In two years with Shigeta, Eugene had learned that change in Japan could be an interminable process. Eugene had also learned that that grinding process often needed a jolt to set it moving. The end of Japan's feudalism and the nation's turn toward the West began in 1853 when Commodore Perry anchored off the coast of Shimoda and announced to a stunned Japan that the United States wished to trade. Eugene, too, would try setting Shigeta on the path to change by using a different form of coercion: his departure. If Eugene left, the access he had brought Think to the American market would go with him.

On the Monday of the Golden Week holiday, a week of two national holidays during which almost every company shut down and Japanese set off for Guam, Honolulu, or mountain hot springs, Eugene rode his motorcycle to Yokohama. There he met Ikuo Umebayashi, who had introduced him to Shigeta and who had therefore assumed a great stake in their relationship. Think had only two and a half days off. On Saturday, when the trains heading away from Tokyo were jammed with vacationers, Shigeta had walked among his employees, joking, telling them that they were the hardest-working company. People did not laugh about this, not with their friends off having fun.

Monday was a sunny day and Eugene sat at a low table in the Umebayashis' den. Mrs. Umebayashi fed him. Mr. Umebayashi listened.

"Mr. Shigeta's goal is to be number one in Japan," Eugene said. "But there is potential to be great in the world. I don't want to stay forever. Not for twenty years. You understand my goals."

Umebayashi had understood Eugene well enough to believe that he and Shigeta would be good for each other. He was a business journalist who now ran a center for small businessmen. Shigeta was a member of Umebayashi's group. It was through the group that he had met Eugene.

Umebayashi believed that Eugene could help Shigeta at a time when Think was on the verge of bigger things. After twenty years of growth built upon small steps, Umebayashi felt that the time had come to attract investors, and with the investors, new people to manage Shigeta's company. There were risks; but Umebayashi believed that it was the only way for Shigeta to grow. If he did not grow, he risked being overtaken by those with the money to eclipse him. Think could become rich and perhaps a player of consequence on the world printing scene. It would still be called Think. But it would no longer be Shigeta's company, not the way it had been.

Umebayashi held seminars which Shigeta dutifully attended. But when he arranged for a consultant to visit Think for a few days, Shigeta sent the man away. Umebayashi understood what a new sort of Think Laboratory would mean for a man like Shigeta, who had made himself indispensable.

Umebayashi also understood that Shigeta was well aware of the risks of change. Failure was all too common for those who tried pushing their small companies onto a higher plane. As high as the failure rate was in the United States, it was higher still in Japan, where the good money and the best people were still drawn off by the big companies. Shigeta's peers were, like him, cautious men. If venture businessmen in America were often young and restless people—people like Eugene—who might take their companies public in five years, in Japan they were almost always prone to the slow route. Eight years was the fastest known time for any Japanese venture company to go from inception to public ownership. One company had done that. In the United States twenty firms had done it in three.

Eugene knew only too well how much Shigeta resisted letting go. But he also believed that the first step toward profits abroad could come less painfully. All Shigeta had to do was give Eugene permission to set off in search of the American market.

"I must know the future of the company," Eugene said. "I can go my own way."

Umebayashi told the story of the Nobushi Gata, a band of samurai who lived in the mountains and whose loyalties to feudal lords lasted only as long as that relationship was useful. These samurai, he explained, had to decide whether they'd stay in the mountains where they were strong, or come down into the towns where they might become stronger—or where they might lose everything.

He drew a diagram, showing the samurai on the top of the mountain. Eugene said, "Damn, I'm in the mountains."

"The idea was to move down from the mountains, take over a town, get bigger, make more people work for you," Umebayashi said. "Slowly they got bigger. It's very difficult to live in the mountains. You have to come down to the town. But you have to know what's in the town."

That was Eugene's idea all along, knowing what was "in the town" and knowing how he could turn that knowledge to his advantage. He had learned important lessons about loyalty and hard work and the bond that could exist between employer and employee. Now, as he learned about change, he saw much that displeased him. His disappointment was not limited to Shigeta, although with Shigeta it was most acute because it was Shigeta for whom he cared. Eugene saw how skillful Japan could be at deflecting attempts to change it, especially attempts to get it to buy as much as it sold. Eugene's disappointment escalated to anger the day he watched Dennison, the American company he had introduced to Japan, discover just how inaccessible—how resistant to change—Japan could make itself.

Dennison came to Japan to do business. Eugene and Shigeta helped arrange meetings and introductions. One plan was to seek a contract for printing cigarette packages from Nihon Tobacco, the former government tobacco monopoly. Dennison was among the best known American printers. It was experienced at printing cigarette packages. A meeting was arranged, and Eugene and Shigeta accompanied the Dennison officers. The meeting did not last long.

"Are you as big as Dai Nippon printing?" asked one of the six Nihon Tobacco representatives.

Dennison's vice president admitted that his firm was not.

Shigeta jumped in and said that he knew all the big Japanese printing companies because they all used his machines. He vouched for the quality of Dennison's work and printing methods. He assured them that Dennison's printing system was even better than the one Nihon Tobacco was using.

Dennison asked if it could submit a sample of its work. It asked for Nihon Tobacco's pricing list.

"You can't give us the same quality," said Nihon Tobacco's representative. "You can't do it on time. You can't do it at a competitive price. So there is no sense in our giving you criteria for submitting a bid. You cannot submit a bid."

"Are you saying we can't compete?"

Nihon Tobacco said that was just what it meant.

Eugene had never seen a company told that it could not submit a bid because it was presumed incapable of competing in the market. The Japanese market was closed to Dennison, just as it had been closed to the foreign companies that tried submitting bids for the new international airport near Osaka and were told only Japanese firms could get the airport done in good time; the American aluminum baseball bat-maker who was barred from selling in Japan because the government decided its bats did not meet the safety standards of Japanese bats; ski equipment manufacturers who were told that because Japanese snow was unique, foreign skis could not pass local certification tests.

The commercial counselor's office at the American embassy kept a thick file of cases in which foreign competitors were (not very mysteriously) kept out of markets in which Japanese firms had an interest. Congressmen came through Tokyo, talking of the protectionist mood in Washington and warning the Japanese that unless their markets opened, there could be serious consequences. Sometimes, after considerable pressure, those markets did open. And sometimes Japan's trade officials let it be known—off the record—that the Americans were great talkers and second-rate doers, and that the Japanese did not quake at the sound of their threats.

Eugene acknowledged that Americans could be not only blustery but ill-prepared. American firms often came to Japan unschooled in the market and unwilling to work the way they had to work to make a place for themselves. There were companies that did not understand about service and relationships and taking years—not months—to build secure positions in the market. Yet while there were many American firms that looked only to turn quick profits, there were many other foreign companies who found themselves mired in a thick bureaucratic web when they tried coming into Japan.

Eugene watched and swore that he would come back, perhaps as a trade negotiator, and play the same game the way the Japanese played it, burying their imports under tons of regulations, offering windy explanations about the special character and needs of the American consumer, and in all ways showing the Japanese that two could play at the game of obfuscation.

"I'm gonna get 'em," Eugene would say, when he saw Japan at its most unfair.

But first he had the more immediate concern of Tatsuo Shigeta. Eugene wondered about Shigeta's life, about what filled it aside from work. After two years, Eugene understood that there was nothing in Shigeta's life but work. Mrs. Shigeta, knowing how much her husband talked with Eugene, hinted to Eugene that he suggest that her husband exercise. But Shigeta did not exercise. He worked, and when he went home—sometimes bringing Eugene with him—he pulled a tape from his vast video library and educated himself on technological matters. There were no diversions, and this made Shigeta no different from most of the people around him.

Work was so much at the center of people's lives that the government found it necessary to extol the pleasures of rest. Encouraging vacations and weekends away from the office, the government judiciously avoided using the Japanese word *yoka* because it implied wasted time. Instead it spoke of ree-zha—"leisure"—opting for a Japanization of an English word. Newspaper editorials called upon the nation's workers to have fun, to go on vacation. Most people used only half of their two weeks of vacation. Taking more time, salaried workers explained in endless surveys on the quality of Japanese life, would make things harder for everyone else, and so it was better to stay and work.

Work meant that families could be separated for years if the company decided that a man was to be posted far from home. These men were called *Tanshin Funin*, or "Lone Voyager Away from Home." Their wives stayed behind with the children, especially if the children were in a good school. For all the hours and sacrifice and talk of loyalty, work did not always make people happy. Polls reported that many men did not like their office spaces, their bosses, their hours, and the demands of having to go off with workmates at the end of the day for drinking and mah-jongg. Female employees admitted, anonymously, that they did not like being forced to join male colleagues at drinking parties because the men sometimes touched them suggestively. Still, they went to the parties and poured the men's drinks. They did so because, as with the men, it was expected of them, just as it was expected of everyone to work hard and long and without complaint.

Eugene did not mind working hard, but he believed that life offered more than any office could provide. He wanted Shigeta to see this. When they were planning their trip to Israel for the contract signing, Eugene suggested a day trip to Jerusalem. Eugene had not been to Jerusalem and was excited by the prospect of the trip, and perhaps a visit to Bethlehem. Shigeta did not want to go to Jerusalem. There was no business to do there and so no point in wasting time with the trip. When Shigeta spoke like this, Eugene called to complain how Shigeta cared about nothing but work, and that all his self-taught technical knowledge could not make him a worldly man.

On the Tuesday night before Eugene and Shigeta left for Israel, we all went to the sushi bar with Hanan Drory, who worked for Scitex, the Israeli company with whom Think was embarking on its new venture. Drory had been in Japan for a month, working on the technology for the new machine. He and Eugene enjoyed each other's company. Drory was candid and Eugene liked talking to him, especially about the company. Drory could not understand how Think could function as it did, with one man doing everything. He mentioned that to Shigeta at dinner.

The conversation had been drifting along. Drory, Shigeta, and Eugene toasted each other and their new project and the international market that awaited them. I had heard it too many times before. I was no longer moved to envy by the sight of Eugene and Shigeta beaming at each other. The talk now seemed little more than platitudes. I checked my watch and wondered how long I'd have to stay before my exit could be graceful.

"Maybe we celebrate too early," Drory said. "Now the big work starts."

"Yes, yes," said Shigeta.

"But you're on the right track," Drory said.

"Mr. Drory, my thinking is the same as yours," said Shigeta. "Our technology can create a bigger market. Scitex and Think by themselves cannot create a bigger market."

"But at the moment, you're doing all the running around in Japan," Drory said. "Is that sufficient for you, one man? In Scitex our president used to do this at the beginning and he didn't see what was coming far enough in advance."

Shigeta tried interrupting, but Drory continued and Eugene, excited by what Drory was saying to Shigeta, kept interpreting.

"He thought he could do everything himself," Drory said. "He found out that he couldn't do all the selling with all the customers. He had no time to manage the company."

Then Shigeta spoke. "I respect your president. I understand his trying to do everything. Scitex is a very big company. We have only sixty people, one-twentieth the size of Scitex. But I have a lot of power in this market in Japan. But only in Japan right now. The market is growing in Europe. I have been to Europe. I know what's going on. Eugene knows what I'm going to say. America and Europe are a sleeping market with big possibilities. . . ."

He went on about the way the market would have to change, how jobs unfortunately would be lost, but that a new age for printing was coming. Theirs would be the task of educating this vast new market. It was not merely a matter of selling machines. The world of printing was changing. They were the vanguard of change.

As for the world of Think Laboratory, Shigeta did not say. He did not dispute what Drory told him. He simply did not address it.

And as Shigeta spoke, I looked at him, sitting next to me at the small, low table. He talked in his easy, friendly manner. He did not argue. He just turned the conversation back to where he wanted it.

✐ ✎ ✐ ✎ ✎ On the train to the Rural Gospel School I saw the Hutterites sitting together near the front of the car. They were a family, a mother, father, and young daughter. They were dressed in dark blue and black, plain colors cut in the simple fashion of the Amish, a group to whom they, as Japanese members of a German sect, were akin in faith and exclusivity. The father, a pastor, wore a black fedora. The mother wore a blue bonnet and a dress that came down to her ankles. The daughter wore a white bonnet and snow boots. She was perhaps five years old but still retreated from strangers. She ran to her mother and cried when she went away.

Armin Kroehler had invited the Hutterites to the Rural Gospel

School to speak about the good things people could bring from the earth when they worked together. Armin hoped that the farmers of the Aizu district might see what the Hutterites had done with their meager tract of land, and apply this knowledge to their own work.

I went to the Rural Gospel School anticipating success, for this would be a gathering of Christian farmers searching for answers at a time when their farms were dying. Yet just as success for the Kroehlers had come subtly, so too, I was to learn, did failure: there was no rejection of the Kroehlers or their message. In fact, there was a good deal of acceptance, so much so that I sensed that the only people who believed that the school had somehow failed in achieving what Armin and Evelyn had hoped for were the Kroehlers and myself. The farmers who gathered in the Aizu-Takada church listened all day. They asked questions, made comments, and talked about themselves. Armin spoke about the need for cooperation between man and God and the earth. The farmers had no quarrel with the message, no quarrel save for a specific point on the nature of cooperation: the farmers at the Rural Gospel School, Christians, churchgoers, could pray for their deliverance from difficult times, and then dismiss the suggestion that their deliverance lay with each other.

I left the Rural Gospel School feeling as if I'd been watching people nod approval to a man speaking in tongues.

The sign outside the Aizu-Takada church read, "Joy and Hope for the Farmer." One farmer carried in a big can of fresh milk. Another brought vegetables. Pumpkins were in season, so Evelyn made pumpkin bread and pumpkin cookies. She and Armin loaded these into the trunk of the car, along with a vat of oxtail stew.

The night before we'd sat up, talking about Armin's sermon. It would be a hard sermon, in keeping with the times. The future held little for the nation's rice farmers. The government, which had been buying the farmers' rice—and getting their votes—for years, was reducing the amount it would purchase. Imported rice was cheaper.

Families that had farmed for generations now watched their eldest sons, traditional heirs to the land, leave for the cities. The aging farmers worked the land themselves, and when they died, the farms died with them. After the harvest, the men left for construction work in the cities, leaving their families behind. There were stories told of farmers who left, found new wives, began new families, and were never seen again.

"I think we're going out into an unknown, uncharted area now and people need encouragement and they need the courage," Armin said. "Like Jesus said, 'Seek God's Kingdom first and all these things shall be given you.' "

There was, however, a caveat. Farmers, he believed, could no longer work alone, each making a living without regard for his neighbors. Armin wanted to believe that this spirit of cooperation could transcend the rice and grain cooperatives where harmony was institutional. It could be a matter of the heart, of wanting to work together because it was the right thing to do. Obligation would not be the force that brought and held them together; instead it would be a feeling among the farmers that their lives could be better by sharing, on equal terms, with their peers.

The issue was not restricted to Aizu or to farming. Rather, Armin said, it had everything to do with the way Japan saw itself in the world. He mentioned a study that the education ministry had conducted on the qualities that embodied "the ideal man." There were four: man as individual, as family member, as a member of society, and as a member of the Japanese nation.

"And then they stopped," Armin said. "They didn't go beyond that. I thought it was so strange that that was where the thinking stops. It has to be a step further. Japan working for the good of the world, not just for the good of Japan."

A new Japan, Armin explained, could turn from being an exploiter to a bridge between enemies; that Japan had the first constitution renouncing war meant that the nation might one day become a true leader in the cause of world peace. "Japan could set a new direction," Armin said, hoping that that new direction could begin, for Aizu, the next day, when the farmers would come to church and hear from the Hutterites, and from each other, all the good that could come from harmony of the spirit, not just of the word.

It was February and bitterly cold in Aizu-Takada. The mountains were powdered with snow and the sky was gray. The fifty-second annual Rural Gospel School of the Aizu-Takada church would fall on National Foundation Day, a holiday for the nation to celebrate its mythological founding by the Sun Goddess.

Armin introduced the Hutterite pastor by reading from the Book of Acts: "The group of believers was of one heart. No one said that any of his belongings was his own, but they shared with one another everything they had."

People began arriving as Armin spoke. At nine o'clock the bustle in the downstairs kitchen subsided and ten men took their seats in the small sanctuary. The women and their children would join them later. The room was pale blue and lined with hard benches. A gray heater filled the center of the room, and people sat as close as they could without perspiring. Rikie Yamauchi, the veteran of the Philippines campaign, sat next to the heater, and behind him sat younger men, in their thirties and forties, dressed in blue jeans and fashionable ski sweaters. Armin wore a blue plaid suit and under the jacket a rust-colored sweater with a loose turtleneck collar. He stood at the front of the room, beneath the plain wooden cross. Pastor Endo—this was the son of the pastor who had brought the Kroehlers to Aizu-Takada; after his father's death, he had become the town pastor—led the farmers in "A Hymn in Time of National Trouble." Armin spoke about man's stewardship of God's earth.

Then the Hutterite pastor, Reverend Kikuta, rose and came to the front of the room where he faced the farmers. He told them how he, the son of a naval officer, had turned away from the military and found a new life among the Hutterites, a sect with a 450-year history of devotion and insularity. The Hutterites of Japan—who, he added, were being pressured to speak German like all the other Hutterites in the world—lived on six acres of not terribly arable

152

land. There were twenty-six of them, twelve adults, three teenagers, nine primary school children, and two infants.

"We twenty-six live where three can't make a living," he said. The Hutterites had two goats that provided their milk and 1,800 chickens that produced the eggs they sold. The Hutterites supported themselves by selling their eggs. Commerce was one of their very few links to the outside world.

Reverend Kikuta explained how the Hutterites' eggs brought a good price because their chickens were not fed chemical additives. He took great pride in telling about the independence they had achieved because they worked together. The community was made up of people from all over Japan. The oldest was a woman of seventy.

"We have plenty," he said, "because we are a community."

When he was done, one of the young farmers raised his hand for a question.

"What is the significance of your movement to people in general?" he asked. "You isolate yourselves and become independent and self-supporting. But what significance does that have for the people outside?"

Reverend Kikuta was silent for a moment and Armin said, "That is something they're facing. It's a kind of model, an experiment on how people can work together. Whether to copy every aspect of it is another thing."

Mrs. Kikuta spoke at lunch. Everyone gathered at the low tables of the church kindergarten. They passed the plate of Evelyn's pumpkin bread and the bowls of oxtail stew. People chatted and laughed until Mrs. Kikuta rose to speak.

"All we buy is sugar, salt, rice, and a little fish," she said. She smiled a modest smile. "We make our own bean paste, and we're studying to make our own tofu. Our son always says he can see what season it is by his lunches. We have lots of carrots. We had kiwi fruit and lots of potatoes this year. Our children eat cucumbers for snacks. We work together in the kitchen morning, noon, and night."

Every night the community gathered for prayers. The children knew that they could not linger after school for sports and clubs because they would be late for prayers. The Hutterites hoped to have their own elementary school so that their children would not have to go to school with children who were not Hutterites. Sometimes other children threw mud and stones at the older Hutterite children.

"Our most difficult problem is relating to the society around us," Mrs. Kikuta said.

The panel discussion was to be an exchange of ideas. The panelists sat at the front of the sanctuary. Each spoke for six minutes and then a bell rang, signaling the next speaker. The first to speak was Shimpei Hori, a church elder and a prominent man in town.

"I have four hectares of rice fields and thirty beef cattle," said Mr. Hori. "I want to have ten hectares and in twenty years, thirty hectares." Mr. Hori wore a blue, three-piece suit. He said that he was very busy, attending a meeting or two a day as a member of the town council. "If I had more free time to think . . ." Mr. Hori said, making it clear that he did not.

Kenju Sato wanted more roads in the mountains. He had eight and a half acres of walnut trees and hoped that when the prefectural recreation center opened near his farm in the mountains, city people might want to come to his place and pick their own walnuts. Mr. Sato thought this might be a tourist attraction.

Farmers needed wives, said Kunio Ukawa. Marriage prospects were so bleak in the farm towns that one village had dispatched its headman to hire a matchmaker. Another farm district had begun importing women from Sri Lanka. The Sri Lankan women were brought before the farmers wearing numbered tags. The farmers chose the women by number. The Sri Lankan women were said to be good and useful wives because they were "obedient."

"The problem is to get young women to come and marry," Mr. Ukawa said. "If they could look forward to an enjoyable future, they'd come."

Mr. Ukawa was a youngest son who had returned to his parents' farm because his older brothers did not want to farm. He was forty-two years old and the youngest farmer in his village. Mr. Sato said that none of the forty families in his town could make a living by farming alone. "We do it now, my son and I," he said. "But I wonder whether we can continue with my grandson."

Armin, sitting on a hard bench near the wall, spoke up. "It takes so long for one family to do everything," he said. "How can people cooperate in production, harvesting, and selling?"

Mr. Hori answered Armin. He said, "It's difficult for farmers to work together on an equal level."

Mr. Hori, after all, with his ten hectares that might become thirty, did not consider himself the equal of a farmer with less. Mr. Hori had no equal. In a sense, no one had an equal. Each farmer existed on a separate plain, distinct by income and acreage. No one disputed Mr. Hori's assertion. It was so obvious. Farmers, like everyone else, could cooperate only by accepting the premise of inequality. This way each knew his place. If they were all brothers and sisters in Jesus's eyes, that was fine. But that was limited to their relationship with God, not each other. With each other they were ranked.

"I want to stay optimistic," Mr. Hori said, as the talk drifted back to laments about hard times. He wanted to know how he could increase his rice acreage so that his son and grandson would have a worthy farm.

The discussion ended without answers. The men and women and children who'd been twisting in their seats rose, and together they prayed: "To those whose hearts are disturbed be strong. Be not afraid. God will save you. Your God will come with recompense."

Armin and Evelyn drove me to the station. "I was happy for the turnout," Armin said.

"Several of the women said they'd like to go and visit the Hutterites," said Evelyn.

"But we're talking about it before doing something about cooperative marketing. People from elsewhere come in here and sell."

"And we're raising the same thing they're selling."

"I don't know why these young guys can't get together."

"Maybe they're better friends when they're not working together," said Evelyn.

"We've talked about this before," said Armin. "I don't know how to convince them. They'll have to come to the point of realizing the limitations of everyone for himself."

Armin spoke about how hard it was for the churches to work together because of jealousies and rivalries. Evelyn pointed out that just by becoming Christians, the farmers at the Rural Gospel School had shown they were strong people, leaders, and that it was not easy to get leaders to work together.

"I don't know. If they had some kind of boss who'd come in, some sort of father figure, then it would be possible," Armin said.

"The Japanese always have to know who the leader is," said Evelyn.

"Pastor Endo tells me I should be more forceful in my leadership. Tell people what to do. But that's not me."

They talked about the elder Pastor Endo, who had been a strong leader, a man with big ideas. People listened to Pastor Endo, and so devoted were some of his parishioners that when he died, they left the church and no longer practiced Christianity.

Always, it seemed to the Kroehlers, faith—like cooperation— was contingent upon personal relationships. While that sort of particularism was not unique to Japan, it was especially central to the way the Japanese saw the world and themselves in it. Abstract concepts were acceptable as ideas but inapplicable if they came from the mouth of one with whom there was no *kankei*, no connection. Parishioners told Armin and Evelyn that they had become Christians simply because the Kroehlers had attended their spouse's funeral and that this gave them a good feeling about Christians. Others agreed with everything Armin said about God, man, and the love between all people, and then told him that joining the church was out of the question because their local pastor had not shown true sincerity in answering a question about the omnipresence of God.

Perhaps if they all lived in the same town, and all grew rice and had equipment that each could use but that only one or two owned, they could cooperate at planting and harvest time, as farmers had when they were tenants on the land of wealthy families. But the farmers at the Rural Gospel School lived in different towns; though they lived in the same district, they were not neighbors. Their acquaintanceships were based upon familiarity at church functions—if indeed they even went to the same church—and, to a lesser extent, upon a belief in the same God. That shared belief, however, did not necessarily qualify as a binding relationship. That belief was strong. But it was also tailored to Japanese needs.

Those needs dictated why, among many other constraints, an elder in the Aizu-Takada church could come to services only every other Sunday. On the alternate Sundays he was obliged to attend historical society meetings. The elder had a relationship with the historical society's members. The Kroehlers did not doubt his faith, but they were dismayed by its place in his life. They would have liked to see him at church every Sunday but knew that that was expecting the inconceivable.

In the weeks that followed, people from the church began planning a visit to the Hutterite community. I thought of them coming to the bit of land the Hutterites farmed, seeing how the Hutterites worked as a unit, how they isolated themselves from the world around them. In the Hutterites Armin had found a mixed blessing—one that promoted cooperation, but in a narrow sphere. They were a microcosm of Japan within Japan. They could work together, as neighbors could, because everyone understood the basis for that cooperation and made the necessary adjustments. Others were peripheral. Others were people to whom you sold your goods and from whom you bought when it was necessary.

I wondered whether the Aizu farmers would in some way see this as confirmation for their lives, lives built in equal measure upon faith and separation.

When I left Japan in 1985 for my first visit to America, I did not want to leave my wife, but I could not wait to go. I stopped in Chicago, where a friend met me at the airport.

We ate lunch in the airport coffee shop and for the first time in my life I was excited at the prospect of leaving a tip. In Japan there was no tipping; I was not in Japan.

I returned ostensibly for work. I could have pushed and finished in three weeks and gotten back to Japan, but I took my time. As much as I missed my wife, I was not ready to leave. I went with friends to the Russian steam bath on the Lower East Side of Manhattan and afterward we ate thick sandwiches and potato knishes. I played football with my brother and sister. I went to movies and to new restaurants. Everyone looked as happy to see me as I was to see them. I put my head on my father's shoulder. I let my mother feed me cake.

Talking was the best part about being home. It was fun hearing gossip and reports of pregnancies and romances and even of break-ups. I cannot remember what we talked about after we'd filled in the gaps in each others' lives. But I do recall how that talk pushed lunches well into the afternoon and dinners late into the evening.

I delayed my return flight a week.

Only afterward did I learn how much I'd talked about Japan. I talked about it all the time, or so I was told by a friend who teased me about my professed distance from the place. He said, "That's all you talk about. Don't tell me you don't care." But I wasn't hearing the stories I was telling, stories about batboys playing catch in the outfield of the Giants' stadium after the players had gone home; about getting drunk one night and eating blowfish, a lethal dish when prepared incorrectly; about sitting with legs crossed for eight hours, watching the sumo matches—stories of Japan as I thought it should be, gentle and exotic, stories about people I watched but whom I did not know.

Between stories I was hearing a voice that told me that home was good and Japan was not.

Home meant feelings I could anticipate. I knew who loved me and missed me when I was gone. I knew when I was pushing a joke too far with a stranger, and when I was sealing a friendship. For a month I basked in familiarity, a realization that disappointed me because I wanted to think myself more adventurous than that.

I wanted to believe I could go off and adapt and make people in a new place like me because I could sense their needs and moods.

My wife met me at the airport. Tokyo was cold and rainy and she knew when she looked at me how sorry I was to have left New York. I tried chatting on the bus, filling her in on the details of friends' lives. Then, using fatigue as an excuse, I fell silent.

I woke the next morning without jet lag, which was the worst way to feel. I wanted to be tired so that I might have an excuse to stay in bed. But at ten o'clock I was at my desk, looking out the window. The trees were leafless and the sky was gray and I was back in Japan, angry and bewildered at the realization that I was no less lost than I had been that first sunny day when I rode in from the airport, looking out the window, hoping my illusions would be fulfilled.

I was angry because I wanted to talk. Home reminded me how much I had missed the tension of conversation. I missed raised voices and loud laughter, interruptions and wisecracks and disagreements.

In the months that followed, I met people to talk with; and because I almost always met them through work, I could ask many questions. I heard thoughtful replies, as I did with the Kroehlers at the Books and Tea Club. But I wanted, needed, the talk to move beyond questions and answers to conversation. I was out of step with Japan, where silence was the preferred mode of interaction and where the talk I overheard was filled with the sound of people agreeing.

I went back to language school but the language came agonizingly slowly. Each day I listened for the squeak of the mailman's bicycle, hoping that when I opened the box I would find a letter from home. I laughed at the businessmen who fell down drunk in the street. I was huffy with sales clerks who took forever to wrap a package because they were trying to do it the way they were taught. Boys on the subway tried talking to me in English and, assuming they just wanted to practice, I told them to get lost.

Maybe they wanted to talk. Maybe I had dismissed them too

hastily, squandering a chance for conversation. I could not be sure. In the absence of the words I needed I was left to guess, hoping that I had guessed correctly. If signals were being sent my way, I never saw them. I was not sure I would have recognized them if I had.

At home I knew what people were telling me. In Japan I did not even know how to distinguish kindness from curiosity. In my anger I shut my eyes, closing myself off from both.

After the spring rains ended and the days turned sultry and the air still, Lafcadio Hearn bade his wife and family good-bye and set off for a brief and painful return to the Western enclaves. First he went to Kobe, an open port. Then he went back to Yokohama. What he had once scorned and rushed to escape he now embraced. The trip was painful because it made him happy.

He had left Yokohama five years before alone and enchanted. He returned not only a married man and provider for his extended family, but a father. The previous fall, his wife gave birth to a son whom he named Leopold Kazuo. The Leopold was dropped and Kazuo shortened to Kaji. Hearn was mystified by the way his son clung to him.

Desperate for a way out of Kumamoto, he set off for the big cities in search of publishers and work. He was gone six weeks. As much as he missed his wife and son, Hearn did not want to go back to Kumamato.

The West of the open ports felt big and forceful and Hearn felt foolish for once having belittled it. He swam, ate steak, and drank beer and gin and lemonade. He made instant friends who made him feel warm, because he had no friends in Kumamoto. "How small my little Japan became!—how lonesome!" he wrote. "What a joy to feel the West!"

Five years before, Hearn had stumbled upon a small temple, hidden from the street by shops and by the banner of a secondhand clothing store. On the walls inside he had found a framed print of the Philadelphia Exhibition and of the actress Adelaide Neilson as Juliet. The incense box was an empty Pinhead cigarette tin. Hearn had not minded the Western touches. He assumed that they had been gifts from people who thought the offerings exotic.

He had liked the temple and especially its priest, an elderly man who was writing a history of religion in Japan. He had writen 230 of the 300 volumes he planned. The priest told Hearn that he was eighty-eight years old and hoped to finish his work before he died.

They talked about the Buddhist concepts of good and evil and how those qualities existed in all acts. They talked about past lives and whether sex and love were a hindrance or aid for those seeking enlightenment. They talked for a long time. When it was time to leave, the priest gave Hearn two gifts—a package of white sand from the temple where good souls went after death, and a small white stone said to be a relic of a Buddha's body. Hearn asked if he could come again. The elderly priest said that that would please him.

Now, after knowing the joy of Matsue and the disappointment of Kumamoto, Hearn went looking for the temple. New houses had replaced the older houses of the district, but Hearn still found it. At the entrance he met a young priest. The old priest had died during the cold of the past winter.

Inside, Hearn saw the same portrait of Adelaide Neilson. But the room had lost its appeal. The young priest brought him into the study where he had sat five years before. The old priest's books were gone. In a cabinet, Hearn saw his memorial tablet. The incense box was the same Pinhead cigarette tin.

Hearn lingered and then, as he was leaving, the young priest asked his name and whether there was anything he wished.

"Only a prayer," Hearn replied. "My name makes no difference. A man of forty-four. Pray that he may obtain whatever is best for him." But he did not tell the young priest the prayer in his heart.

"I knew the Lord Buddha would never hearken to any foolish prayer for the return of lost illusions."

4

Kobe

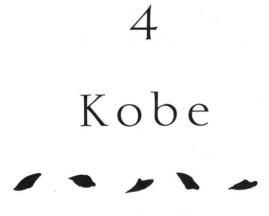

*H*earn ran. He quit the school, gathered his family, and fled Kumamoto. They headed north, for Kobe, where he had stepped, happily, back into the West. But in Kobe the troubles did not go away.

He thought he wanted to be back among Westerners. Yet in their company, Hearn longed for the Japanese: "I am happy only out of the sight of foreign faces and the hearing of English voices. . . ." Among the Japanese he missed the West: "I have been obliged to recognize the fact that I can never become a Japanese, or find real sympathy from the Japanese. . . ."

Yet even among the Japanese he saw too much of the West: "Carpets—pianos—windows—curtains—brass bands—churches! how I hate them! And white shirts!"

He longed to be among others "with the same color of soul." Nothing had changed. Japan was good when it presented itself as a series of woodblock prints come alive. It was bad when it was real—a country rushing to catch up with the rest of the world; refitting itself; rejecting its art, music, and dress in favor of borrowed ideas that bore no resemblance to the past; a country emerging from a cocoon.

He found a two-story house. The bottom floor was Japanese, the upper floor Western. He was not entirely pleased. "Kobe is a nice little place. The effect on me is not pleasant, however." Kobe was a city. Hearn had lived too long in the country.

He was hired to write editorials for the English-language *Kobe Chronicle*. He worked for a young man he liked, which was a pleasant change from Kumamoto. Newspaper work was familiar and left him to write his books at night. By day he dressed in Western clothes; at night he wore kimono. He dreamed of living in Kyoto, with its famous temples and shrines. His wife wanted to move to Tokyo. The idea repelled him. "I want to see and feel Japan," he wrote; "there is no Japan in Tokyo."

If not Kyoto, he decided, then Matsue. He longed to go back to Matsue.

He wrote, "I am in a perpetual quandary."

He did not know whether he wanted to stay in Japan or leave. He thought that if he left he could still come back from time to time.

Japan, meanwhile, was ascending. Hearn was impressed. He was also aghast.

The nation was defeating China. It was showing the West that it was not going to be another Eastern country ready for carving and serving. Hearn was proud of Japan and its might and wrote about that in his editorials: "She may be able not only to win her goal, but to go far beyond it,—not only to place herself as a confessed equal in the great family of civilized Powers, but to take a higher ranking among them than even she herself ever deemed possible."

But in the street, children called him mocking names and Hearn felt the rise of antiforeign sentiment. Foreign teachers were losing their jobs, having been deemed no longer useful.

He wrote to Chamberlain (but not in his newspaper), "Life will be made wretched for Occidentals—in business—just as it is being made in the schools—by all sorts of little tricky plans which cannot be brought under law-provisions, or even so defined as to appear to justify resentment—tricks at which the Japanese are as elaborately ingenious as they are in matters of etiquette. . . . The nation will turn its ugly side to us—after a manner unexpected, but irresistible.

"The future looks worse than black." He thought again of returning to New Orleans, and yet he believed that leaving Japan would be "like tearing one's self in two."

At home, Hearn, a man in love with big ideas and fanciful dreams, lived among people he barely understood and who were incapable of sharing his thoughts. But home was also a reminder of Japan as it was supposed to be, perhaps because home was a place built around the needs of a child—"My whole family are always caring for the boy: his interests and necessities rule the whole house . . ."

Hearn wanted the world for his son. He wanted him educated in English as well as Japanese. He wanted him schooled in the classics. He wanted him provided for, as he did for his wife. And there he sensed a problem. Only Japanese could own land in Japan. If Hearn died while still a British subject, his wife would lose claim to her family's lands.

The future could be made secure only by his becoming a Japanese. So for his family, for the sake of those who sustained an image he could not find elsewhere, Hearn decided to become a Japanese citizen.

The authorities came to the house to ask many questions of his wife—whether Hearn was a good man, a kind man, and a good provider. Though committed to his family and their future in Japan, Hearn still wrote of finding a place—perhaps Manila—that moved and tantalized him and filled him with the excitement he had thought he would find in Japan.

The government completed its investigation. It was satisfied with Hearn. It granted him citizenship. It decreed, as it did to all new citizens, that he take a new name, a Japanese name.

Hearn became Yakumo Koizumi. He took his wife's family name—the name of the family that adopted him.

For the first time since he was a boy, since his father went away and his mother left him behind when she returned to Greece, Hearn had a family of which he was truly a part. Yet he could not find peace, peace with himself and his peace with Japan. For the former,

I pitied him. But for the latter, I empathized, especially as I learned how others made theirs.

⟋ ⟍ ⟋ ⟍ ⟍ Eight months had passed since Kathy had stood before Mr. Yamada and refused to be fingerprinted. Now Mr. Yamada, looking to Kathy as uncomfortable as he had the day of her refusal, took the stand as a witness for the defense.

Kathy's trial had assumed the endless quality that characterized the Japanese legal system. Lawsuits dragged on for decades; criminal trials took years and almost always ended with convictions. Kathy's showed no signs of speedy execution. Hearings were months apart.

Shunsuke Nomoto, Kathy's lawyer, called on Mr. Yamada to explain to the judge, since jury trials did not exist in Japan, what the Yamato city office did with the fingerprints it gathered.

Mr. Yamada testified that it did nothing with them. The tax office sometimes came by to check them. Mostly, it was the police who came to see the files kept on foreigners, although the immigration bureau insisted that alien registration prints were not used in criminal investigations.

"You said the city office does not use the fingerprints to confirm the identity of foreigners," Nomoto said. "Does the city office have any equipment to examine them?"

Mr. Yamada said it did not.

"So we can say the fingerprints preserved at the city office are in fact going completely unused. Is that right?"

Mr. Yamada said it was.

"In that case, then, isn't it a complete waste of time to carry out a print-taking procedure and store prints that are never even used?"

"That's right," said Mr. Yamada.

Mr. Yamada was not criticizing the procedure; he was merely stating a fact. Others, aware of the same fact, were criticizing the system.

The association of alien registration desk workers called for reform of the Alien Registration Law. So too did the All-Japan Federation of Prefectural and Municipal Workers. The National

Association of Mayors called for the abolition of fingerprinting. Even the Yamato City Council wrote letters to the prime minister and justice minister asking for changes in the law.

But the Ministry of Justice and National Police Agency were still arresting and prosecuting those who refused fingerprinting. Mr. Yamada testified that when his office delayed sending its report of Kathy's refusal to the police—"not an agreeable job," he admitted—the justice ministry had called several times, asking, "When are you going to report her?" Finally, fifty days after her refusal, Kathy's case had been turned over to the police.

The government was still harshest with Koreans. There were reports of Koreans being arrested, having their fingers pried apart and forcibly printed. One Korean sociologist had reportedly been arrested by thirty policemen (after being followed by plainclothesmen for weeks), forced to strip naked, subjected to a full body search that included an anal examination, and then held in jail for three days. Rightist groups sent him anonymous letters threatening to "try" and punish him. Among the hate mail he received were letters demanding that he be fingerprinted because Koreans were known to be criminals and were now insulting Japan.

Through it all, Prime Minister Nakasone continued speaking out on the virtues of homogeneity. At Hiroshima, on the anniversary of the atomic bombing, he told the assembled survivors that "because we have been living on these islands for over two thousand years with no different ethnic people present, ours is a country where such a good aspect remains [and] robberies and murders are among the fewest in the world."

Kathy was ready to leave. It was August, which was always the worst time for her. She suffered the pain of an arthritic back made all the worse by the humidity. Kathy had been in Japan for ten years and now doubted the wisdom of staying. She had Jun and her friends. But she felt no more accepted now than she had when she first arrived. Jun's teaching schedule permitted six months of independent study, and for a while Kathy thought that they should move to the United States. Jun would return to Japan only to teach.

Kathy was weary as well of the pressure to conform from those who insisted that they had her best interests at heart. A group of lawyers who'd taken an interest in the fingerprinting issue formed an organization of their own. One of their members, a professor, sought out Kathy. He told her he wanted to meet with Jun. Kathy said that Jun was not available, so the professor met her for lunch.

The professor wanted Kathy to slow the pace of her trial. It was moving too quickly, he said, and Kathy stood too good a chance of being convicted before anyone else. The professor told Kathy that if she delayed her conviction—a judgment he thought inevitable—others could join "the movement."

Kathy said again she was not interested in being part of the "movement." She told the professor that she would not slow the pace of her trial. Moreover, she told him that she had not given up on acquittal.

Afterward, Kathy asked Nomoto why this professor had taken such an interest in the case. "He's not even a foreigner," Kathy said. Nomoto gave her a quizzical look, one that made plain to Kathy that she had fallen too easily into seeing the world in terms of "us" and "them." It was a joiner's thinking, the thinking of someone whose identification was bound to the company he kept and the side to which he was aligned. Kathy wanted to believe that she was a different sort of person, a person whose agenda—both in thought and deed—were her own.

Her trial abruptly picked up speed the day *The New York Times* ran a story about Kathy; the article made a passing reference to the "tortoise-like" pace at which the trial moved. This brief characterization of the judicial system only served to make Kathy the first Westerner convicted of violating the Alien Registration Law. The judge saw the reference as "international criticism" of his handling of the trial. He scheduled four more hearings in quick succession.

It took only another ten months for him to reach a verdict.

On the day of the decision Kathy came to court wearing a new blue and gray dress she had found after a day of bargain-hunting. She'd had her hair done. The night before, Kathy had gone to church and prayed.

Seating in the courtroom was determined by lottery. When Kathy arrived, the gallery seats were filled. People fanned themselves with handkerchiefs in the sticky heat. The photographers waited in the corridor.

The judge appeared just after one o'clock.

"Will the defendant take the stand?" said the bailiff.

Kathy rose and took her place.

"The court finds the defendant guilty as charged," the judge said. Her fine was ten thousand yen—then forty dollars. If she did not pay she would be sent to the workhouse for five days.

"The system is administratively necessary to identify foreigners," said the judge, explaining his decision, dismissing Kathy's arguments about the human rights covenants as well as the testimony of those who took and kept the prints. Kathy and Jun went home undecided about an appeal.

It would take many more months and a new round of court appearances before they found a way for Kathy to win. But before she would win, Kathy would have to accept defeat, because only by losing could Kathy triumph.

Not only would Kathy play by the government's rules. She was going to make the government play by them, too.

"The reason most go along with the rules is that nobody wants a blot on their record," Kathy said. "But after this set of circumstances evolved, my whole existence was a blot on the record."

Jun said, "I try to tell my students, 'Instead of getting a different haircut or a Marlon Brando T-shirt, instead of trying to be different, just be different. Be a human being instead of a robot.' "

"But what if you've been programmed?" Kathy asked.

"I tell them, 'I'm not going to give you knowledge. I'm going to give you a shock treatment,' " Jun said. " 'You are like bonsai trees— your roots are so tangled and tight and trunks are so twisted. I want to put you in ordinary soil, not bonsai soil, so that you are able to see things on your own, to look at the world, to look at society, or even at an interesting fact that you've never heard before.' "

The rules were not a series of prohibitions—"Thou shalt

not . . ."—but rather a compendium of suggestions for suitable responses. The rules were, in a sense, highly democratic in that they
had been settled upon by consensus. The minority was entitled to
differ in private.

Japan was a reactive society: people were reactive not to faith
or doctrine but to one another. To react differently was to be
suspect. To be suspect suggested selfishness, willfulness, and a general unwillingness to be a good and productive member of society.
It was possible to be different—as the various groups critical of
fingerprinting had been—as long as you could be different together.
By being different together, you were still reacting the way the
others around you were reacting, and were thereby spared the pain
of being not only different but also alone.

Indoctrination in the virtue of conformity—and the threat of
separation from the group—began at a tender age: I remember
watching a Japanese child throw a tantrum at a party. The child lay
on the floor, screaming, crying, and kicking at his mother, who
stood above him. She did not pick him up, or in any way try to
restrain him. She simply said, "Everyone is going to laugh at you."

And that was all she had to say.

Kathy's early education about Japanese thinking and feeling had
introduced her to the concept of *amae*, the need for indulgence.
So crucial was the satisfaction of this need, that the threat of its
withdrawal was often all that was needed to keep people from stray-
ing too far in their reactions. People did what they did not want to
do because they feared the withdrawal of affection.

At first I did not believe that an entire society could be so moved
by a single need. My confidence began eroding the night I sat in
the bar of a Japanese trading company—the bar made the requisite
drinking with workmates only an elevator ride away—and listened
to a middle-level manager bemoan his fate.

He hated his job. He hated his boss to whom he could never
refuse a request for a drink or game of mah-jongg. He hated having
to go to the plant and make believe he enjoyed the lewd jokes he
heard over drinks.

"Do you ever talk about this with your wife?" I asked.

He laughed, more a sneer than a guffaw.

"I cannot talk about anything with my wife," he said, explaining that he had not sought a conversationalist in a wife, but rather someone adept at laundry and breeding.

He dreamed of returning to his village to teach.

We met again a few weeks later. I was excited about talking with him, sensing that I had found the crack in the national armor, the flip side of the rising gross national product fueled by fifteen-hour workdays.

We drank a few beers. The alcohol relaxed him, or at least gave him the excuse for being relaxed. I raised the question of his apparent misery.

He smiled, more in bemusement than pleasure. He explained that surely I did not think he was miserable. Of course, he did not like his boss and their mah-jongg games, or the trips to the plant, or anything else about his work. But he got so much in return. His father was proud of him. His wife bragged about him to her friends because he had a good job with a big company. His hated boss was good to him because he worked long hours and was always available for mah-jongg. Everyone was kind to him.

He was not about to give that up, not to go back to his village and be a teacher, not if it meant giving up all that *amae*, all that indulgence.

He may not have liked the rules. But he was not about to do something rash, such as disobey them.

Kathy filed her appeal and waited. She did not have to wait long. The chief of the appellate court, the three-judge panel of the Tokyo High Court, wanted a quick proceeding.

Nomoto wanted to call on two justice ministry officials to testify. The judge refused him.

When Nomoto told the judge that he wanted to call on Kathy to testify at the next hearing, the judge insisted that she testify on the spot. Nomoto told the judge that he could not question Kathy because she was not prepared. The judge said that that was fine with him and that he and the prosecutors would question her themselves.

Murakami, Kathy's other lawyer, rose but before he could open his mouth, the judge ordered him to sit. Kathy took the stand. The judge asked her what she thought of her conviction.

"I thought the decision made implicity clear the unfair distinction the law makes between foreigners and Japanese," Kathy said.

The judge asked if there was anything else she wished to say. Kathy said if the law was fair, the justice ministry should feel confident enough to come to court and defend it.

A prosecutor asked Kathy if she had ever heard of the concept of rule of law.

"I am not a legal scholar," Kathy said, wondering whether she would have been better off simply saying no.

"Well, simply put then, it is the idea that if there is a law you follow it. Don't Americans do this?"

Kathy explained Thoreau's philosophy of good and bad laws. When she began explaining Thoreau's influence on Mahatma Gandhi and Martin Luther King, the judge interrupted and said, "That's enough." Even the reporters in the back of the room were laughing.

Months later, at the final defense summation, the judge wanted the brisk pace maintained. Nomoto still wanted to call two mayors who were not reporting fingerprint refusers to the justice ministry. The judge refused the request.

Nomoto rose and formally protested the judge's handling of the trial. The motion was denied. Nomoto asked for a five-minute recess to confer with Kathy. The judge refused to recess.

Kathy rose and announced, "I withdraw my appeal."

The judge said nothing. He looked at Kathy with his jaw slack and eyes wide open.

He asked Kathy to repeat what she had just said.

"I withdraw my appeal," Kathy said.

The judge called for a recess. He disappeared for two minutes to confer with the two other judges.

"Did you prepare this beforehand?" he asked when he returned.

Kathy and her lawyers said nothing.

"Did you prepare this beforehand?"

"Why, yes. Why?"

The judge shook his head. He asked Kathy if she was sure she knew what she was doing. Kathy told the judge that she was sure.

The appeal had been doomed to failure. Kathy and her lawyers saw that. The proceedings had not been fair. The supreme court was unlikely to hear the case because no new evidence had been submitted. If the appeal was rejected, other appeals would likely be rejected because a precedent had been set. So Kathy and her lawyers decided that their only chance for victory was to withdraw the appeal and force the government into the embarrassing position of throwing her into the workhouse for five days.

"I have completely lost faith in receiving a fair hearing," Kathy told the reporters assembled outside the courtroom. "I intend to follow the decision and serve my five days in prison in order to protest the unfair nature of the trial."

If the government was so intent on punishing Kathy for her crime, she was not going to make things easy for them by paying the fine. She was going to take the government up on its threat.

The government's first postcard to Kathy demanding payment of her fine read, "Failure to comply could mean that you will be forcibly apprehended and have to serve time in the workhouse."

Kathy ignored it.

Her lawsuit was still inching along. After yet another hearing she stopped by the prosecutor's office to let them know she was not going to pay her fine and that as long as she was there they could take her off to the workhouse immediately.

The secretary had Kathy put this in writing and told Kathy that the prosecutors would get back to her once they had time "to study the form."

The next postcard, demanding immediate payment, arrived the following month. Kathy ignored it. The next postcard set a final date for payment, underlined in red. Kathy ignored it. The prosecutor's office called and asked Kathy to come in and "discuss" the matter. Kathy said she had nothing to discuss. The prosecutors said they needed a new written explanation from Kathy because the previous one was not "official enough."

"If you do not want to allow me to serve my sentence, why put a criminal penalty on the offense?" said Kathy, who was now being featured in the weekly gossip magazines. "Is it only to scare and intimidate foreigners?"

The deadline for payment came and went and the police did not come to take Kathy away. Instead, the fine was taken out of her wages. The government had bluffed, and Kathy had called it.

Jun was right. The foreign population was untrustworthy: it could not be trusted to behave as expected. It could not be trusted to obey the unwritten rules.

Kathy was not supposed to make the government look foolish by daring it to throw her in jail. She was supposed to apologize, express understanding of her offense, and then make believe that nothing had happened. But Kathy had realized that in breaking the rules she had nothing to lose. She could not be deported because she was married to a Japanese. She would not be thrown in jail because the government did not want the embarrassment. She could not be denied *amae* that she had never received. So don't like me, Kathy told the government of Japan. The government did not know how to reply.

◢ ◥ ◞ ◥ ◞ The missionaries, those who were left of all the ones who had come, gathered once a year to remind each other of the value and purpose of their work. A generation before, at the end of the war, there had been five hundred United Church of Christ missionaries in Japan. Now there were perhaps two hundred. The missionaries met for two days at a modern meeting hall in a convention center far from any town. The center was surrounded by woods.

Some of the missionaries were new. They were young and eager and talked about the excitement they felt in bringing God to Japan.

"I try to encourage the students to think for themselves," said a young woman who had been teaching English in Hokkaido for several months. She spoke with the ebullience of someone telling about the best thing that had happened to her. "My students ask, 'Can we visit you?' I say, 'Sure, bring your friends.' "

Evelyn Kroehler smiled and thought of the young English teacher's home overrun with students, the way her home had been overrun years before with all the people who wanted to see what a Western house looked like on the inside. She remembered the day the oil heater caught fire and the town fire brigade rushed over. The downstairs was filled with smoke, but the limited damage was confined to the living room. The firemen wanted to check upstairs. Evelyn, knowing that what they really wanted was a peek at the living quarters, told them that that would not be necessary.

Evelyn spoke at the meeting, too. She told the missionaries about the Books and Tea Club, Rikie Yamauchi's visits to the Philippines, and the children from the church kindergarten whose parents had begun coming to church.

"Many a little child has brought his whole family to Christ," Evelyn said. "God is at work far beyond the comprehension of our thinking or imagination."

In the back of the room were tables filled with tools and aids—books on the Burakumin; videotapes on minorities in Japan; a scripted slide show on the Koreans; selected Bible stories compiled by Evelyn's father and edited by her mother, Cornelia Schroer, who sat with Armin and Evelyn.

After the speeches the missionaries hovered near the tables, looking at the books, putting their money in the coffee tins for the ones they bought. Armin and Evelyn had not seen many friends in a long time. A woman who had known the Kroehlers for years told Armin, "Is it okay to tell you that your wife looked just beautiful today?"

Armin beamed.

"I can't tell her but would you please tell her?" she said.

"I do tell her," said Armin, who looked proud.

After lunch a young man with a guitar led the missionaries in song. They rose at their seats and sang, ". . . We must be ready for risk and for sacrifice." When they sang the words, "raising our hands in worship to Him," they slowly raised and opened their arms like a sunrise.

When the song was done the missionaries honored those who were leaving. One of the older missionaries spoke to those who were newly arrived and bewildered: "Some of you come and are not greeted warmly. The people you're supposed to work with don't know what you have to offer. There are times of loneliness and discouragement. But we're grateful for your coming to work with us and explore yet unforeseen possibilities of the church here."

After the war, when all the beliefs upon which the war was built were, like Japan's cities, reduced to ashes, the nation had been receptive to new ideas. Their assumptions had failed them. They were starving. If, in their conquests, they had proven themselves the superior nation, in their defeat the Japanese saw themselves as their conqueror's inferior. During the American occupation, Douglas MacArthur was said to have asked for a thousand missionaries for Japan—not necessarily to spread the gospel, but to go into the countryside and show the face of America. Cornelia Schroer and her husband returned. Their daughter Evelyn and their new son-in-law Armin were already there, as were many others who would become their friends.

Early in 1955, Armin wrote: "Since coming to Japan almost five years ago, we have grown to love this country and its people. . . . Interesting as was the large city, we have found rural Japan even more fascinating and have come to feel that it holds the key to Japan's future."

Now, in the break before dinner, the Kroehlers, Mrs. Schroer, and an old friend from Tokyo, George Gish, drove into the countryside. And there, unexpectedly, they found a bit of a past remembered as a time when they were younger and Japan was filled with promise.

They were looking for a paper maker, an artisan so famous that he was deemed a Living National Treasure. They drove into the mountains, following a river. They talked as they drove, remembering meetings after the war that five hundred missionaries of different denominations attended. Mrs. Schroer reminded them that before the war there had been few missionaries in Japan, and hardly any in the countryside.

As dusk approached, they found the home of the paper maker. It was a long wooden farmhouse with a thatched roof. The paper maker, small and robust, sat near the door with his son and grandchildren. Armin drove up to the door and the paper maker invited everyone inside.

He said his name was Uchino and he was seventy-eight years old. Evelyn said, "This is my mother," and Uchino asked her age.

"Eighty-eight," said Cornelia Schroer, in her strong voice.

"Oh, you're so well," Uchino told her.

"But you, you're so well," said Mrs. Schroer.

Uchino took them into the work room. The floor was earthen. The walls were thin and wooden, and the room was dim. Uchino's daughter-in-law stood at a wooden vat, pulling pieces of paper from the murky water.

Uchino said that he was a seventh generation paper maker. When Uchino was a boy there had been five hundred paper makers in the town. But now only three families made paper.

He showed them the stalks that were ground to pulp and then boiled into the mash that made the paper. Armin examined the reeds and Evelyn stood by the tank where they were boiled. Armin tried positioning himself so he would have enough light to take a picture. Uchino's daughter-in-law lowered a wood-framed screen into the water. She brought out the screen and on top of it was a sheet of paper. She gently pulled the sheet from the screen and laid it on a thick, neat stack of papers.

She pulled sheet after sheet as her father-in-law told their guests what he had done in the war. The military, he said, came to him with the idea of making giant paper balloons that would be flown across the Pacific laden with bombs. Uchino went to work making the balloons.

"I made those. I worked all night," he said. "They wouldn't let me sleep."

179

They went into the living quarters for tea. Uchino's wife sat at a low table, wrapped in an orange blanket. Under the table was a recess where coals burned. Uchino joined her and gestured for the others to sit. Mrs. Schroer tucked her legs under the blanket and let her feet hang over the coals.

"Americans are more interested in making paper than the people around here are," Uchino said, lamenting the slow death of his art. He told them that he had been to Hawaii where he was honored for his paper making. American artists bought his paper. "They say 'Look at the wonderful paper we got,' and it's my paper."

Green tea was served, along with homemade pickled radishes.

Uchino continued: "Foreigners are getting to be more adept at it than Japanese. Japanese lose interest. They don't have patience to go through the many, many stages. It takes ten years to learn. Young people aren't doing it anymore. But then the Westerners come who have good brains and they stay and learn."

"What about your son and his wife and your grandchildren?" asked George Gish.

"The grandchildren get bored with it," said Uchino, who did not want to make paper either when he was young. He wanted to go to Brazil.

"I heard it was the thing to do," he said.

"Why didn't you go to Brazil?" asked Mrs. Schroer.

"There wasn't any other work to make a living," said Uchino. "So I had to make paper to eat. When I was a boy we'd make ten yen a month."

"About five dollars," said Armin.

"The richest homes had bicycles," Uchino said. "When I was twelve, Japan was so poor that people talked about going to Brazil. It was a great dream. We gave our rice to the landlord and ate the leftovers. We made our own bean paste and soy sauce. We learned how to do it because we couldn't buy it."

"It took three years to make it," Mrs. Schroer said, remembering the same Japan. "They'd have great big barrels."

"I remember that people sold their daughters up in Iwate Prefecture," Mrs. Schroer said to Uchino. "They got three hundred yen for them."

The wind blew hard against the thin walls and rattled the door. The light over the table was harsh in the dark room.

"During the war we were prisoners of war, and my husband was in prison," Mrs. Schroer said.

"You suffered during the war," said Uchino.

"Yes," said Mrs. Schroer, "but not as much as other people. And now we're back in Japan."

In the car, going back, the missionaries could not get over their luck in finding Uchino, who not only had shared part of his life with them, but had also reminded them of the Japan that had first welcomed them. "The human relations seemed so much more genuine and deep," Evelyn said.

"People invited you in," said George Gish.

"People today are so busy," Evelyn said. "I was amazed at how open Uchino was, telling us about himself."

"It's so much harder today to get beyond the surface," said Armin. "I don't know that it was any easier then."

But people, they agreed, had at least been listening. "After the war," Armin said, "there was more of a search. I don't feel that there is that much of a search today."

That search had been an aberration: the nation had long before settled upon a role for faith. When Japan began regaining its strength and self-respect, religion was restored to the periphery.

There are 120 million Japanese, of whom 112 million declare themselves Shinto, 89 million Buddhist, and 1.5 million Christian. Affiliation is unrestricted, which is why conversion numbers are a meaningless statistic. The Kroehlers believed that placing Christianity's system of beliefs at the center of a life had to be a matter of choice. But in Japan, people did not feel compelled to choose. "With so many good religions around," a bemused Japanese Christian theologian once said of his countrymen's thinking, "why choose just one?"

The Kroehlers worked not against rejection but against acceptance, the sort of undiscriminating acceptance that in the West would be dismissed as absence of character. But in Japan multiple affiliation did not imply contradiction, just as the acceptance of two kinds of truth did not imply deceit. Different sorts of truth served the greater purpose of smooth relationships and harmonious feelings, just as different religions provided the ritual for celebrating the one great faith that had no competitors.

That faith was Nihonkyo, "Japanesism." Christianity, like Buddhism and Shinto, provided the way of worship. It was possible to be many things, as long as you were one thing—Japanese.

Shinto explained, through its millions of gods, nature's mysteries: why trees grew up, rain fell down, and fish swam in the sea. Buddhism was the religion of death and remembering. They sometimes overlapped: straw hawsers and white fringes of Shinto worship appeared in Buddhist temples. No one complained. No one thought it sacrilegious. The faiths stood together in people's hearts, where there was also a small corner for Christianity.

Christian missionaries had been coming to Japan since the sixteenth century. They made many converts. Then, in the seventeenth century, the missionaries were sent away and their followers killed. For hundreds of years, Japan forbade Christianity. After the nation opened itself to the world, Christianity returned. It enjoyed only a modest following. Insisting upon exclusivity, Christianity struggled to compete.

Still, the faith, with its music and holidays, did offer ritual with a Western flavor. Among its gifts, Christianity gave Christmas to Japan. Department stores wrapped their outside walls with miles of red ribbon and lined their aisles with holly, baby pines and "Merry Christmas" posters. Community choral societies performed Beethoven's Ninth Symphony, which was deemed appropriate Christmas music. Bakeries churned out "Christmas cakes," which fathers brought home on Christmas Eve so that the family could gather around the cake and sing "Silent Night." In Japan there were no calls for putting "Christ back in Christmas." He had never been included in the first place.

Christmas was like National Foundation Day, the Festival of the

Dead, the emperor's birthday, and Vernal Equinox Day—festivals with vague attachments to sets of beliefs. The holidays provided the songs and dance and occasional prayer that celebrated the greater belief, the belief in one another.

After dinner the missionaries gathered to sing and dance and play. It was cold outside and they hurried to the center's gymnasium, where they slipped off their shoes and gathered in a big circle in the middle of the floor. They called out in Japanese, "One-Two-Three, Let's Play."

They danced the Bunny Hop and played Scissors, Paper, Stone. The winners clapped with their hands over their heads and the losers smiled and went to the sidelines. The leader told them that in the next game, everybody would have to make animal sounds, the sounds of sheep, cows, frogs, dogs, and lions. The game began and the missionaries, laughing, made animal noises at each other. Armin walked around, scratching his head. A woman dressed as a clown came over to Mrs. Schroer and hugged her.

Armin joined me and said, "I've evolved into a person." He was smiling. "It's crazy. It's good. You want to blow off a little steam once in a while."

Jan Landis put on her puppet show. She had been doing her puppet show for twenty-five years. Armin and Evelyn remembered how they and the other missionaries brought their children to meetings and how Jan Landis's puppet show was the highlight. The missionaries' children had grown up, but their parents still gathered in a semi-circle in front of the puppet stage. They sat cross-legged on the cold floor watching, with the eager eyes of children at camp, as Jan Landis's puppets performed. They laughed at such familiar spots as Jan's train whistle. Jan always did a good train whistle.

Evelyn's shoulders were getting stiff. Armin gave them a squeeze.

A young woman sang, "Father we just want to praise you . . ." and the other missionaries hummed along. Mrs. Schroer sat with a friend, who put an arm around her shoulder. Armin and Evelyn sat close together on the floor.

They closed their eyes as the woman sang. Her voice got soft, as did their humming. The song got softer and softer until the last, long note, when it disappeared.

The second morning of the conference, the gathering ended with prayer. The missionaries rose from their seats and came to the altar at the front of the room. I sat in the back, searching out Armin and Evelyn, finding them together, with Cornelia Schroer. I listened as the missionaries' voices came together in harmonies that had not been planned.

The song was simple, like a children's song, just as the morning speaker's message was simple. It was a Japanese message, a reminder to persevere. I admired the missionaries' dream, just as I found myself admiring the Japanese resistance to the missionaries' work.

I had no quarrel with the idea of one world without distinctions between better and lesser peoples, although my tradition did not believe in Christ as an answer. But in its rejection of the missionaries' doctrine, Japan had shown once again that it would accept the West not on the West's terms but on its own. The West had ruined once-great nations in Asia. It had used the East. In its wartime colonization of Asia, Japan had replicated what the West had been doing for centuries.

Japan was alone among the nations of the Far East in losing little—if anything—of itself in the coming of the West. Japan had defined the terms of the encounter. It had preserved its integrity. I may not have liked the values that defined that integrity; but then who was I, or the missionaries, to impose alien concepts of right and wrong as if those beliefs were better? It was the nation's place to choose. If the missionaries had a new idea to present, then they were free to present it, just as the nation was free to reject it, which is just what it did.

The missionaries heard a poem written by a foreigner who had lived in Hokkaido for thirty years. The poem told the story of three Japanese boys on their way home from school. The boys spotted the foreigner. But instead of calling him "foreigner" they called him "uncle." The boys had made the man happy, calling him something other than "foreigner."

The missionaries put their arms around each others' shoulders for communion. The Kroehlers stood at the edge of the circle, their heads bowed.

"May we all give birth to spiritual children. May thousands come pouring in," the leader called out in a passionate voice. "Today we have received what it takes to go the second mile. We, in turn, bless Japan. We thank you for Japan. What a beautiful nation."

"Amen," answered the missionaries.

✐ ➤ ✐ ❧ ➤   The odds of changing Tatsuo Shigeta did not favor Eugene Matthews. But Eugene was not dwelling on the odds. He was thinking of the future, and the future, according to Eugene, was in America, with its manifold printing needs. Eugene wanted to sell Think Laboratory's machines in the West. He wanted to be Shigeta's agent, selling Think's Boomerang machines and Japanese printing systems. Eugene had a partner established in the American printing industry.

But first Eugene would have to sell America to Shigeta. To do this he would take the president by the hand and show him physical evidence that the president could not dismiss or consign to the black hole of further study. All the lessons learned in two years with Shigeta, all the indirect instruction acquired through twenty-four months of weekends at the office and late nights together at the sushi bar, had brought Eugene to this understanding: if he was going to change Shigeta's thinking he would have to do so by Japanese rules. American tactics, bold tactics that might have come more naturally to Eugene, would surely fail. He had to pressure Shigeta in a way that did not feel like pressure. He had to push without seeming to push, cajole without being obvious, all the while taking Shigeta to the point where he could see things in no other way than Eugene's.

And while Eugene had to be gentle—or at least appear to be gentle—he had to take a position from which he would not budge.

If Shigeta sensed indecision on Eugene's part he could turn the uneasiness to his advantage, keeping Eugene suspended in eternal negotiations, promising a decision that would never come.

"I'm worried about the time," Shigeta told Eugene when Eugene explained why he wanted Shigeta to come to America. Eugene mentioned that they could visit companies in three countries.

"I'll think about it," Shigeta said.

Eugene sent him an itinerary. Eugene was already in Boston, tending to the details of Think's splashy entry into the American market, the unveiling of the Boomerang machine at the headquarters of Dennison, the Massachusetts printers.

Shigeta called Eugene in Boston and asked that he meet his flight in Los Angeles. He did not want to fly on to Mexico alone. Mexico would be the first stop on Eugene's Selling of the Americas tour.

First they visited plants. They saw expensive machinery and saw, too, where Think's technology could fit into other people's plans. Eugene translated when the printing company men told Shigeta, "We need a representative here. We want someone to be here."

Eugene let these men speak for him and did not embellish their words. Shigeta nodded and said, "Yes, I understand."

They flew to Monterrey, where the message was the same. Then they flew north, to Canada. In Toronto, a printing company executive who wanted to buy looked at Think's sorry brochure. The brochure was a thin, lifeless booklet, bound in white and pea-soup green. It was filled with creative spellings and photographs of the backs of heads. Eugene had pestered Shigeta about changing the brochure, but Shigeta had ignored him.

"I've got people on my board from major companies," said the printing executive. "You think I'm going to show them this?"

Shigeta said, "Yes, I know. Eugene told me this two years ago."

From Toronto, they flew south again, to Tennessee, where Eugene rented a car and drove Shigeta to tiny Rogersville, a lonely town where Dennison had a plant. The vice president in Rogersville told Shigeta that he had a wonderful representative in Eugene. He also said that he wanted to place some orders and that he might be interested in Think's new laser as well.

From Rogersville they went to New Jersey—more complaints about the brochure, but more encouraging talk about market potential, talk they heard every place they went.

No one discouraged them. No one was tepid about the prospects for Think in America. Eugene was introducing Shigeta to people with money who wanted to buy. From New Jersey they flew to Boston for the unveiling.

Eugene and Shigeta had traveled together thousands of miles, spending every day and every meal together. Eugene did slip away for workouts in the hotel health clubs; Shigeta passed on the exercise. They heard the same messages of potential, the need for an American representative, and the fine job Eugene had done for Shigeta in the West. They talked only about machines and markets and what they had seen that day. In all that time they did not speak about the future, even though the subject was always with them.

It went unmentioned until the night before the opening ceremony for the Boomerang at Dennison. They were coming back from dinner and Eugene decided that the time had come to heighten the pressure.

He told Shigeta, "I want to be the agent for Think in America."

"No agency," Shigeta said. Instead he wanted to establish a subsidiary. He would call it "Think America."

This, for Eugene, was a revelation; he had never before heard Shigeta talk of a Think America. Eugene had the president leaning his way. But he sensed that the talk should go no further just yet. Eugene wanted Shigeta to be able to discuss his company's future when he was at home, not far away, helpless without Eugene to lead and speak for him. Still, Eugene wanted the president to understand the boundaries of any future talks.

"I don't want to talk about it now," Eugene said. "But I want to go back to the States at the end of the year and establish an agency."

Shigeta made believe he did not hear him.

"I'm serious," Eugene said.

"I don't like agency," said Shigeta.

"I just want to tell you that at the end of the year I'm going to America," Eugene said, not as a threat or an ultimatum, but as a statement of fact.

They retired to their rooms, the advantage, seemingly, Eugene's.

The people at Dennison had never before conducted an opening ceremony for a new machine. They asked Eugene, who'd pushed them to do it, what was called for. Eugene suggested gifts and a ribbon cutting. In Japan, white gloves would have been required for the ribbon cutting, but Eugene did not think them necessary. Donuts and coffee were served.

Eugene wanted Shigeta to see Dennison as a firm to which he was bound, not simply as the place where Eugene had sold a machine. Eugene wanted Shigeta feeling responsible for what happened at Dennison. If things went wrong, he wanted Think to fix them quickly, just as it would for a Japanese company. The opening ceremony would cement Think's relationship with Dennison.

In the morning, representatives of the two companies gathered at the big machine. Dennison gave Shigeta a leather briefcase. There were wallets for the Think employees who'd installed the machine. Having learned the Think basketball team's name, Dennison also made gifts of Los Angeles Laker T-shirts and caps. Shigeta, in return, gave framed artwork that had been drawn by a computer—circular rainbows that also decorated the cover of the much-maligned brochure. Dennison's president came downstairs and together he and Shigeta cut the ribbon, sealing their bond in business.

The next day Eugene drove Shigeta to the airport but kept his distance. Then he went back to his hotel, to finish writing a formal business plan for the future of Think. The plan was ready for Shigeta two weeks later, when Eugene returned to Japan.

He did not hand the plan to Shigeta immediately. Instead he said that he wanted to talk. Shigeta said that he could not talk because he had people coming in.

The visitors came and left.

"Let's talk now," Eugene said.

"I have things to do," said Shigeta.

"Later," Eugene said.

"Lunch first," said Shigeta.

"For your benefit and everyone else's we should talk," Eugene said, knowing that in Japan delay was often the route preferable to commitment.

"I don't have time now," said Shigeta.

"We have to talk now," Eugene said.

He handed Shigeta the report. Shigeta looked at the report and, knowing what Eugene had in mind for America, said, "When?"

"Read this, then we talk," said Eugene, who sensed in Shigeta's question not curiosity but discomfort—the discomfort of not knowing how much longer he could delay.

The plan was a detailed, fifty-page analysis of the company's technological strengths and administrative weaknesses—both of which Eugene and Shigeta were quite familiar with. The highlight was the cover letter. In the letter Eugene addressed the ingredient essential for his success with Shigeta: feelings.

Eugene thanked Shigeta for bringing him to Think and for teaching him so much. He wrote that no matter what the president decided to do, he wanted nothing to jeopardize their friendship.

Shigeta thanked Eugene for the plan, and especially for the letter.

It was as if Eugene had his hand firmly on the back of Shigeta's head. Before them was a window, wide and clear. Eugene stepped toward the window, bringing Shigeta with him. Together, they took longer steps until they came close to the window. Then Eugene felt resistance. He countered by pushing harder. Shigeta stiffened. Eugene wanted Shigeta's nose pressed to the window, because then, with the world as Eugene saw it spread out before him, and with the strong hand of Eugene at the back of his head, Shigeta, unable to turn or back away, and with no view left but the view before him, would smile and say, "I like what I see."

Eugene had done almost everything he could. Now he needed to establish a timetable. Without one, talks would proceed at Shigeta's pace—interminably. And here too, Eugene showed how well he had learned.

Anxious for a speedy resolution—the end of the year was still months away—but careful not to make Shigeta feel too hurried, and therefore unreceptive, Eugene told the president that he needed to improve his Japanese. Although his conversation was all but fluent, it was not refined. His reading was limited. He needed to go back to school. School was beginning in three weeks.

Playing upon the Japanese passion for self-improvement and the always appropriate belittling of one's own skills—the correct response to a compliment was not thanks, but a fawning insistence that it was not deserved—Eugene explained to Shigeta that he would have to have an answer soon so that he might be allowed to go off and make something of himself as a Japanese speaker. Shigeta could not argue with the logic, even if it did make things feel a little rushed.

Shigeta said nothing for a day. Eugene took the next day off. That night, a Friday, he went to Tokyo on a date with the sister of his best friend from work. On his way to the city, he passed his sushi bar. Outside, he saw Shigeta's black van with the Think logo on the side. Eugene knew that Shigeta was waiting for him in the sushi bar. But Eugene went on his date and left Shigeta sitting.

Shigeta called him at eight o'clock the next morning. He said, "Let's have a meeting."

At the office Eugene joined Shigeta on the leather couch where the customers sat. Shigeta opened. "I read this three times," he said of the business plan. "It's a very good report."

He commented on the report for fifteen minutes. Then he stalled. Eugene stayed silent while Shigeta stressed the need for further consultation with all parties before he made any move toward America. This could take two or three months, Shigeta said. Or maybe a year.

Finally, Eugene said, "Thank you."

Then he said, "Do you want to do it or not? There are a lot of things to discuss. I'm leaving soon for language school. I'm not

Think Laboratory. You are Think Laboratory. Maybe in your opinion it is not the best time."

Shigeta smiled. He looked at Eugene, who had been trying so
hard to play the game of manipulation according to Japanese rules.

"You know much about Japanese people," Shigeta said. "But you
are a real American."

A customer appeared. Shigeta called for a recess. Eugene sat at his
desk, reading a trade magazine. Just before lunch Shigeta stopped
by and said, "I'll be back at three. We'll talk then."

At three o'clock Eugene heard someone say that Shigeta was not
coming back. Eugene decided to give Shigeta until six and then go
out for the evening. Shigeta returned at four and summoned Eugene
back to the meeting area.

Now, Eugene led. "The most important thing is the last point
I made in the letter about our being friends and colleagues."

"I liked the letter," Shigeta said. "It was very important."

"It was from my heart," said Eugene.

They chatted for a few minutes. Then Shigeta began asking
questions.

"Where will you set up offices? Boston? New York?"

Eugene said he was leaning toward New York.

"Let's go through the business plan step-by-step," said Shigeta.
"How should we go about this?"

Eugene, weary of indecision, rose and walked to the display
board. In big letters he wrote the words Risk and Potential. He said,
"There is a lot of potential and little risk. Yes or no?"

Shigeta looked at the board. He sat back, turned his head to
the side and squinted, as he always did when he was concentrating.

"Okay," he said. "We do it."

Shigeta grabbed Eugene's hand and pumped it. "Let's go eat
dinner," he said. "Let's call Umebayashi. Let's tell him. We're going
to make a lot of money."

That night, at the sushi bar, they ate and drank and shared their
good news with the sushi bar owner. "I am so happy now," Shigeta

said to Eugene, in halting English. They stayed until Eugene, who had not slept in two days, could not stay awake.

The sushi bar owner got his car keys so he could drive Shigeta home. Shigeta and Eugene walked outside. Shigeta turned to Eugene.

He thanked him. Then he hugged him. Eugene, exhausted by the day, excited by the result and shocked by a hug he never expected, crossed the street and headed home.

✂ ✎ ✐ ✎ ✎ A pop fly rose high and lazy and fell fast into the big mitt of the new third baseman of the Yakult Swallows, Leon Lee. It was summer, and Leon was back in Japan, practicing and wilting in the midday sun. The rainy season had passed, but in its place came heat that baked men as well as the outfield's artificial turf. Leon, sweating and sucking air, came in from the field to drink cold water. "Japanese water," said one of the coaches to Leon, who wisely nodded in agreement.

The Swallows were a refuge for Leon. The team, desperate for hitting, had hired him within days of his release. In March he was in Yuma, Arizona, where the Swallows trained. The training, however, did the Swallows little good: they were the worst team in the league. They had finished last the past three seasons. Their following was limited to relatives and close friends. The players called the manager "Airhead."

The Swallows' inefficiency worried Leon, who sensed that it might portend a brief stay. Leon needed a better finish than last place if he wanted to ensure his coming back for another season. Leon hoped for fifth place, reasoning that if the Swallows finished fifth, management would be reluctant to break up their best team in years. Fifth place would likely mean a job for Leon for the coming year. Fourth place would clinch it. Maybe fourth place was asking too much.

In July the Swallows showed signs of life and fourth place did not seem unreasonable. The Swallows won games in bunches, at one point eight in a row. Leon Lee hit home runs and made important catches and even helped win games with his baserunning. Leon was having a terrific season.

But that was July. This was September and the Yakult Swallows were going to Osaka, for the final road trip of the season, buried in sixth place, the cellar.

Sixth place assured him nothing. Blame would have to be assigned. And while in America the manager was the one to go, in Japan it was often the foreigners. Last-place teams ended their seasons by announcing searches for new foreigners, strong foreigners. The losing teams looked at the winning teams, saw what their foreigners had done and looked for something similar. Randy Bass, Leon's friend, had won the league home run, batting, and runs-batted-in championships two years in a row. Bass had raised expectations. He was the new standard. Everyone wanted a Randy Bass. And if they did not want a Randy Bass, then perhaps they'd want a foreign pitcher, like Brad Lesley, who made faces on the mound and entertained the people with the overly emotive behavior that had earned him the nickname "Animal."

Leon was neither. He hit home runs, but not as many as Randy Bass. He kept his feelings in check, which made him not nearly as much of a show as Animal Lesley. Leon wondered whether the Swallows would want him back.

The Swallows assembled on the bullet train platform just after ten in the morning, having played a game the night before. They wore gray slacks and knit blue blazers with YS stitched over their hearts. Leon was exhausted.

The players lounged in their railway car, waiting to go. Two young women slipped into the car and asked the players if they might have their pictures taken together. Leon stood on the platform with Mark Brouhard, the Swallows' other foreigner. It was Mark's first season in Japan and he was struggling. He could not seem to hit the Japanese pitches, even though he had played for five years in the major leagues. Leon tried helping Mark and shielding him from the coaches who, unlike American coaches, did not regard batting slumps as inevitable but rather as lapses in consistency that called for experimentation and perhaps a brand-new batting stance. Mark smiled his boyish smile and seemed agreeable, which made the coaches think he was receptive to many suggestions.

One of the coaches told Mark, "If you hit twenty-five home runs and drive in eighty runs, I'll buy you a steak dinner."

Leon, who often interpreted for Mark when the coaches suggested new techniques, asked, "What about me?"

"You don't count," said the coach, who expected better things from Leon.

On the platform an autograph-seeker approached Leon and Mark. He looked up at Mark. He asked for his signature.

Leon did not exist for the autograph-seeker. It had been that kind of year.

The year began with bad dreams. In Yuma, Leon dreamed of Kondo, the Whales' manager. He dreamed that Kondo was chasing him. In the dream Leon turned and shot at Kondo, trying to stop him. But the bullets did not stop Kondo and he gained on Leon. Leon had the dream over and over.

He could not hit in Yuma.

"I'm out there thinking home run every time up," Leon told me, remembering the spring. He wanted to hit home runs to show everyone and to show himself that he was not a bad player, that the Whales had been wrong to fire him. Leon felt that people regarded him as damaged goods. Unable to accept being spurned, Leon tried fighting back, swinging his bat against rejection that took the form of a small, white ball. He swung often and hard but with little success.

Mark, who was having a good spring, told Leon that he was sorry about what had happened to him.

"Don't worry about me," said Leon.

He vowed that he would not get close to his new teammates, not the way he had with the Whales.

The Swallows opened their final road trip in Osaka, on a Friday night, against the Tigers, Randy Bass's team. The year before, when the Tigers won their first championship in twenty years, their stadium had been filled three hours before game time and the faithful had cheered during batting practice. The Tigers were Osaka's team, the second city's team, and the people took great pleasure in beating the Giants, Tokyo's team. The Tigers became the team of those who felt they had never won. Their following was national, blue-collar, and passionate. Fans came to the Osaka zoo trying to collect tiger hairs as good luck talismans. The Tigers had loyalists even in Tokyo, where one Tiger fan beat another to death—the killer had fallen asleep during a Tiger victory party; the victim had questioned his loyalty.

Several people in Osaka also rooted for the Swallows. They called themselves the Yakult Swallows Cheering Party, Kansai Chapter (Osaka was in the Kansai region). At the ballpark they changed into pale blue Swallows road jerseys and navy slacks, stuffing their civvies into shopping bags. They brought the tools of cheering: flags, whistles, horns, drums, and plastic megaphones. Like all other fans of all the other teams, the Yakult Swallows Cheering Party, Kansai Chapter, cheered as one. They cheered when their cheerleaders signaled them to cheer. Otherwise they were silent, just like the many thousands who did not sit in the designated cheering sections and who, without cheering instructions, watched the game without comment.

There were a dozen chapter members at the stadium on Friday night. They pulled their flagpoles from the Yakult Swallows flagpole bags, unfurled their Swallows flags, pulled on their blue Swallows caps, spread themselves across a meager two rows of seats, and assumed the role of gadflies—pests and irritants to the tens of thousands who defined happiness by the fortunes of the home team, the Tigers.

Leon came to bat with one out in the top of the sixth and the Swallows down by a run. The head cheerleader assumed his position on the railing, facing his charges. He looked over his shoulder at the playing field. He held a whistle between his teeth. Arms extended, hands in white gloves, he began blowing his whistle in a steady cadence. Together the cheering party repeated after him, "Home run, home run, Leon Lee."

I once made the mistake of calling to an outfielder, "You bum!" I was stared at, not with anger, but in disbelief. There was no "bum" cheer and there had been no order that an epithet be bellowed. Fun at the ballpark, I quickly learned, was a shared experience. You came to the park to be together, in one voice, and in joint adoration.

For a while I wondered how people could possibly be having any fun if they could not feel free to do so spontaneously. But people smiled when they cheered. Sometimes, when their teams lost big games, they cried. They cried together, sharing the pain. I did no more yelling on my own. Sometimes I sang with the others when Leon came to bat.

The Swallows made a run at the Tigers. They tied the score and briefly led. But the lead did not last. When the Tigers went ahead, the stadium vibrated with the sound of their faithful singing the team song, "The Wind That Blows Down from Mount Rokko." The Swallows cheering party began gathering the litter from their dinners. The two women among them retired to the ladies' room to change out of their uniforms. The men pulled off their Swallows jerseys and bade each other good night. They shrugged and smiled and shared the sadness of defeat. They headed for the exits. Out of their uniforms and no longer together, they were lost in the thick crowd, which swallowed them up, one by one.

The Swallows lost again on Saturday. That night, after the game, Randy Bass had the foreign players to his house. "Animal" Lesley was in town, as was Leron. Nine foreign players whose teams were in Osaka for the weekend came to Bass's big house, which sat on a hill overlooking the harbor of Kobe.

Animal Lesley lounged in front of the television, watching a tape of an American football game. He yelled at the good running plays and the dropped passes. The men helped themselves to beer from the refrigerator. Bass served them steaks.

The talk was loud and rowdy and filled with innuendo. The men laughed and teased each other as if they were mates on the same team, celebrating. Bass lamented their not having had the chance to get together like this sooner. The season was ending and the men understood that some of them would not be back.

This was a night, however, for jokes and too much food and football on television, for being together after a long season with only one other man to talk with on the road, the other foreigner.

The party ran late, even though the Swallows and Tigers had a game the next day. The men had to leave to be up in time for their games. The crowd thinned. At two in the morning, the Lee brothers, Bass, and Mark Brouhard walked out onto the patio and looked down at the harbor.

The lights glistened against the water. The night was still. Mark said the view made him feel like he was home, in California. The stillness made Mark think of the country. Bass, who came from Oklahoma, teased him about the country he might find in California. They laughed.

Mark said he wished they didn't have a game the next day so that they could stay up and talk. They could sit outside on the grass and look down at the harbor and talk till the sun came up.

In the morning, Leon and Mark were back with the Swallows. The players, as always, were on the bus half an hour before it was scheduled to leave. Young girls crowded by the doorway, hoping for snapshots and autographs.

Leon joined his teammates on the bus. He talked with the ones who had become friends. Leon had broken his early-season vow of distance. Teammates who lived in his apartment complex had stopped over. They had tried Pam's lasagna and when Leon saw how much they liked it, he had brought some for them. The players had called Leon and asked him to go out with them.

Mostly, it was the older players who became Leon's friends. He had them over for barbecues. Early in the season Leon and Pam had invited over a group of players and their wives and children. It was a Monday, a rare day off for the team. Leon had wanted his new teammates to feel comfortable in his home, so when they arrived, he told them there would be no bowing.

"Let's forget all the bowing tonight," Leon said.

Pam made her lasagna, as well as chili and meatloaf to go with the steaks that went on the grill.

Everyone arrived together. Places were taken. The wives congregated near the coffee table. The men went off together. The girls followed Raya, the Lees' eldest daughter, and watched her run the home computer and play the piano. Derek, their oldest son, played catch with the other boys.

The lasagna went quickly; the meatloaf followed. Pam sat with the wives, who rose to serve their husbands. Leon, who wanted everyone to feel like a guest, said, "Nobody waits on anybody here."

The men stood outside by the grill. And as men will do when meat is being grilled out-of-doors, they held cans of beer and shot the breeze. Their talk surprised Leon. They spoke about the coaches they disliked, and the long hours of practice that left them limp and ragged by August. They asked how things were done in America and how Americans might respond to certain baseball situations. Leon had known his teammates as endurers, not as complainers, and their talk was filled with uncharacteristic carping.

The talk made Leon feel that his teammates were comfortable with him in his home, as comfortable as he was beginning to feel with them. In the weeks after the party they asked Leon if he could bring them more lasagna.

The Swallows lost again on Sunday and then went home. They continued practicing every day for two hours. They played their remaining games with little passion. Fifth place had vanished from view. The cellar was theirs. Leon wondered whether he or Mark would be the one to go. There was talk that the general manager was going to America to bring back a major leaguer with a famous name.

The major leaguers came over in November to play a series against a team of Japanese all-stars. Kondo managed the Japanese team. The Whales had fired Kondo. He was going to become a broadcaster; this was his last managing job. I saw him standing near the dugout during practice and went over to talk. He was a pleasant-looking man, tall, thin, and bespectacled. We talked about the coming series, and he thought it would be a good experience for the Japanese players "to meet a superior team."

We talked about the differences between American and Japanese players and Kondo noted the closing gap in weight and height. The Japanese, he said, were getting bigger and stronger.

"The Japanese practice a lot more than Americans," Kondo said. "Since the Japanese practice more they are improving in technique."

We chatted a while longer about the traditional Japanese sports, sumo and judo.

Then I asked, "Why did the Whales release Leon Lee?"

The question did not upset him.

"He couldn't hit in the clutch," Kondo said.

"How can a man drive in one hundred ten runs and hit thirty-one home runs in a one-hundred-thirty-game season and not hit in the clutch?" I asked.

"He was not a good batter against good pitchers."

"But how can a man hit so consistently and only do well against weak pitchers?"

"The statistics are good but if you analyze those one hundred ten runs batted in, he did not do well against good pitchers. In one game he drove in ten runs. But that was because the pitcher was not so good," Kondo said of Leon's great game for the Whales against Hiroshima, which had the best pitching in the league.

"I knew that Leon had a place to go," Kondo said. "I knew that other teams wanted him. He was a very good player. But he was satisfied with his position and he didn't grow. I felt that Leon had been with the Whales so long that if he changed teams he'd be a better player."

"Do you mean that Leon considered himself too much a part of the team?" I asked.

"There is no discrimination between Japanese and foreign players. Foreigners are considered helpers."

"Foreign players say that that is all they are, helpers. They say that they never feel they are part of the team. Was Leon naïve in thinking he was part of the team?"

"If you stay with a team too long you become selfish. Players demand too much if they have been on the team a long time. Leon's wife is very strong and Leon demanded many things from the front office, like fixing the kitchen in their home. Such demands came from Leon but she was behind it. It happened because Leon had stayed in Japan too long."

This was absurd. First it was Leon's hitting that had led to his release. Then his overweening sense of "comfort." Now it was his wife.

The Whales had wanted to replace Leon. That was a business decision. Foreigners were paid a lot more money than their Japanese teammates. The team had a right to expect a lot for its money. But in searching for an excuse for firing its best hitter, the team had made matters very personal. The Whales had questioned Leon's enthusiasm, not just his productivity. His relationship with his wife was ridiculed. Leon had been deemed a nuisance.

Leon was a loser no matter how he acted. If he was remote, he was not fostering team harmony. If he was warm and close, he was overstepping the limits of his role. The Whales had reminded Leon that he was never more than a helper, and that the team wanted the help to know their place.

Leon knew it, too. He had seen it early in the season, when the Swallows played the Whales in an exhibition game in the northern city of Niigata. Leon hit a home run. He had thought the home run would satisfy him, the way meeting an old flame when she is available and you are not is satisfying. But when Leon had gone out to the stadium and seen his old teammates, the men who had taken him out for dinner and singing, who had told him how sorry they were that he was not with them anymore, he had lost the desire for revenge.

After the game both teams had assembled on the train platform. Leon was talking with his old teammates when Kondo approached. The players grew silent and stepped back to let Kondo come to Leon. Kondo smiled and shook his hand. Leon did not refuse the hand. He said hello. That was the moment when Leon understood that the feelings had always been one-sided. On Kondo's part, it was as if nothing had happened between them. There was no overly solicitous behavior that might have masked discomfort. There was no apology, which would have wiped the slate clean. Although the dismissal was an issue that would never have been raised—too tense, too uncomfortable—Leon looked at Kondo and recognized that the event which had so upset him had meant nothing to Kondo.

There had been only Leon's feeling for the team, never the team's for Leon. There was no awkwardness on Kondo's part because there was nothing to feel awkward about. To have felt uncomfortable would have implied that Leon's position was as intimate as he had imagined.

"I guess I had this illusion that I was really part of the team," Leon said. "And that's what it came down to, an illusion. As much as they want to accept you, it can't happen. They only see you as an image, an image of a faraway world. You fight so hard sometimes to say, 'I'm from another country. Please accept me.' And they're saying, 'We're trying, too.'"

✦ ✦ ✦ ✦ ✦ Peace came to Lafcadio Hearn when the light was dim and the view hazy. Then he could see what he was looking for. Inevitably, however, the lighting grew bright and the world Hearn lived to see did not so much fade away as vanish in a flash.

Hearn welcomed the sensation. In Japan, he believed, the short life of pleasure was defined by fragile elements—light, clouds—coming together in just the right way just long enough to create not only a view but a feeling, "the feeling of Japan." The pleasure was not supposed to last.

The week after he arrived in Kobe, Hearn went to Kyoto, for the festival commemorating the city's 1,100th anniversary. He took the morning's first train. His car was crowded and people had to stand. Among the travelers were geisha who sang and flirted with their escorts. Hearn loved when geisha sang; their voices reminded him of birds.

The streets of Kyoto were lined with paper lanterns. The lanterns on each street were the same size and hung at the same height.

There were streets where each lantern was topped with a small paper umbrella.

The festival parade would not start until the next morning, so Hearn went to the imperial summer palace to look at the exhibitions. There, among the calligraphy samples, he saw a poem on display. The handwriting was so beautiful that people came to stare at it. The poem was signed not with a red-inked seal, but with a child's handprint. The child, Hearn learned, was five years old and had performed his writing before the Emperor.

"Still, it was not the beauty of the thing in itself which impressed me," Hearn wrote. Rather, it was the feeling that this child was writing from experiences a thousand years old. "Generations of dead calligraphers revived in the fingers of that tiny hand. The thing was never the work of an individual child five years old, but beyond all question the work of ghosts,—the countless ghosts that make the compound ancestral soul."

That night Hearn walked along the lamplit streets. He stopped at a show where "mermaids" sang Japanese songs and at another where a man drew Buddhist texts and pictures of horses with his feet. Then he stopped in a toy store, where the pleasures were more understated.

Hearn marveled at the toys, at paper chickens that could be made to peck by the simple device of a bamboo spring; at a clay and paper mouse that scampered at the pull of a string; at a paper butterfly that could fly.

He stepped back outside. The shops were closing. The streets were dark. Now, "This sudden coming of blankness and silence made me feel as if the previous experience had been unreal,—an illusion of light and color and noise made just to deceive, as in stories of goblin foxes."

It rained as I read about Hearn's trip. When I was done I went to the room in our house that overlooked a garden. The room had a tatami-mat floor and paper screen doors.

The day was gray and chilly. I kept the lights off so that the room was dim, almost gray. I wrapped myself in my *hanten*, my thick house jacket, and sat facing the garden. I framed the view between the paper screen doors and kept my hand alongside my face to block the view of the air conditioning unit from the Western house next door.

The rain fell on the gray tile roof that rose above the garden. The rain made the roof shine. In the garden the branches of the thick shrubs and trees swayed, but just barely, in the breeze. Three birds lighted on a branch. A toad croaked. Rainwater ran off the roof and onto the garden.

That was all that happened. I sat for a while, knowing that soon the vegetable peddler's truck would drive by playing calliope music. But now, in the silence, I told myself to note each element in the tableau—the light on the wooden walkway leading to the garden, the deep green of the vegetation, the way the rain fell straight down—sensing this was a scene I might not find anyplace else.

Of course I was wrong. I could find the rain and the light and the trees and maybe even the toad. All that would be missing would be the qualities I ascribed to them, the belief—the desire to be-lieve—that I was being transported. This self-conscious attempt at romance with Japan made me uncomfortable, as if I were watching myself make love.

Hearn was right: the moment was best when short-lived. That way, when I rose and turned away, I kept a picture unsullied by loud sound or harsh light, a picture that lived as a picture because it stayed with me as still and as silent as it was during the brief life my fanciful imagination gave it.

After his night in Kyoto, Hearn wrote: "Happiest he who, from birth to death, sees ever through some beautiful haze of the soul, — best of all, that haze of love which, like the radiance of this Orient day, turns common things to gold."

But then comes the light, intrusive, sobering, and painfully in-structive. For Hearn it came in Tokyo where he went, after the year of mixed blessings in Kobe, dreading what he might find, hoping that the past was not gone. For me, closer now to seeing what Hearn had seen in Japan, it would come in Matsue.

5
Tokyo

The second time Kathy Morikawa refused to be fingerprinted, Mr. Yamada was sitting at a new desk, in a new division of the Yamato city office. When he saw Kathy and Jun come into the city office, Mr. Yamada lowered his head, averting his eyes so that the Morikawas might not be tempted to come by and say hello. The Morikawas had been nothing but trouble for Mr Yamada since the day Kathy had first refused to be fingerprinted.

Five years had passed. Kathy needed to renew her alien registration booklet. A fingerprint was still required. Though the government now talked of fingerprinting only once, rather than periodically (it still could demand more prints if it had doubts about the original), and replacing the registration booklet with a card (thereby raising questions about governmental responsibility: Which body would do the laminating?), the print itself still was deemed necessary.

Kathy and Jun stopped outside the city office, a modern building draped with a banner that read, THE CITY HAS PROCLAIMED ITSELF FOR PEACE AND WANTS TO RAISE BRIGHT AND STRONG YOUTH.

"How does my hair look?" Kathy asked Jun. Jun took their baby daughter Julie and Kathy brushed her hair. They headed inside, past Mr. Yamada, who tried not to notice.

It was August, the week before O-Bon, the Festival of the Dead, a time of sticky days and sleepless nights, of rain that brought no relief from the heat. The air was heavy and so still that it felt as if it had settled over the country with the passing of the rainy season and had not yet moved. Jackets gave way to white, short-sleeved shirts and string ties as acceptable business attire. The blocky clerk at the alien registration desk had his sleeves rolled up. Kathy handed him her printless card and the clerk grew nervous.

Kathy sat alone at the plastic-topped counter. Nearby was a set of English-language pamphlets, including one entitled "How to Get Japanese Nationality for Your Children."

Kathy filled out the alien registration application form and returned it to the clerk, who took it and disappeared.

He returned with ink and cotton swabs. He asked Kathy, sheepishly, for her fingerprint.

"I refuse," said Kathy, who sensed she was not surprising the clerk.

The clerk nodded, acknowledging her action. He called over another clerk to witness the proceedings. Jun, sitting with Julie, who was playing with her toes, looked up. Kathy beckoned to him. There was nervous laughter. Kathy looked at the form and tapped the counter with her fingertips.

"Under the law I cannot issue a new card," the clerk said.

"I didn't think I needed one in the first place," said Kathy, who was not trying to be difficult but who wanted to make her feelings clear. Clerks at nearby desks turned from their work to watch.

"You will get a temporary card," said the clerk. "Once a month, for the next three months, you must come in so that we can talk to you."

Kathy, having no use for attempts at persuasion, said, "I'm not coming in anymore. Send over the police now if you like." The clerk said nothing.

Jun said, "I know you have no control over the situation, but play fair. Whatever you do, be above board about it."

The clerk handed Kathy her old card. Attached was a form that read, "Your attention is invited to the fact that if you fail to receive the said certificate within the said period you will be punished."

Kathy and Jun tried catching Mr. Yamada's eye on the way out. He did not look up.

Newspapers, meanwhile, were calling on the nation to "internationalize." Ethnic food became fashionable. Taco stands appeared in the entertainment districts and Domino's pizza could be delivered at home. Budweiser became the beer of choice. Young people who could no longer afford down payments for apartments in Tokyo—land prices had virtually doubled—were vacationing in California and coming back with gift cartons of Häagen-Dazs ice cream and with Mickey Mouse dolls too big for airline overhead bins.

Yet Kathy, in her role as television critic, still noticed such offerings as *Foreigner Watching*, snide comments about a Japanese actor's "blond wife," and the occasional "stump the foreigner" quiz show. Just as truth in Japan could be either meant or spoken, so too, it seemed, was "internationalization" an effort that looked wonderful on billboards and in travel advertisements, but in reality was as empty as a promise made for the sake of convenience.

The message of "internationalization" was that Japan should get to know foreigners better. Implicit in the message, of course, was the concept of the foreigner—as in "Think better of the foreigner," or "Make friends with a foreigner." When Tokyo held its first international film festival, Victor Banerjee, the Indian star of *A Passage to India*, was brought onstage at the film's premier. He wore a kimono. He was asked whether he liked Japanese food.

Every so often, however, Kathy saw in the often-reactive medium of television signs of an awareness of the dangers of parochialism. One drama that particularly moved her told the story of a Japanese boy who had spent several years in the United States with his parents. Shortly before his high school entrance examinations, he returned to Japan to study. His parents would join him later. The boy moved in with his grandfather.

On his first day at school he was teased because he spoke English and had lived among foreigners. The boy said that he had lived in Florida and had seen the explosion of the space shuttle Challenger. His classmates tormented him all the more. His teacher resented him because his English was better than hers. His classmates burned him with cigarettes, sprayed his eyes with hairspray, and stabbed him in the crotch with a pencil. When the boy was hospitalized with a bleeding ulcer, the grandfather came to school to talk with the teacher.

The teacher said that such problems were unavoidable. The boy, she said, disrupted the class. Besides, she told the grandfather, he wasn't really Japanese. The grandfather, once a policeman but now sensing he was powerless, could not argue with the teacher. He accepted her assessment and went away.

When the mother returned to Japan and saw what had happened, she announced that the boy was returning to America, where children who knew the world beyond Japan could live happily.

Kathy was once asked to take part in a magazine's panel discussion about fingerprinting, and Japan's place in the world. "Those Japanese who want to be international are supposed to go abroad," Kathy said of the thinking and obstacles to "internationalization" she saw manifest around her. Still, when Kathy called the network after seeing the drama about the boy and asked if there might be a repeat airing, she was told that many others had already called and that the drama would be shown again.

In the absence of change, there was at least awareness. And sometimes, from that awareness, came change. In the spring before Kathy's second refusal, a Japanese court, for the first time, ruled that a naturalized Japanese could drop the Japanese name he was "advised" by the justice ministry to take when he became a citizen, and use his given name, his Korean name.

Yet fingerprinting endured. Ron Fujiyoshi, the Japanese-American missionary who'd wanted Kathy to join his movement, went on a hunger strike to protest the government's unwillingness to give him a reentry permit without a fingerprint. Fujiyoshi wanted to visit his dying father-in-law. He fasted for twenty-five days. He was hospitalized in Japan, where he remained without a reentry permit.

Kathy's reentry hearings continued into the fall, without a ruling. She did not seem concerned. There was too much else to think about: Jun's dream, the seminar house where visitors from different countries could gather and talk, had been completed. The house was three hours north of Tokyo, in the Japan Alps, an hour's drive from Chino, the town where Kathy and Jun had lived just after they were married, where Kathy had never been happier.

Kathy and Jun brought sleeping bags, two cups, a saucepan, and several days' supply of diapers for Julie. Furniture would have to wait until the end of the year, and Jun's bonus. They subsisted on tuna sandwiches. Jun brought his guitar, but was too tired at night to play. He was up each morning at five, clearing the brush and fallen branches.

Kathy and Jun visited the local elementary school. The principal offered them a tour. He explained that his school was different from other schools: children did not have to wear uniforms; classes were small and not regimented; elderly people came to the school to show the children the games they had played when they were young and to tell them stories about the past. In the courtyard was a large compass that showed the names of the nearby towns. The children could stand in the middle of the compass and turn to face the towns. There was a second ring, with names of cities in other countries so that the children could turn to places outside of Japan.

Kathy and Jun liked the school so much that they decided that this was where Julie would go to kindergarten. They were thinking that they might move back to the country for good.

Jun wanted to hold the first seminar in the summer. The topic would be Japan and the Third World. Jun planned to invite the exchange students from his university to the town. The students were from Southeast Asia and from Africa. Jun hoped that people in town might let his students stay with them. He wanted the townspeople to feel that they were a part of the seminar house— that it was not a place that an outsider from Tokyo had imposed upon their town. Jun thought people might be skeptical of his plans at first, but that would pass. Even if it took three or four or even five years, Jun did not mind: he had time.

People had been receptive to him and Kathy before, in Chino. Ten years later, the grocer from Chino remembered Kathy and Jun. He still sent them a box of apples when the crop was good.

A few weeks before they left for the country, Kathy stopped by the Yamato city office, not to be persuaded to relent, but to pick up her temporary alien registration booklet. But when she went to the office she was told that the booklet was not ready and that she would have to come back.

Kathy took the free blood pressure test offered by the city, borrowed some municipal stationery, and wrote a letter to the head of the immigration bureau, criticizing both the tactic of making her come in for repeated visits and his bureau's failure to meet with those who refused fingerprinting.

The bureau director, who was leaving for his new appointment as ambassador to Pakistan, noted his busy schedule, and then replied that by refusing to be fingerprinted Kathy was "doing a disservice to the basic framework of the society from which she and her family are daily benefiting."

Nothing had changed. Only Kathy had changed, from first refusal to second. Anticipating the predictable response to her unpredictable act, Kathy decided that if the government was going to be foolish enough to embark on yet another court case against her, she would point out that foolishness in her response. If the government wanted a trial, she would represent herself. Kathy thought the weekly scandal magazines would get a kick out of that. And if they simply wanted to fine her, Kathy had devised an appropriate form of payment.

Her penalty would come in coins, one-yen and five-yen coins. The fine might be upward of 10,000 yen. Kathy already had three coffee tins of coins saved. The one-yen coins were an inconvenience; the five yen coins made a statement. In Japanese, the words for five yen—*go en*—sounded the same as another set of

characters with a very different meaning: "a long and fruitful relationship."

Kathy would pay her fine with a smile, and with thousands of
coins to symbolize her commitment to a future together.

✔ ❥ ✔ ❧ ➤ The cold days came early to Aizu-Takada, earlier
than they had in years. The rice crop was harvested, and the fields
were barren and mustard yellow. With the cold came rain and with
the rain the mist that settled over the mountains. Summer green
turned to dull orange, and sometimes to red. The sun set early and
the nights were cold. Armin and Evelyn Kroehler brought out the
electric blanket and sweaters, and lit the heater in the living room.
It was late October and the snows were a month away.

The Kroehlers had spent August at a lakeside retreat with no
telephones. But fall brought the return of requests and obligations.
Open dates on the calendar over the phone disappeared. There was
the kindergarten children's field day, the Books and Tea Club, the
Christian art exhibit, and the seventh annual Walk for Nepal at
which ninety-five people hiked to raise money for charity. A new
English teacher from Delaware needed introductions. Evelyn went
on a women's retreat. The tourism association was ready for a dry
run for its *sake* factory tour for foreigners. Rikie Yamauchi, the
veteran of the Philippines, was organizing a tea party at the Kroehler
home for all the elderly Christians in the area who had fallen away
from the faith.

Then there was Christmas. Armin and Evelyn cleared the furniture out of their living room for the sixty-five children from the
church kindergarten who came, in two shifts, for a party. Evelyn
served Mandarin oranges and sugar cookies shaped like stars and
Christmas trees. The Kroehlers had hosted the party for years—for
children whom their children had played with and for the ever-
declining number of children who years later would still come to
the church, but only for after-school English conversation class with
Armin and Evelyn.

The coming of the holiday also meant the Simon Shoe Com-

pany's joint Christmas party and company gathering. The company
had been founded by five Japanese Christians who named the firm
after Simon the Tanner, of the Book of Acts. The owner came up
from Tokyo and listened with eyes pressed closed and hands clasped
tight as Armin told the story of the doubter whose eyes were opened
to God by Saint Francis of Assisi. The employees, in blue company
uniforms, dozed during a speech by a local pastor who told them
that a town without a railroad station was a town without a heart.

Armin and Evelyn wore the big red corsages of guests of honor.
They sat in the front row and applauded each presentation in the
talent show: the display of ballroom dancing, the dance of the fishermen, the two young men who sang "Jingle Bells", and the spirited
"Dance of the White Tiger Company" commemorating feudalism's
dying moment in the Aizu district. Awards were given for Best
Artist, Valor, and Nice Mrs.

The lights were dimmed for "O Come All Ye Faithful." The
Kroehlers rose to sing. Behind them stood the predominantly non-
Christian employees of the Simon Shoe Company, each holding a
candle and singing in the dark.

"I just hope that maybe somehow, not the words but a spirit can
be conveyed," Armin said, when we stopped for coffee after the
party.

"There are longtime Christians in that group," said Evelyn.

"Not many."

"Not many, but a few. The name of the factory is taken from
the Bible."

"But what impact has that had? It has never struck home to them
beyond the surface."

"But if they ever wanted to find out, they could come to a
Christian."

"It always takes some explanation. 'What kind of God is that
God of the Bible?' "

Mistaking frustration for bitterness, I had assumed that day that
the Kroehlers were despondent in their work. But I had since learned
that they were neither saddened nor, in moments when they felt

their faith becoming part of people's lives, naïve enough to think that Christianity's time had come at last in Japan.

Japan pleased the Kroehlers. At times it bothered them. Their moods swung in a narrow arc. Comfort with mixed feelings came for Armin and Evelyn when both the crush of disappointment and the sunburst of happiness abated and limitations became acceptable.

Evelyn would say that she saw Japan as she saw her parents: there were qualities she admired and others she did not. She and Armin were home in Japan. Armin may have still doubted himself when he saw that he was not living what he called a "Christlike" life, a life that might exemplify his beliefs. Luckily, Evelyn could still make him laugh. They could even laugh about their home, not out of anger or vindictiveness, but because it was home, and home has its funny moments.

Christmas, with all that it meant to Armin and Evelyn, was also a time for laughter.

Their two eldest daughters, Kaye and Iris, had come for the holiday. The children were scattered. Iris and her husband lived near Tokyo. Kaye, who lived in Hawaii and worked with the handicapped, was spending a semester at Hiroshima University. Ken was at Harvard, working on his doctorate. Margaret worked in New York for a foundation that worked to foster good relations between Japan and the United States. Chris was at the University of Washington. He wanted to be an artist. He, Ken, and Margaret got together for the holidays. The children maintained a steady correspondence with their parents. Armin and Evelyn covered the refrigerator door with snapshots of their children.

Kaye and Iris arrived in time for the forty-first annual Aizu-Takada town Christmas. In the years after the war, before television and radio and choices in distractions, a thousand people had come to the town Christmas because there was nothing else to do in Aizu-Takada. Now only a few hundred came.

We ate heartily at breakfast—eggs, hot cereal, toast—because it was not only cold outside but indoors too, at the town gymnasium, which was heated neither for basketball games nor for the Christmas pageant.

In the frigid gymnasium the children ran in the random, breathless, gleeful way that comes when there is room to play, folding chairs to knock over, and other kids to run with and from. The youngest children huddled in the corridor, shivering in the tights they would wear for the pageant. The teenage boys sat in the back rows of chairs, hands deep in their pockets. They wore looks of sublime indifference. A few, hair styled in ducktails and waves, tried to look mean. The teenage girls sat close by them, rapt.

Evelyn, Kaye, and Iris pressed close to each other and sang "Joy to the World" with everyone else. Young Pastor Endo, trying to keep the children at bay, told the story of "Silent Night."

The little girls in the dance class danced to a racy samba, their faces spotted with rouge and eyes lined with thick mascara. Parents ran to the stage with flashing cameras as the girls lay on the icy stage, kicking their lacy, pantalooned legs over their heads. Armin, who'd had to attend a meeting of the town fathers, arrived and took his place next to one of three space heaters.

The lighting director waved a penlight at the boys working the spotlights. The lights dimmed and the pageant began with the evening stars—the kindergarten children in white capes and star headbands. "This is the story of two thousand years ago . . ." they intoned in the uniform singsong of words committed to uncertain memories. The children looked in every direction except straight ahead at their beaming parents.

The pageant was followed by music, provided by the teenage boys who had been too cool to applaud. They hooked up their guitars, tuned in a rude cacophony, and played a raucous number, heavy on the bass. The Kroehlers, bemused, looked at each other. The teenage girls ate it up.

Then the band played "White Christmas." The lead vocalist read the words from a little piece of paper he held in his hand. Although more familiar with angry music, they still played most of the notes correctly. "I'm dreaming of a White Christmas . . ." sang the vocalist, sounding like a tenor in a regional opera troupe singing Italian lyrics only vaguely understood.

The fractured rendering of English, however, did not matter at all to Armin. Sitting by the heater in gloves and hat and heavy coat, he sang along quietly, privately, almost to himself.

Eugene Matthews did not know why he was bothering to go on the company weekend. He was leaving Think Laboratory. Friday would be Eugene's last day.

The agency plan was finished. In truth, it had never been. The celebration at the sushi bar had been short-lived. Eugene came back to work and discovered that Shigeta had meant something other than the agency when he said to Eugene "Okay, we do it." Shigeta had meant a subsidiary, Think America, where Eugene would work for him.

Eugene asked Shigeta to reconsider. He would give Shigeta a week. But even a short delay seemed foolish to Eugene, who believed that Shigeta would not agree to any arrangement that he could not control.

Shigeta said more discussion was needed. Eugene replied that a simple yes or no would do. Shigeta said wait, and Eugene agreed. As long as he was waiting—as long as there was hope, scant hope— Eugene thought he should go on the company weekend and take me with him. We were going to Sado, an island off the western coast.

Eugene tried to be jolly. On the train from Tokyo two of the wise guys from the cylinder plant, playing their game of "touchee," tried pinching his penis. Eugene smacked away their hands, and laughed with them. It was ten in the morning and the beer cans and *sake* bottles were well on their way to emptiness. Eugene abstained. Still, he tried to be a good sport. When the young men from the machine design division insisted that he follow them to the end of the car to ogle a woman with large breasts, Eugene smiled and said he would join them later.

Eugene sat back and the smile slipped from his face. He took a swallow of orange soda and told me about the disaster of a dinner in Tokyo the other night with Shigeta and Umebayashi, their go-between. They talked for two and a half hours, most of which was spent trying to convince Eugene to go to America not as the independent agent he thought he would be, but as the lone employee of Think America. Eugene thought this unwise, both for himself and for Shigeta. Eugene believed that unless Think's technology was packaged with Japanese printing presses—presses that had no place in Shigeta's Think America—the new business would languish. Eugene and his partner wanted to represent Shigeta through a company of their own, and reasoned that this could save Shigeta the hundreds of thousands of dollars he would have to invest in a subsidiary.

As illogical as the situation was—the risk, after all, was primarily Eugene's, not Shigeta's—Eugene recognized what had happened since the celebratory night at the sushi bar two weeks before: Shigeta had assumed that any American venture would be under Think's aegis. Eugene had assumed that Shigeta understood that his interest in the Americas would be as a minority partner. Eugene wanted control. So too did Shigeta, who had never had to share it.

"We have to have discussion," Shigeta said late in the evening. "I'll do a plan. Mr. Umebayashi will do a plan."

"Look, I'm going back to America in December," said Eugene. "Maybe you don't think this is in the best interests of the company. If you don't think so, let me know."

"You think we have a big gap? There's no gap between us," Shigeta said, optimistically, erroneously.

They did not talk on the train from Tokyo or on the ferry to Sado Island. Eugene and I sat with Yamaguchi, the plant manager, who told stories of his boyhood in Nagoya, during the bombing at the end of the war, when there was no school or buildings or food. Eugene tried getting Yamaguchi to teach him a Sado Island ballad. Yamaguchi tried a verse or two, but gave up when Eugene could not quite master the melody.

Sado Island was covered with clouds. At the ferry pier we boarded a bus. I asked Eugene where we were going. Eugene, knowing the answer but wanting to hear it again, asked the trip's organizer, Matsuzaki.

"Ma-chan," Eugene said, using a nickname, "where are we going?"

Matsuzaki sighed with the weariness of answering the same question eight hundred times. In English, he replied, "Fishing festival."

"What is the fishing festival?" I asked Eugene, assuming the event might feature a parade with floats bearing smiling, papier-mâché recreations of prawns and blue gills.

Eugene hadn't the faintest idea.

For half an hour we rode on a bus too small to permit all sixty Think employees to sit. We drove along the coastline, passing fishing villages where the boats had been pulled ashore in anticipation of rough weather. A light rain fell. A typhoon was heading our way.

We reached a bend in the narrow roadway and stopped. We disembarked and looked out at the gray sea. We stood high above the thin beach, leaning against the rusting guard rail.

No parade. No floats.

The organizers called us together.

One by one, we were handed a fishing rod, hooks, a bag of worms, and a can of beer.

We were told to fish for an hour and a half.

"Is this the fishing festival?" I asked Eugene, who laughed, took his rod, and headed toward the rocks.

One man fell in the water up to his knees. Another caught six small fish. Eugene climed out on the rocks with the fellows from the cylinder plant. The man who had not talked to Eugene for six months baited his hook for him. Eugene cast his line twice and got his hook caught in the dense seaweed. The rocks were crowded and it was only a matter of time before someone caught a hook in the ear. The rain was getting heavy. Eugene and I looked for cover.

People filtered back from the rocks and ducked into the doorways of the shops along the road. Eugene and I stood by the roadway railing, cast our lines, propped our rods against the rail, and sat under an umbrella, eating potato chips. On distant rocks, just beyond a red wooden footbridge, stood Shigeta, alone, reeling in his empty line.

Soon, most everyone but Shigeta and Yamaguchi wanted to know when the bus was coming to take us away to the hotel. And when it arrived, mercifully, half an hour early, we dropped our rods in a pile and hurried aboard.

"Fish," said Yamaguchi, in English, carrying someone else's catch. He smiled, as everyone did. This was the company weekend, an event rain could not spoil.

Catcalls heralded Eugene's arrival in the bath. But this year there was no parade or gathering to witness Eugene's disrobing. Shigeta left as we arrived. A prankster from the cylinder plant offered to wash Eugene's back and did not even try to pinch him. Scrubbed clean, we sank to our necks in the hot, communal tub. Eugene sang, "Amen." His voice reverberated off the tiles. Eugene wanted the others to join in, but they smiled instead.

All of us, man and woman alike, wore matching blue and white cotton robes to the banquet room—all except six young men in jeans who wanted to be different. Over the robes, underscoring the uniformity, we wore short blue jackets. We gathered at the front of the room for the group picture. Shigeta sat in the middle of the first row. Yamaguchi sat at his side. It mattered less where the others stood.

We blinked at the flash and then assembled in neat rows on a tatami-mat floor, each of us before a small table laden with crab, tuna sashimi, and tempura. The room, brightly lit and undecorated, was long and wide. Eugene and I sat in one corner; in the far corner sat Shigeta, whose lottery-assigned seat placed him as far as could be from Eugene.

We lit the Sterno cans that heated the dinner stew and poured each other's beer and *sake* for the opening toasts. Eugene, citing great hunger, began eating before the eating formally began. Perhaps, under different circumstances, he might have waited with everyone else. But Eugene was indifferent to disapproving stares. His heart was elsewhere, in a future now undetermined.

Yet just when Eugene thought he understood the state of his affairs with the company, Shigeta came to the front of the room for his speech. The president's company-weekend speech traditionally provided a brief review and forecast. Names were not mentioned. When Shigeta singled out Eugene for the work he had done for Think in America, Eugene stopped eating, and a pained look came over his face.

"I'm going to have to go over and thank him now," Eugene said, dreading the delay in their breakup.

Six local women danced traditional dances. Hostesses, mostly older women in kimono, appeared to pour drinks and laugh at jokes. Shigeta's employees circulated. They carried bottles of beer and warm *sake* and stumbled about, addled but happy. When they came to a friend's table, they sat on the floor and insisted upon topping the glasses. The room, quiet at first, was now noisy with sounds of fellowship.

Eugene sighed and rose, having spotted Shigeta nearby. He sat himself next to the president and talked close to his ear.

"It's nothing," Shigeta said as Eugene offered thanks. "Don't worry. You did well. Don't worry about bad communication. We have good communication. We're going to do the business in America. We'll have better communication. You have your idea. I have my idea."

Eugene, though warmed by the president's goodwill, did not think it possible for Shigeta to relent.

The drinking brought on the singing which brought Shigeta to the microphone. He announced that Eugene was going to sing a song that he, the president, especially liked.

Shigeta sat himself near the front of the room. Eugene sang "The Star Spangled Banner" for him. The room was hushed as Eugene sang. Eugene had his audience. He sang slowly, drawing effect from the longer notes, embellishing the song with grace notes and tremolo.

Shigeta's men answered first with applause and then with a song of their own, unrehearsed and spontaneous. They sang the "Kimigayo," Japan's brief but mournful anthem. Eugene, who had never before heard Japanese break into the singing of their anthem, did not move from his place until the song was done.

I woke the next morning with my thumb throbbing and remembered that I had smacked it on the top of Yamaguchi the plant manager's head when he insisted that I play Ginger Rogers to his Fred Astaire. Yamaguchi, shorter than me by a foot, had pulled me from my seat, wanting to dance. We had all retired to the "snack bar," where videos of ocean sunsets accompanied the sentimental songs.

The banquet ended at ten o'clock with the customary announcement that the banquet was over and the rhythmic clapping of hands that ended all happy gatherings. By then inhibitions were drowning in a rice-wine sea. Three men in the back tried piling dishes as high as they could. When the stack fell to the floor, the men fell too and burst out laughing. Eugene and I sang "When the Saints Go Marching In" without accompaniment or shame. A young man and young woman slipped off together. Shigeta rose on unsteady legs to fetch an ice bucket for the whiskey. Singers sang ballads and Eugene danced slowly, like a geisha, behind them. A hostess, still young enough to be coquettish, sat herself across from me, asked where I was from, how long I'd been in Japan, and whether I could eat Japanese food. Then, caught up by the intoxicated spirit of the room, she reached across to pull my long nose, checking if it was real. Not satisfied with the nose alone, she reached her hand under the fold in my robe and rubbed the hair on my chest. She giggled, brought her fingers to her nose, and took a sniff.

"Eugene," I called, shocked and panicky—like Alexander Graham Bell to Mr. Watson. "Come quickly. I need you."

By the morning the typhoon was five hours away. If we did not leave the island now we might be stranded for a day or two. Plans had to be changed, which meant that Shigeta had to be consulted. The organizers waited until he appeared before making preparations to flee. No one dared take the initiative in his absence. Shigeta gave the order and we caught the last ferry to the mainland.

The sightseeing tour of the island was replaced by a sightseeing tour of Niigata, a dismal city made prominent by deep, crippling snows and by a native son, a former prime minister, who had brought the bullet train to town. We drove past beige apartment blocks set against a gray sky. The guide, chirping dutifully, noted the heights of buildings and the ages of roadways. She stopped talking only to sing Niigata folk songs. Most everyone slept. We stopped at the house of a man who collected carp. We stared at the pool where his carp swam and at the pictures of famous people who had come to see the carp. We got on the bus and went back to sleep.

Shigeta sat in the middle of the bus, packed tight with his people. The bus motored through the forlorn streets of Niigata carrying, in a single load, the world that jumped at Shigeta's command.

I looked about the bus and decided that Eugene did not have a chance.

Eugene was not asking too much. He was asking the impossible. Whatever financial incentives Shigeta had for change could not compete with the single emotional obstacle that stood in its way: fear. Eugene saw excitement in change. But that was Eugene, the American, who welcomed excitement and the joy of surprise. Change for Shigeta would mean the end of certainty. Predictability in Japan was built upon the premise of uncertainty—of earthquakes, tidal waves, and the less catastrophic but more ominous belief that luck was all that stood between man and disaster. The gods existed not for forgiveness but for the watchful eye they might provide.

Surprise was all well and good for places with significant land masses built primarily upon bedrock. The people of thin archipelagoes stretched across fault lines needed to impose sameness, the sense of stimuli evoking reliable responses. If the earth and sky were uncontrollable, then people—presumably people united in understanding the tenuous nature of life—could be predictable, or could be made to be. Environmental unreliability could be balanced with human efficiency—in reactions, more so than in productivity.

I was quick to dismiss Japanese laments over the fragile nature of existence until my first earthquake, when the house felt as if it were being picked up and dropped, for sport. I shielded my head and looked up, not knowing what I was looking for except what might be coming down. I was helpless and afraid. The next day I went out and bought bottled water, six cans of tuna, a flashlight, and extra batteries, and stuffed them all into a backpack that sat by the door. Having had my hint of catastrophe, I was taking no chances.

Buildings could be built to sway. Seismologists might even be able to forecast the big quake long overdue. But in the end, when the earth began moving and the sea churned, you were stuck, on your own, like everyone else, trying to stay on your feet, losing control. In Japan handwringing talk of natural disaster was too often the excuse for social rigidity—rigidity that could tyrannize the spirit and sap the life from what I still saw as the pleasure in spontaneity. Though I wearied of the tiresome talk of a people bonded in their understanding of the way things were done, that belief was none-theless rooted in a historical fear of death from above or below. It was not environment alone that had made Japan resistant to change. The environment only accentuated and gave credence to what I had come to see as the very natural human inclination to wake up every morning knowing where the world began and ended. My nation's myths may have told of endless possibilities built upon the promise of change. But those were myths; and in the everyday business of living I recognized that the Japanese were not alone in seeking sameness. They had simply used the valid concern over their shaky homeland as the basis for attaching virtue to predictability.

Yet once, twenty years before, Shigeta had changed on the strength of his considerable will. He had left his job, setting off on his own without benefit of a bachelor's degree. He had been un-predictable. He had remade his world, at the same time insulating it from change he could not control. Now, threatened with change from beyond, from the foreigner, from Eugene, he held up his arms, put out his hands and said, Wait.

Wait, but not no. Not yet.

On Monday Eugene began cleaning out his desk. Shigeta did not ask what he was doing. On the train back to Tokyo from Niigata, Eugene had sat with Shigeta and told him that any more discussion would only jeopardize their friendship. He would be leaving at the end of the week, and would appreciate a response by Thursday.

On Tuesday, Eugene came in just as Shigeta was finishing his morning speech. He heard his name mentioned and asked Matsuzaki what Shigeta had said.

"He said, 'Eugene and I disagree. We see things differently.' "

Eugene took the words as a death knell. Shigeta was establishing an explanation for his imminent departure.

On Wednesday Eugene, feeling he had nothing to lose, told Shigeta he would review the outstanding overseas contracts with Nagase, the international salesman. Shigeta said he appreciated that.

"Mr. Shigeta," Eugene said, "Friday's my last day." He went home to pack his clothes.

Eugene was on the telephone at nine o'clock. The apartment was all but empty. There was a knock on the door. Eugene asked who it was and heard Shigeta's voice.

Shigeta asked if he could come in. He did not waste time with explanations. He had come with a decision.

Shigeta stood before Eugene and looked into his eyes.

"We do it," Shigeta said. "We do your plan."

"Really? My business plan, the agency?" asked Eugene, trying to make sure of what he was hearing before the glee began bubbling up.

Shigeta nodded. This time Eugene reached to hug him.

"I'll still do negotiating for you," Eugene said. "I'll still come to help you out."

"I thought about it," Shigeta said, "and when you said Friday was your last day I couldn't imagine not seeing your face anymore."

Eugene would leave on Sunday, not for language school—not now—but to set up an office in New York. But he would be back in a few weeks. He would come back often.

"Let's go out and eat," Shigeta said. "I'm hungry."

They walked out together into the chilly night, onto the gravel walkway, past Eugene's red motorcycle, the one he had once been so eager to show Shigeta. Shigeta had never been comfortable with the idea of Eugene on the motorcycle. There were so many fast drivers on the highways, especially late at night.

"I want to meet with this Japanese girl you were dating," Shigeta said. "I want to talk about your marriage. I will talk to her parents for you."

Eugene, soaring, decided that battle could wait.

◢ ◣ ◢ ◥ ◢ The Yakult Swallows wanted a big April from Leon Lee. If Leon had a big April, a month of home runs and key base hits, then he, as the team's strong foreigner, could carry the Swallows, who might even finish fifth. The Swallows worried that if Leon did not have a big April their season would be over as soon as it began. The team would be in the cellar by the emperor's birthday.

At the Swallows' annual preseason banquet the president himself told Leon how much the team needed a big April from him. The team had had its preseason strategy session—an attempt at imposing predictability on a game built around a round ball that bounced unpredictably—and its preseason visit to a Shinto shrine where a priest asked the appropriate gods to look after the Swallows. The banquet featured videotapes of spring training, women singers, and a television personality who served as master of ceremonies. The master of ceremonies invited some of the players to come onstage and sing with the women. He asked Leon, "How did you like the singing?" and Leon said he liked the singing. He asked Leon if he wanted to sing a song with one of the women and Leon said thanks but no.

The president was in a rare chatty mood. He had had a bit to drink when he approached Leon to remind him of the importance of a big April.

"How are you?" the president asked. "How is your condition?"

Leon said he was fine.

"It's really important we get off to a good start," said the president.

Leon said he agreed.

"And that depends on you."

"But I'm only one player," Leon said to the president, who, not hearing the answer he wanted to hear, nodded and walked away.

The Swallows also wanted a new foreigner. Even though the Swallows had finished the previous season in last place, Leon believed his job was safe, considering the expectations of his big April. Because a team was permitted only two foreigners, Mark Brouhard would have to go. Mark, with modest results in his first season, had nonetheless gone home with assurances that he'd be back. Soon after he got home, Mark got a call from his agent telling him that the Swallows were letting him go. Mark went fishing. When he returned his agent called again to say that the team had changed its mind.

But now Leon heard that the Swallows' general manager was in the United States scouting and talking, reportedly, with George Foster, who had once hit fifty home runs for the Cincinnati Reds but who was finished in the big leagues.

"What is it they're looking for?" Leon said one day over lunch. "Do they want a well-known foreigner coming over here when his career is over, or do they want someone younger who will come over and hustle?"

Leon had been that sort of younger player, the same sort of player as Mark Brouhard, who worked hard and tried to please. Logic dictated that a team was best off with someone young and potentially productive. In the years just after the war Japan brought over men from whom others could learn, major leaguers whose names, forgotten at home, could still draw in Japan. Now those once-great American players were rarer in Japan, where they were not needed anymore. Yet the lure of a major leaguer, though years past his best years, endured—less for practical reasons than for what he represented, which was the image of something better.

Mark knew he was finished when the manager started talking to him. The new Swallows' manager was Sekine, who had managed Leon on the Whales in the years before Kondo, and who always seemed to be smiling. Sekine, however, had all but ignored Mark during the spring. He had batted Mark only against left-handed pitchers, an ignominious fate in a country where children were taught to be right-handed.

"We know how you feel," the coaches told Mark, who told them they didn't. When Sekine began patting Mark on the back and encouraging him, Mark told Leon, "Now I know something's going to happen."

The season opened on a chilly, overcast day. Mark played center field. He hit well. He was batting over .360 when, after a week, the team learned that the new foreigner was coming, a foreigner unlike any they'd ever seen. This was not a faded major leaguer or a young man with promise, but a star—Bob Horner of the Atlanta Braves, the first American all-star ever to come to Japan in his prime.

A free agent in the States, Horner wanted more than Atlanta was offering. Hoping that the American owners might be found to have colluded to stop the bidding wars for expensive free agents, Horner decided to come to Japan for a year, earn $2 million, and wait for the arbitrator's decision.

Mark, meanwhile, called his agent, searching for work in the minor leagues. The Swallows players waited for the new man, first with curiosity and then resentment when they learned that his salary had doubled the payroll. News of all the money being thrown at Horner—the highest-paid Japanese player earned perhaps a third the salary—prompted stars of other teams to accuse the Swallows' owner of madness. The owner, enraged, demanded that these stars apologize to him over the stadium public address system.

Suddenly it did not matter if Leon had a big April. Horner was coming and he was going to hit fifty home runs. The team even put the number fifty on his uniform back. Concessionaires began selling Horner flags, Horner buttons, and little Horner noisemakers to be sounded for each home run. All the Swallows' stars had buttons, and some had flags—all the stars except for Leon, for whom there never seemed the need.

Leon heard that Horner, a third baseman, was going to play first, where the running was minimal. First base was supposed to be Leon's, but accommodations had to be made. Leon watched his teammates sag, not only because of the unprecedented disparity in wages—foreigners were supposed to make hundreds of thousands of dollars more, not millions—but also because the jobs they'd worked to win were suddenly gone in the interests of fitting Horner into the team.

"Leon, during game, you and me, three-hour coffee break," said an infielder, who was losing his place in the lineup.

The general manager, thinking he was appeasing but doing just the opposite, told Leon, "If you have a really good season you can make as much money as Horner."

Horner hit a home run in his first game with the Swallows. He hit three more in his second, and the panic was on. Newspapers began running daily Horner reports—one was called the "Horner Corner." A hundred photographers camped outside his new apartment to record his coming out the door and getting into a car. Television stations ran features on the best ways to get Horner out, showing with diagrams and videos where pitchers had thrown balls he had actually missed.

The photographers waited for him at the ballpark, there to record batting practice. They formed a semicircle around him, and waited in silence for him to enter the batting cage. Horner, who did not chat during practice, blew into his batting gloves, adjusted his glasses, and tried not to notice.

His new teammates, meanwhile, came to Leon when they wanted to talk to Horner. They asked Leon to ask questions for them because they were afraid to approach him themselves. Leon insisted that they try without him.

Even Sekine and the coaches were humbled in Horner's presence.

Sekine, who once would have stopped to chat with Leon, now only nodded on his way to Horner. The general manager did not even nod as he went to Horner to shake his hand. Leon, however, was expected to take Horner to the ballpark, to take him home, and to make himself available when Horner needed him. When Leon complained that he was a baseball player and not a chaperone, he was offered cash.

"Like you sell your pride for some money," Leon said.

Irked as he was at the way Horner's ascent had come, in part, at his expense, Leon was all the more disturbed by the nature of the fawning. Admiration quickly escalated into sycophancy as the nation's celebration of itself turned to self-degradation. "They feel so intimidated by this big major leaguer," Leon would say. "They're looking down on themselves."

It was as if Japan wanted its suspicions confirmed: that in Horner it saw evidence that perhaps it was not such a great nation after all—or at least that there were people who were bigger and stronger, and by extension, greater. The phenomenon was the flip side of the nation's ongoing love affair and general fascination with itself, when the talk of "poor island nation with few natural resources" sounded less like a backhanded self-congratulation ("yet look at all we have done with so little") than like genuine resignation over an inferiority that no rise in exports and gross national product could undo. As much as the nation was keen on itself, so too was it capable of looking in the mirror and bemoaning its reflection—a reflection that looked sad and fragile compared to that of the people from the larger places.

That Horner spoke no Japanese and showed little inclination to relate to the nation other than in the arena—more out of personal habit than design; he was a private man—only heightened the sensation that the nation had before it something very new and wonderful and worthy of a look before it went away. Gripped by what was dubbed "Horner fever," fans flocked to the Swallows' Jingu Stadium in numbers not seen in years. The nightly television baseball news shows featured segments on Horner's performance of the day. And foreigners such as myself, who stepped to bat in casual games, now heard "Horner, Horner," as if to categorize the genus of the batter. The year before I was "Randy Bass," when Bass was the terror of the league. Now Horner was to Bass what the panda doll was to the stuffed koala bear: this year's model.

The Swallows may have shied from Horner, but not from Leon, to whom they could always talk. In the spring, when the team was in Yuma, Arizona, for training, Leon had gone out in the evenings with his teammates to watch as they tried to strike up conversations with the local women. The men had wanted to ask the women to dance but did not know how. They had asked Leon if he would ask for them. Leon had spoken on their behalf. He had looked on as his teammates took turns dancing with the women and, between turns, dancing with each other.

Back in Japan the players called Leon and invited him out. They came to his home in twos and threes for dinner. And, at the ballpark, in the lazy time between the end of practice and the start of the game, they huddled around Leon at the dugout steps and talked baseball.

Horner kept hitting home runs, but not at the rate of three a game. From time to time he was hurt and missing from the lineup. But his presence was missed more for attendance figures than results: the Swallows had become winners.

They were not losing by the embarrassing scores of the past. In fact they won almost as often as they lost. By midsummer they were in fourth place, a position they would not relinquish. Though a championship was unlikely—the Giants were in first place, where the Giants were supposed to be—fourth place was the stuff of puffed chests and happy times.

Leon, though still assigned the Horner watch, grew closer with his new teammate, with whom he sometimes went out after games. Horner, who showed no desire for the intimacy Leon felt for Japan, asked Leon why he played hurt, why he cared so much what other people thought of him.

The question, which had no answer, made Leon smile. Caring so much about what other people thought was as natural to Leon as it was to his teammates, who placed him at the center when they gathered by the dugout steps.

Leon had a strong April, which was good, even if it was not as important as it might have been before Horner arrived.

He had a better July. In July he was the Central League's player of the month. He hit for power and average and, with Horner now at third, played where he wanted to play.

In July Leon was in a groove, the zone to which all ballplayers aspire, when every pitched ball arrives looking like a beach ball, fat and slow. A ballplayer in the groove knows when a curveball is coming and when the pitch will be inside; he can feel it. The feeling can vanish just as easily as it appears, but while it lasts, a man of thirty-four feels like he's nineteen and capable of anything. One day during his month in the groove Leon was in the batting cage, taking his practice swings. The photographers had abandoned Horner, who was delighted to be left alone.

Leon, batting helmet off, sweat running down his forehead, was taking his big swing and following the balls as they flew to center field. The balls landed in the bleachers, distant enough for the thud of their landing to take a second to travel back to the batter's box.

A coach leaned against the cage and watched as Leon drove the balls over and against the center field wall. The coach turned and smiled.

"So strong," he said. "Foreigners are so strong. A Japanese could never do that."

Late in the season Leon fouled a ball off his leg and missed several games. He did not hit well when he returned. But by September he had brought his batting average back to .300 with nineteen home runs. He was looking forward to coming back for another season. He was wondering what the team would offer him. He was home, in California, when the Swallows released him.

✐ ✦ ✐ ✦ ✦ Lafcadio Hearn once wrote to a friend that as he looked back upon his life he could remember no happy times.

Perhaps he was unfamiliar with the sensation and assumed that happiness was an unwavering emotion, a sustained peak. Or perhaps he recognized happiness and did not want to compromise, did not want to risk settling for a lesser pleasure for fear that that greater one might be lost to him forever.

Hearn, in love with an idea imposed upon a country, would not let go of his dream. He had been in Japan six years. At forty-six he felt himself growing old.

The Imperial University in Tokyo offered him the chance to teach English literature. He wanted to move back to Matsue, even if its winters were bitter cold, but his wife, Setsu, longed for life in the capital. Hearn accepted the offer.

"Probably on my way to Tokyo comes the very last apparition of Old Japan—the charming Japan that must remain eternally young in the story of human faith and art. . . . For me the New Japan is waiting; the great capital, so long dreaded, draws me to her vortex at last."

The streets of Tokyo had turned to bog after three months of rain. Roadways were split open to lay the city's new water main. Reservoirs were dug but not yet flooded. Telegraph lines ran high above rice fields which sat near barracks, military parade grounds, and the foreigners' colony that reminded Hearn of an "American suburb." Beyond the parks and bamboo groves were the factories, railway stations, and warrens of shops that periodically caught fire and burned to the ground.

"The Holy Ghost of poets is not in Tokyo," he wrote to a friend in America.

His commute to work took an hour by ricksha over two miles of muddy roads. He taught Milton and Tennyson to students who showed no particular academic rigor but who recognized that simply by attending the prestigious university they had secured their futures. Still, it was not all bad: he was treated kindly by his colleagues and was back home in time for lunch.

His wife and servants welcomed him at the door. Hearn changed from his suit and tie to kimono. He took his seat by the garden of his Japanese home, lit his Japanese pipe, and assumed the pose of the contemplative gentleman. Sometimes he muttered to himself; sometimes he walked out, past the garden, to the temple on the hill overlooking his house. The path took him through a forest of maples and cedars and pines, to the temple and its cemetery.

In the evenings, when supper was done, the family and servants gathered for singing and dancing and then for a ghost story, told by Hearn in his fractured Japanese. When the story was done all went to sleep, except for Hearn, who went to write.

He wrote to tell more stories. He told about life in a shop in Osaka where workmen assured him that even though they were paid miserable wages they were happier than if they were working for well-paying foreigners. Hearn saw nobility in their acceptance of hardship, a trait he ascribed to Buddhism's influence. He wrote about the songs the washermen sang, sentimental songs of women lost or never won, songs made especially appealing to Hearn for their simplicity, their "artlessness."

But more and more he wrote to tell stories that told about a world removed from the world around him. At the desk in his small study, his nose pressed low to the paper, Hearn wrote about headless demons, spirits that returned to the world of the living, and beautiful women who disappeared from their loving husbands because they had only been ghosts. Above his desk hung a portrait of a woman he had once loved but whom he had never told.

When his wife returned from Kabuki, Hearn had her tell him the plots of the plays. He wrote down the stories he liked, adding them to the collection of legends and myths he wanted to retell. He asked his wife to tell him ghost stories, and dimmed the light when she began. After she told him the story of the blind singer who sang for the dead, she came upon him secretly, outside the paper screen door of his study. She called to him, "Hoichi, Hoichi," which was the name of the blind singer.

"Yes, I am a blind man," Hearn replied, imagining himself as the singer. "Who are you?"

He missed meals. His wife sent the boys to fetch him. When Hearn did not come she called out, "Wake from your dream."

234

"Indeed," Setsu Koizumi wrote, "sometimes I thought he was mad, because it seemed that frequently he saw things that were not and heard things that were not."

Friends died, friends such as Sentaro Nishida, who had been his protector in Matsue and who had introduced him to his wife. Others, like his longtime correspondent Basil Hall Chamberlain, were cast out of his life, as had happened so often before, for unexplained offenses or slights to his pride. He welcomed the out-of-the-wayness of his home because it kept people from visiting.

In his solitude, he worried. He worried about his health, which was fragile, about Japan, which was at war with Russia, and about his eldest son, who was being buffeted between two worlds. The boy, Kazuo, while reared by his mother and grandmother with the indulgence accorded Japanese sons, was being educated by his father to be a young man of the West. Hearn taught his son English, written and spoken. He did so with a ferocity that left Kazuo shattered. Hearn wanted his son to know the glories of Western civilization as much as he wanted him to be a proper Japanese. He tried cramming into his young son the quality that had eluded him, the middle ground. Kazuo stood at his father's desk, trying to please, but failed and ran off in tears.

Kazuo was thin and gentle, nothing at all like his wild and hardy younger brother, Iwao, who struck his father as infinitely more Japanese in appearance and manner. Hearn wanted Kazuo to be a good swimmer. He took him far out into rough water that terrified the boy. Hearn believed such lessons prepared his son for life's cruelties.

And when the lessons were over, Hearn locked himself away. Late at night and well into the early morning—keeping hours that removed him ever more from the life of his family—Hearn secluded himself in his study, to pace and worry and then to write down his dreams.

It was not only Hearn's illusions that betrayed him. After six years at the Imperial University, the government-run school decided that he would henceforth be paid not as a foreign professor but as Yakumo

Koizumi, a Japanese. His salary would be reduced by half. When Hearn protested, he was reminded that, like a Japanese, he could subsist on rice. His sabbatical year had come and Hearn asked to be given time off. The request was denied. The message clear, Hearn left the school, even though the students rallied, to no avail, on his behalf.

He asked friends for help in finding something new, something outside of Japan, in America or England, where Kazuo might be able to complete his education. He thought he could stay away for two years, in the hope that the climate for foreigners might become more receptive. Perhaps he might again write for a newspaper, so long as the work was not too strenuous. The sight in his one eye was worsening, his health was fading.

Friends long removed from his life interceded on his behalf. One approached the president of Cornell University, who invited Hearn to give a lecture series on Japan. The lectures would be testimony to his understanding of what was taking place around him—even if that understanding was useless in lessening his disappointment. He prepared lectures on the rise of militarism; the roles of ancestor worship and Buddhism; the historical clannishness of Japanese society; and pressure on the individual to relinquish his wants for the sake of the group. He would argue that democracy, as the West knew it, had no place in Japan, a society equipped with the coercive powers necessary for governing itself. Japan, he would insist, had changed only in ways that did not compromise its soul. It endured— unlike ancient Greece, which did so only in writings—as living proof of its resilience.

He would have said all these things to an American audience now familiar with his writings, had an outbreak of typhoid on the Cornell campus not caused the series' cancellation.

Rejected by the Imperial University, fearful of the future, Hearn despaired, briefly, until he saw that he was still wanted. Tokyo's Waseda University, a private school free from government intervention, offered him a teaching post, and London University invited him to give ten lectures. In the spring of 1904, fourteen years after he had sailed into Tokyo Bay, marveled at the sight of Mount Fuji, and announced that he had found the place where he wanted to die, Hearn prepared to return, temporarily, to a world he once could not wait to escape.

He spent the summer, as he had spent almost every summer since moving to Tokyo, in Yaizu, a fishing village. Yaizu was small, undistinctive, and unsullied, just as Matsue had been. Hearn stayed with his family in a room over a fishmonger's shop. He minded neither the fish smell nor the fleas.

That summer his wife remained in Tokyo with their youngest son Kiyoshi and infant daugther Suzuko. Hearn swam with Kazuo and Iwao and then drilled them in their lessons. Together they visited temples. They walked along the beach, picking up pebbles, which they stored along a windowsill. The boys caught crabs and dragon flies and grasshoppers. Their skin got dark in the sun. In the evenings, Hearn took his sons to the arcade, where the boys took their turns at the shooting gallery. The gallery was called Port Arthur, after the site of Japan's great victory over China.

Hearn sat outside the fishmonger's shop with the townsmen. He told his stories and the men listened because Hearn was a professor and writer and therefore a man of distinction. He wrote to his wife almost every day, telling her how the boys were doing with their swimming and their lessons. In simple letters, he reported on the power of the waves, the visibility of Mount Fuji, and the changes in the weather. When the weather turned cold, she sent him warm shirts.

"I feel lonely sometimes," Hearn wrote to his wife. "I wish I could see your sweet face."

In his letters he called her a pet-name, "Little Mama." He signed the letters, "Papa."

In the fall, he returned to his teaching and writing, and to a home that adjusted itself according to the seasons. When new life appeared in his garden, Hearn asked to be told, no matter how mundane. The family came to him with news of a new anthill, a butterfly, a frog.

"Perhaps," Setsu wrote, "if anyone happened to witness, it would have seemed ridiculous. Frogs, ants, butterflies, bamboo-sprouts—they were all the best friends to my husband."

In late September, on a morning when an unseasonal blossom appeared on the cherry tree, Setsu came to her husband, fearful that the blossom portended evil. She found him in his study, smoking his pipe. He told her about the dream he had had the night before.

"I had a long, distant journey. Here I am smoking now, you see. Is it real that I traveled or is it real that I am smoking? The world of dream!"

Hearn went with her to the balcony. He looked at the blossom and said, "Now my world has come—it is warm, like spring."

The cold weather was not far off. Hearn told his wife that before it came they should free their caged night-singing insect. He stopped in her sitting room and looked at the picture on the wall. The picture was of the seashore in early morning.

"A beautiful scenery?" he said. "I would like to go to such a land."

The pain came to his chest at dinner. He hurried to his study. Setsu followed. He lay down with his hands on his chest. He was calm. And as life slipped from him, Hearn was smiling.

He had not wanted guests at his funeral. He had wanted his death to go unnoticed. But many people came to Hearn's funeral, even the fishmonger from Yaizu, who remembered how Hearn would come each summer and swim in the ocean.

His death, at age fifty-four, was noted in the American newspapers. Two more books were published, posthumously. But slowly his name stopped mattering in America, where people dismissed his Japan as a fantasy.

But if he was forgotten in the West, he was remembered in Japan, where children still read his books. Most especially, he was remembered in the Izumo district—in Matsue—where he had returned, just before moving to Tokyo, for a final visit. "I felt curious in advance as to the nature of the impressions I was going to receive on revisiting, after years of absence, a place known only in the time when I imagined that all Japan was like Izumo." His steamer sailed up the Ohashi River, toward the dock by the bridge. He looked out at the rice fields and the farmhouses. Woodsmoke rose from the houses toward the sky, where wild doves flew between sailing kites. The sun slipped behind clouds, a brief rain fell, and Hearn remembered that this was just the way summer was in Matsue.

The bridge, white seven years before, had turned gray. The fishermen were out on the river, in boats that reminded him of crescent moons. The streets seemed smaller, narrower, but Hearn reasoned that he had gotten too used to the look of cities. The shops still sold fans, porcelain, and bronzes different in design than any he had seen in Japan.

He found his home. The owner, treating him like a friend, invited him inside and took him to view the garden, with its lotus pond, chrysanthemums, and small shrine to Inari, the fox god. He climbed the hill to the castle. Rotting beams had been replaced, as had the roof tiles. The inside of the turret had been converted to a museum of booty collected by local soldiers in the war with China.

At the middle school, the new director brought him to his old classrooms. The new students, like his old students, rose to salute.

In the evening Hearn was invited to a banquet. He sat with friends from the past. Poems were recited. Women danced. One, dressed like a samurai, with two swords and a white headband, sang a fighting song, one of the popular songs of the day. Hearn remembered the woman. He had seen her dance when she was a girl. He asked if she would perform a dance she had done as a child.

The woman danced the dance, but with a mask. The mask was of the face of old age. When the dance was finished she came to Hearn and gave him the mask.

A friend handed him a cup and said, "Tonight we must think only of happy things." Hearn wanted to be happy, too.

"But, after all," he wrote, "nobody can visit with absolute impunity a place once loved and deserted. Something had vanished, something immaterial, of which the absence made a vague sadness within me. I tried to think what it could be. Old friends had entertained me. The city had remained beautiful for me in the light of the fairest summer days. The queer street vistas, the familiar

239

shops, the quaint temples . . . were unchanged. The landscape looked as it used to look. . . . Was not the lost charm something that had evaporated out of my own life,—something belonging to the first irrevocable illusion of Japan?"

The bridge across the Ohashi River is concrete gray now. The steamer dock is gone, and in its place is a Mazda billboard. The Mon Cheri coffee shop is across the narrow street, as is a beauty salon. There is also a tea shop where an old woman sits, tapping the kettle as the water boils.

In Matsue's downtown shopping arcade Mozart plays from loud-speakers. The movie theater is housed in a converted Quonset hut. An Eddie Murphy movie is playing. The inn where Hearn stayed on his first night has been replaced by a hotel, which also looks out onto the river. At the mouth of the river the fishermen, still in long, narrow boats, scrape the riverbed for snails with baskets fixed to bamboo poles. An old woman in baggy pants pulls a cart through the downtown streets. She is the fish peddler and sells her fish door to door. Her face is worn and puffy. When she reaches the wooden temple by the river she lowers the handle of her cart, brings her hands together, and claps to signal the gods.

Across the river are cheap bars promising good times. The bars are named Crazy Monkey and Snack Joy.

Away from the downtown, the streets are empty. The homes are topped with blue tile roofs and their siding is aluminum that has been made to look like wood. In a rice field, a farmer in a broad-brimmed straw hat smooths mud walls with a hoe. He sloshes through the muck, finds a tin can, and tosses it out. The streets are so quiet that from the puddles that connect the shallow streams comes the splash of minnows working their way to the deeper water.

Boys and girls from the junior high school march to the castle grounds for field day. They wear bright green sweatsuits. At the castle gate, a group of middle-aged tourists poses for a picture. On the grounds boys play baseball and girls play badminton. Children bounce a volleyball off the stone base of the castle. The castle

narrows as it rises. Its roof is still topped with dragon horns. The
display from the China war is gone, of course. Instead, there are
helmets, old lacquerware, and a mural showing how samurai put on
their armor.

I climb to the turret and look out at the town, which spreads
out flat in the plain below the castle hill. There are steel-and-
concrete blocks downtown, and apartment buildings with the stair-
ways on the outside. In the distance is a giant bowling pin, next to
the bowling alley.

I come down the stairs and out into the sunshine. The children
call out to me, "Bye, bye."

Hearn's house is owned by a descendant of the man who rented
it to him. The public is admitted for a modest charge. The rooms
have been left unchanged and the doors have been opened to the
gardens. An elderly couple sits on the tatami-mat floor by one
garden. I sit behind them, watching them look out onto the thin
stream, the stone lantern, and the thick foliage. There is a museum
next door, in a new building. I look, through the glass, at Hearn's
Japanese pipe collection, his barbells, address book, pen, fob, and
desk, which was built especially high so that he could hold his weak,
bulging eye close to his writing paper.

In a cabinet is the white suit, black tie, and rumpled fedora he
wore the morning he stepped off the gangway of the steamer *Abyssinia* into Yokohama. He brought one suitcase, never having in-
tended to stay.

It is the 150th anniversary of Lafcadio Hearn's birth. In Matsue
there will be a celebration.

The members of the Yakumo Society—the name is taken from
Hearn's Japanese name—gather for their monthly meeting. Mostly
they are older men, and a few women. The society has 150 members
across the nation. Perhaps thirty are here today. The society pub-
lishes a journal, *Hearn*, featuring essays on its namesake, as well as
historical findings, such as the recent discovery that the *Abyssinia*
bearing Hearn docked in Yokohama on April 12, 1890, not on the
fourth, as had originally been thought. Debate within the society

on matters concerning Hearn is limited to essays and is seldom pointed. Meetings are genial affairs.

In the room next door is a display of Hearn books and letters, as well as Hearn's obituary in the *New York Tribune*, which calls him "the well-known author." There are samples from the junior high school division of the first annual Composition Contest on Reading Lafcadio Hearn's Works. The winner, by Yayoi Abe, is entitled, "Hearn in My Heart." It is a letter to Hearn. In the letter she tells Hearn how he keenly understood the Japanese capacity for seeing beauty in the impermanent.

"But, oh, Mr. Hearn!" writes Yayoi Abe. "What a pity it is that we Japanese are now in an era when we must direct toward our own selves the same kind of suspicion as you had toward Western rationalism. I wonder if the 'Glimpse of beautiful Japan' that you had caught was not the last beauty of Japan in her good old days which is almost lost and gone."

Yayoi Abe need not worry. The beauty endures, the beauty and the ancient spirit behind it. Hearn built a literary monument to it. It is his legacy, and the reason for this celebration.

Today is June 27th, Hearn's birthday, and a hundred people have come to his party. They have come for Hearn, who told what they wanted to hear. That he said nasty things is beside the point. None of the glowing reports that Hearn sent back to America, the florid descriptions of the countryside, celebrations "of the race-soul," and loving depictions of "a land of elves" mattered as much as the essential sentiment that permeated his writing. It was not love, or even admiration. It was confusion.

"I may as well frankly say that the longer I live in Japan, the less I know about the Japanese," he once told a Japanese friend.

"That is a sign," said the friend, "that you are beginning to understand. It is only when a foreigner confesses he knows nothing about us that there is some reason to expect he will understand us later on."

Of course he never can. If he did it would violate a myth far more profound than even the myth of the nation's creation by the sun goddess: the myth of being different. You are unique, Hearn told Japan. You are unlike any other place in the world. And I love you for it. Only, stay as you are.

But Japan was about acceptance; not the passive act that Hearn or I associated with acceptance at home, but an active, forceful, purposeful acceptance of rules as well as of myths. The summer heat was accepted, as was the winter cold, the high yen, the inflated cost of imported food, the crowded train cars at holiday time, and the premise that there were only foreigners and Japanese. Implicit in that premise was the caveat that Japan loved, wanted, accepted only its own. And that was the condition an outsider had to accept.

Japan permitted admiration from a distance, and I marveled at what I saw. As I watched the nation soar ever higher, still embracing its maddening myths and prejudices, I began to understand why Japan moved me. It was its strength. More important than its postwar rebuilding and its economic triumph was Japan's power to define the terms of its encounters, which meant, in turn, the power to remain as it wished. Japan did not wish to change. It never had. And I did not think it ever would.

I knew Japan was strong, and Japan knew it, too, even if the nation still insisted upon disingenuous refrains about the "poor island nation," Japan the "victim" of World War II, and Japan the misunderstood—talk that had all the sincerity of the beauty queen telling her plain friend that she wished she had that friend's cheekbones, seeing as how hers were so poorly defined. What Japanese really felt, the growing contempt for those they had surpassed, was seldom, if ever, shared with outsiders.

Kathy Morikawa could accept the government's endless threats and pestering because she had been through enough—and had paid the price of acceptance—to know that all that mattered was the Japan limited to the pleasant confines of home. Armin and Evelyn Kroehler could accept rejection of their message because their primary acceptance was of a larger truth. Eugene Matthews spent two years learning how to accept what rankled him no end because he sensed that he could profit from the experience. Eugene also got lucky: he found a rare man in Tatsuo Shigeta, a man who did not accept quite as blindly as did most everyone around him.

Leon Lee could even accept official rejection because he knew that his friends cared for him. When I tried to understand why it was that my relationship with Japan had never been more than vicarious, why I lived on the periphery, looking in, never connecting, I thought of what Leon Lee had told me. We were having lunch with his closest Japanese friend, Masumoto, a pitcher from the Whales. Why, I asked, did it take three years for my neighbors to say hello? Why do people get up when I sit down next to them on the subway?

Leon and Masumoto, sitting close together in a booth, smiled at me.

"Just accept it," Leon said.

"Don't ask why," said Masumoto. "This is Japan."

And so I spared myself the rejection Leon suffered, Kathy's trial and threatened jail term, Armin and Evelyn's unheeded message, and the cigarette habit Eugene acquired during his endless days at Shigeta's knee. In return, Kathy's year in Chino lived for me only through her memories, as did Leon's nights out with his teammates, the difference the Kroehlers made in Rikie Yamauchi's life, and the look Tatsuo Shigeta gave Eugene when he sang "The Star Spangled Banner."

The policeman at the neighborhood police booth smiles at me and says good evening. The woman in the stationery store chats with me about typewriters and word processors because she knows that I write. The couple at the vegetable stand wave hello, as do the electrician, the grocer, the dentist and his wife. Japanese friends invite me to their homes. We talk about politics and families. We share worries about work and the future and money. There are conversations like conversations at home, but those are infrequent. Often it is better just to enjoy each other's company.

In Matsue I met, quite by accident, a man who spoke idiomatically fluent English. I asked how he learned to speak so well and he replied, "Singing the blues." We had a long talk about Chicago blues bands and singers. He had a vast tape collection. He played Jimmy Witherspoon songs. I sent him a tape by Junior Wells.

Separated by an eleven-hour train trip, we drifted out of touch, which was sad because encounters like that were rare in Japan. I suppose I might have been better off accepting the unlikelihood of a sequel. Because then, unlike Hearn, I would not have been disappointed. But my curiosity, seemingly walled off by my indifference, had escalated into a desire for more. I could have more, if I could accept.

It was not Japan that was at fault. I did not think it was me. Even if I did not want to accept, I could have just as effectively feigned acceptance by keeping my questions to myself. The rules allowed me that.

All of this meant nothing more than my realization that I wanted the relationship on my terms. Japan, as always, would have it on its own.

It was as if I were standing in the corner of a crowded room filled with the sound of people laughing and others trying to talk over the laughter. I nodded at familiar faces, and they nodded back at me. I was not having a bad time. But I could not seem to have a good time. I took my coat and walked to the door, where I paused to look back at the people in the room. I watched them, just as I had been watching them all night, from my corner. I turned away and walked outside. The night was still. The moon was out and shapes were vivid in its light. I could see clearly. But I could not shake the memory of that crowded room. I stopped and listened for the sound of the party. I heard it, faintly. I wondered whether I should turn and go back. Perhaps I might have a better time.

I stood there for a moment, listening in the darkness, as the sound began to disappear. It was late and time to go home.